Montana treasure

Doctor O. A. Kenck—His Life and Times

HELEN PARSONS NEILSON

RED APPLE
PUBLISHING

GIG HARBOR, WASHINGTON

FIRST EDITION

 RED APPLE
PUBLISHING
Gig Harbor, WA 98329
253-884-1450

Printed by Gorham Printing
Rochester, WA 98579

ISBN 1-880222-51-5

Library of Congress Control Number 20030929332

Cover design by Kathyrn E. Campbell

Cover photo donated by Dr. T. C. Betsner

ACKNOWLEDGMENTS

Only with the help of my two granddaughters,
Joan Marie and Heather Crimson, could I have
completed this biography of Dr. Kenck.
I thank them gratefully for their extensive
work and boundless time.

FOREWORD

Helen Parsons Neilson is a wonderful storyteller and a native Montanan. She is well known and respected too for her generosity, her optimism, and the help and encouragement she gives to better her community. Her love of nature and her grand sense of humor come through in her stories. Her first work, *What the Cow Said to the Calf*, was a classic, and now this one is another.

With his cheery *"Howdy, howdy, what can I do for you?"* and his hurry-up walk, all the local folks knew Dr. Kenck. But none knew him like Helen, his present-day mouthpiece. She figured if she didn't write about these folks, maybe no one would.

Dr. Kenck was as generous as he could be and dedicated much of his life to the youth of Montana—as his work in the Boy Scouts program showed. He was a true man of the land—hiking into the back country to plant fish, for example. His stories are a slice of Montana history. These are true stories of the man, his life, and his beloved Montana.

Helen, as well, is never dull in her storytelling but keeps the reader interested from beginning to end. Her ability and persistent desire to tell these stories has given us a rare insight into Dr. Oscar Kenck, a true Montana Treasure.

—Fay Thompson. R.N.

CONTENTS

9 / STARTING DENTISTRY IN A BOXCAR—1898

13 / ON THE ROAD AT LAST, 1900

20 / ACROSS THE GULLIES AND HILLS TO CHOTEAU

25 / AUGUSTA ON FIRE

29 / HUNTING PACK TRIP, 1901

42 / BACK FROM HUNTING

46 / THANKSGIVING AT THE AUCHARDS

54 / HOME FOR A KENCK FAMILY CHRISTMAS IN HELENA

62 / THE FISHING DENTIST & THE FINGERLING PROJECT

66 / DISCOVERING DEARBORN CANYON

71 / THE VOTE AND A FINGERLING NOTE

74 / RITA AND I LOOK AT DEARBORN CANYON

76 / ORGANIZING A BAND

81 / LITTLE FISH . . . LET'S GO

85 / THE MATCHMAKER

88 / THE STORY OF DR. KENCK'S FATHER'S DEATH,

92 / THE PROPOSAL

95 / TONY PINGS' WEDDING

101 / SERIOUS PLANS—A TRIP TO HELENA FOR THE RINGS

108 / FINDING A HOUSE TO RENT

115 / A LOVE LETTER & THE AUGUSTA COMMUNITY BAND

120 / THE WEDDING

125 / BROTHER VAN

134 / CHOTEAU NEEDS ME

139 / LIFE IN THE BIG TOWN OF CHOTEAU

143 / BACK TO AUGUSTA

151 / A PICNIC IN THE CANYON

157 / AUCHARD FAMILY MINCEMEAT

161 / MORNING SICKNESS AND A MOVE TO CHOTEAU

171 / BABY DICK'S ARRIVAL, JULY 27, 1906

177 / WORRYING ABOUT ALBERT AT THE CABIN

180 / BACK & FORTH FROM CHOTEAU TO AUGUSTA, 1906-1907

190 / CHRISTMAS IN AUGUSTA, 1907, AT THE AUCHARDS

199 / SPRING & SUMMER, 1908, TIME OFF, DOCTOR'S ORDERS

201 / THE CABIN AND FISHPOND

207 / CHRISTMAS WITH GRANDPA & GRANDMA AUCHARD

211 / A LITTLE BIG SURPRISE, OSCAR JR., OCTOBER 3, 1909

218 / HOME AT THE RANCH ON WEEKENDS

221 / THE STORY OF GRANDPA CHARLES KENCK

229 / 1912: RICHARD & HELEN AUCHARD MOVE TO HELENA

236 / THE HARRISON BASIN

239 / THE CLEMONS SCHOOL

241 / SECRET PLANS BEGUN FOR RITA'S CHRISTMAS SURPRISE

245 / MONTANA SNOWSTORMS

249 / MORE ABOUT GRANDPA KENCK

251 / RITA LEARNS ABOUT HOUSE PLANS

254 / THE HOUSEWARMING AT DEARBORN RANCH

258 / THE GREAT NORTHERN RAILROAD—
GILMAN & AUGUSTA FIGHT IT OUT

263 / THE DEATH OF RITA'S FATHER,
RICHARD AUCHARD, MAY 12, 1916

268 / SUMMER PACK TRIP

278 / OSCAR'S BIRTHDAY SURPRISE

287 / BATEMAN'S VISIT AND A POSTMORTEM

292 / YOUNG MEN LEAVE FOR WAR

302 / THE FAMILY TAKES A TRIP TO BENCHMARK

311 / THE INFLUENZA EPIDEMIC—1918

321 / MOVING TO AUGUSTA, THE WAR ENDS,
INFLUENZA ABATES

329 / NEW HIGH SCHOOL, EASTERN STAR,
& THE GREAT NORTHERN RAILROAD

337 / THE CABIN, ELECTRICITY IN AUGUSTA,
& OUR OWN HOME

343 / BIG CHANGES IN AUGUSTA—NEW OFFICE,
NEW HOUSE, NEW SOURCE OF POWER, NEW PEOPLE,
AND HOUSES AND BUILDINGS FROM GILMAN

355 / THE BURNING OF DEARBORN CANYON

357 / DICK, OFF TO COLLEGE

359 / A CUT THUMB, A BROKEN JAW, & GREEN TEETH

367 / RIDING "THE EMPIRE BUILDER" TO CHICAGO

373 / THE PINNACLE OF ALL OUR DREAMS

CHAPTER 1

STARTING DENTISTRY IN A BOXCAR—1898

How in the world did I, Dr. Kenck, get myself into such a box as this? Graduating from the Chicago School of Dentistry is supposed to set me free from the drudgery of studies and school. For what? Now I'm cooped up, boxed in, and stuck in an office. Yes, you bet it's darned kind of Dr. Frary to help me start my practice in his office here in Helena, but I'm no sooner set up and he's off on vacation. Interrupting myself, sorry, one of his patients comes in. He says, "Is the doctor going to be in today?" I can tell he hasn't noticed my new sign right alongside of Dr. Frary's.

"No, but I can help you if you wish," I quickly add.

"No thanks. I'll just wait till the dentist comes back."

I quickly respond, "I'm a dentist."

I can see it goes right over his head but misses his understanding because he says, "You must be learning. You'll probably be a good dentist someday, like Frary. I'll come back when Dr. Frary gets back from his fishing. I know him. That's where he is."

His remarks stick in. I don't even look like a dentist. They think I'm a kid. And, neither will I get to go fishing or hunting. There must be some way.

The next patient standing in the reception room is a tiny, dressed up, young lady.

Right off she asks, "Are you Dr. Frary's new assistant?"

"No, I'm Dr. Frary's new associate. He's taking a vacation. Maybe I can help you." I'm hoping she doesn't think I'm a kid like the other guy. I'm not sure, but I think she giggled.

"Whatever shall I do? I'm from way out at Augusta and this tooth is aching. My father and I are here for a few days. I do need help."

"Now, lady, what is your name? I'll look up your record to see what Dr. Frary has done for this tooth. I'm sure I can help."

"I'm Miss Rita Auchard. Dr. Frary has done some work for me before."

"Please, Miss Auchard, let me take your hat and just have a seat in the chair."

After I had taken care of the aching tooth, my mind went quickly to the fact that this little lady is actually from the fishing and hunting country I keep hearing of.

"Would you happen to know about the fishing and hunting around Augusta?" I ventured.

I ask her if that area could use a dentist.

She responds quickly, "We certainly can. All the folks out there have to make trips here to Helena to get dental work. At times we've had a doctor, but they move away."

"How about Choteau?" I inquire.

"Choteau has one dentist and he is so busy, but Augusta folks often need to come here to the county seat and the state capitol on business."

Our talk about fishing and hunting, as well as dental opportunity, sets me to thinking. I've got to figure some way to get nearer to the good life—hunting and fishing!

The very next day I'm walking along Main Street and see a wagon with a "box" on it. A big sign is painted on the side—MOODY'S PHOTOGRAPHY OF HELENA, MONTANA. As I look at this creature of someone's invention, Mr. Moody appears in his door.

"You interested in my wagon?"

"Yes," I remark. "What an advertising idea! Tell me about it."

Mr. Moody goes on at length about the wagon's origin, who made it, how it gets him business. My mind goes into a spin on this possibility. This is my answer, I'm convinced: a traveling dentist office! Moving and living in it too. I can't wait to get ahold of my childhood friend, Bill Frank. I show it to him and we talk about it.

"Bill, how about working with me to get a box like that made and equipped. Then we'll take it to the ranches and little towns?"

"Oakie, I think you've got something here. I'll help as soon as I'm done with this house I'm building."

"Bill, if you go with me and help, I'll make it right by you."

Soon, I go to a mill near my house on Jackson Street, where I know they do planing, to ask about my idea.

"Yeah, Oscar, aren't you the Helena kid that's made yourself into a dentist? That's a practical idea, a dentist on wheels. Think I know where you got it too! Ya, I can build you a car sorta like Moody's photograph office. Then you can put your dentist chair, cupboards, and workbench in it. I'll get a box ready for you to finish, and you can buy a wagon frame to sit it on." He goes right to work on it. I start calling it *the car* 'cause it does look like a boxcar. Soon the box is ready for the wagon reach and wheels.

While I'm working at Dr. Frary's office, Bill scouts about and finds a wagon that will be right. Together we pull it ourselves from the implement company to the planing mill where we get some more help to hoist the car onto the frame. After the box is secured, we get horses to pull it to the old meat market on Main Street, where everybody will see it. Of course, this is Bill's idea, and it's advertising.

First we paint a big sign on the side—DOCTOR O. A. KENCK—DENTIST OF HELENA, MONT.—with fancy scrolls. Bill is good at that. Constructing and finishing the interior will take time. Bill is also the carpenter. He goes right to work while I'm still working to get money to buy the furnishings. I'll need a small cabinet for larger items—like forceps, towels, and bulk supplies. After I made a trip to the barbershop, I exclaim, "That's it! A barber chair!" It is lightweight and has a short footrest. It will tilt back and be operated by a winding screw that raises and lowers the seat.

For the lab, Bill builds a bench bolted to the wall. The heat for the vulcanizer is a one-burner oil stove. A tripod will hold the sterilizer basin and a wire mat will hold soldering cases.

Bill says, "How about a chest of drawers? Everything we take has to have a place."

"Sure, you're right. Plenty of drawers to hold stuff." Opposite the chest is a clothes and grub closet with shelves and doors.

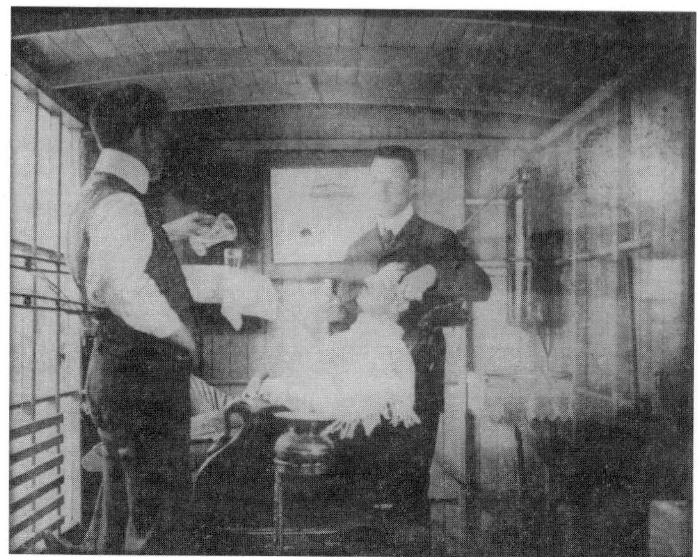

Interior of the boxcar

The front end has a set of double doors that can be fastened open with a bench across where we sit and drive the team. The brake is a hand-rotating lever like those used on railroad boxcars. The water system is a bigger project. Bill and I put together one we think will work. A tinker agreed to make a five-gallon tank that we mount on a frame for gravity. I can dismount it and carry it to a pump or well or even a creek. The sink is a galvanized tub with a hole in the bottom and a hose attached that goes through a hole in the floor to a pool outside. When the pool gets too big, we will move the car. For my lathe, I'll use a special foot-power wheel, and for work at my chair, a special foot engine. For crowns and bridges, I'll take my collection of gold coins and borrow some time at a blacksmith anvil. Also, I'll take cocaine and make my two-percent, local anesthetic. Pulling teeth is too wild without some painkiller.

The day has come. It's taken over a year, actually eighteen months, to get the car made. We are going to get a team from the livery stable and drive to the hay scales to weigh the car. As we drive the horses over the rough street, I couldn't look back but heard all manner of commotion. When we got on the scales, we both looked. Oh, what a mess! All cupboard doors flung open. All drawers upside down on the floor. Everything that could move did move to the floor. After two hours we finally got away from the scales. It takes another day of making bumpers and latches to keep everything in place.

CHAPTER 2

ON THE ROAD AT LAST, 1900

It is early July and we are ready to take off on the first journey of the car. I tell Mutter goodbye again. She says in her German, *"Auf Wiederzehen,"* and I tell her, "I'll not go far. I will be back in a few months." Clothes, grub, supplies, all tied down early at dawn on July 5, 1900. A few people see us off; it's so early. We get our two horses we've bought from the stable, hitch up, and go down across the railroad tracks and out across the valley following the old freight-wagon trail to Sieben and Wolf Creek. Bill is a more experienced teamster than I. When we meet other teams, he can handle the tricky business of passing on the one-lane trail.

John's Ranch at the far end of the valley is the first stop. All the outfits that we meet along the way give us the big grin and wave. Two days there, and then on to Wolf Creek by that evening. Bill complains, "I sure feel rotten. My head aches and stomach too." I reach over and test the temperature of his forehead. He is really hot. When he says his stomach is hurting, I'm thinking typhoid, like many others. By morning, I've decided what I must do.

"Bill, I'm sending you to St. Johns in Helena. I don't have the right stuff to give you for typhoid. Soon as you get well, come back here. I'll wait for you. I need you to finish the trip with me."

For two weeks, I stay in the Wolf Creek area. There is a store, saloon, a planing mill, a blacksmith, and two big barns for stages, horses, and hay. But I can't wait any longer for Bill, so I'll try Rock Creek Stage Stop. A.G. Floweree, a cattle rancher, owns it. It is what I call a big outfit. Floweree owns property in many places. He imports livestock. In 1870 he brought up a big herd from Texas, more in 1873, and many more steer from Utah in 1889. I can see by the house here that he likes nice buildings. The foreman tells me Floweree built the first shingle-roofed house in Virginia City in 1884 and the first two-story house in Montana. Here at Rock Creek, he crosses Cleveland Bay mares with Morgan stallions for good cow ponies. He is also the first in the state to use imported alfalfa seed. He built a reservoir to hold irrigation water about two miles up Rock Creek. All his horses have an "F" on the front shoulder and an "F" on the left neck. His cattle have "F" on their left ribs and a triangle on the left hip.

I wait here for Bill to get well and catch up with me. An outfit like this with horses and such needs a helper. I stay here a month. The ranch crew takes advantage of it. I pull their really bad teeth, fill some cavities, and even make one set of dentures for the horse herder. He calls himself Lucky.

"Sure, I can build you a set of teeth if you can hang around awhile because they'll get loose if you don't wait a couple of months. When your gums heal, they'll shrink some."

"Well, Dr. Kenck, where are you going with this here outfit? I'll just have to find you after the roundup."

"I'm heading now for Augusta and then Choteau. Soon as my helper, Bill, gets well in Helena, he'll catch up with me. He's got typhoid."

"I won't forget you, Doc. Already I feel better."

Finally, Bill gets here, a bit pale and shaky, but we start for Augusta. We aim for the Half Way House, which is twenty-one miles from Rock Creek Ranch and twenty-one miles farther to Augusta. It has bedrooms for travelers and a large barn for twenty horses, they tell me. We make it there all right, feed our team, and bed down for the night. The first twenty-one miles are far enough for Bill. The next day we get close to Augusta. We see several ranches between the Half Way House and Augusta but do not stop yet.

As we come down off the hill near a ranch, we are looking west and see the trees, probably on the South

Fork of Sun River, and it looks like we're getting close. Then I look to my left and the mountains stand out especially inviting. One mountain really jumps into our sight, a butte. It is alone and sharp like a compelling invitation. "What a country," I exclaim to Bill. "See that butte? Wonder what they call it anyway. I'm getting excited. Here is where life can be lived."

When we are close to the river, we stop at a sub-stantial-looking place with a pole gate and big barn. As we drive up to the ranch house, along a ditch and a row of young willows, we see a corral full of horses. A slim fellow comes riding from that direction. At the same time, a tiny lady comes out of the house. She waves and calls out in an unusually mature voice, "Doctor Kenck, I see you finally made it to my coun-try!" I'm astonished. She is the Augusta patient, Miss Rita Auchard. I'm almost speechless, but I manage a greeting. The horse and rider are right beside her.

"This is my brother Will, the one I told you fishes almost every evening." As we are shaking hands, a white-haired gentleman appears in the doorway. "Fa-ther, this is the dentist, Doctor Kenck, who fixed my teeth in Helena. Look what he has done. Brought his office right here with him." I introduce my friend Bill, and we talk about the problems of travel and the road. Finally, Mr. Auchard says, "Follow Will and he will show you where the horse stalls are and the feed. Of course you will stay for supper and the night. You've come a long way." When Will talks to us at the barn, I'm noticing his low voice is like Miss Rita's and Mr. Auchard's.

The Richard Auchard house and barn [built in the 1880s]

After supper, Mr. Auchard tells of his earlier life in New York as a shipbuilder.

"That's what I did before I came west—built boats, houses, and barns. Since I've been here, I've built only houses and barns. My brother Dave has a place on the Dearborn. Together we built a three-story barn with a rock first-story and log upper-stories, pretty good sized too. Probably will last over a hundred years. I believe in building to last! After that barn, I came over here and bought this land." After supper, Miss Rita and Mrs. Auchard show us upstairs where we can sleep. We are plenty glad to turn in. It's a been a long day for Bill and me.

Next morning after a good breakfast we are anxious to see this town of Augusta. Mr. Auchard had told us what to expect. As we go down the road across the creek, I wanted to stop and fish. "Not yet," I tell myself. We turn to the right and soon see a big log house. I wonder about it. Then right again and I can see the town buildings. But for some unknown reason, I turn and look towards the mountains. What a picture! That butte in the morning sun is a jewel. Never can I forget the excitement pulling at me. With difficulty, I turn myself back around and tend to the business I've come for.

We find the hotel Auchard spoke of and the livery stable close by. This is a busy place, like Miss Rita had told us. Three stores! I will unhitch and leave my car by the hotel, because of my sign on the side. The horses we take to Nett's stable. The hotel is willing so we are in business. Now we can eat and sleep at the hotel instead of in the car. Several come in to inquire, and I'm able to keep busy immediately. One fellow says he's the foreman of the ditch crew out on the Bench north toward Choteau. A couple of extractions and he will feel better. I explain some of his other teeth need fillings.

"I gotta get back to the job, but where are you going with your wagon?"

I tell 'em, "Next I'm heading for Choteau, depending on business."

"I'll catch up with you there for those fillings. These toothaches were no joy."

Towards evening I get out my fishing pole and a horse from the stable.

"Bill, I'm going out to the creek. It'll be light for a long time."

"Sure, Oakie. Go right ahead. I'll stick around here in case I can answer questions."

Next morning we have the trout I brought to the hotel kitchen for breakfast. This is the life!

In Augusta I meet important people. The big man who is constable, Treffle Bergeron, has an interesting name but is hard to remember or pronounce. He says, "Smokey Eberle, the blacksmith guy in the log store down the street, give me a nickname. Smokey said, 'Aw, can't remember first part, can't pronounce the rest. You are Joe Bush.' I think it's gonna stick." He laughs and then adds, "My wife, she stay Mrs. Bergeron, even if she is married to Joe Bush."

I take a walk down the street to meet Smokey. He has a store and blacksmith shop and sells coffins in the upstairs. He says everybody needs one sometime or another. He's making one for himself. "I figure to have it done in plenty of time. No hurry," he chuckles.

"Mr. Eberle," I ask, "how come you have these rake spikes fastened to your counter?"

"Well, it's this way. I want fellows to know the counter ain't for sittin'."

As soon as evening arrives, I have an itch to go fishing again. I pay a local boy to catch me some grasshoppers for bait. I take the tobacco can of grasshoppers and head for the creek. Spring evenings are for fishing.

That night, a loud rapid knock at my hotel door.

"Doctor! Doctor! My wife she scream, 'Baby is coming, get help!' I see your name on wagon, Dr. Kenck, please come, please." He keeps hollering, "Doctor, please come!"

Bill says, "Kenck, you better go. He'll wake up the whole town."

I get my shirt, pants, and shoes on. I grab some towels and antiseptic from my supplies and follow the man to a tent by the creek in back of the hotel. Finally we get the baby out, wipe him off, and tie the cord.

I say to the man, "Where are the baby's clothes?"

The mother whispers, "No clothes. We didn't think it would be so soon."

I say to him, "Dad, get yourself to the hotel and get some flour sacks, and fast. This baby will get cold."

Soon he comes with a bundle. I take one and cut two holes for arms, two holes for legs, put it on the baby, and wrap him up in two more sacks. Wow! I'm wringing wet with sweat. The woman is too, but the baby is suckling and the night becomes quiet again.

Haystack Butte

A month goes by fast. More and more I like this life. Every morning I take time to look at the mountains. One is called Sawtooth, and another is Steamboat. But that one butte looms up like a sentinel. It pulls on me. I can't forget it. They call it Haystack Butte.

However, I think I'd better get going if I intend to try out Choteau this fall. Kind of hate to leave this town of Augusta. Seems to have most everything. The big store built by Phil Manix is in itself remarkable. A huge log structure, two stories high. I think his entire family lives upstairs. I see children and ladies on the porch balcony—friendly people—too friendly the night of the Flour Sack Baby, the first in a string of emergencies.

Bill and I finally go to the stable for the team and then hitch up to the car. Mr. Nett at the stable says, "Doc, you don't have to leave. We need you here."

I tell him, "We'll be back."

CHAPTER 3

ACROSS THE GULLIES AND HILLS TO CHOTEAU

Choteau is twenty-five miles away, more or less, so we take off early and head north. Bill is feeling much better, and after the rest in Augusta seems his old joking self again. The road is a wagon trail. Freighters use it at times, but we don't know what to expect. We find that an irrigation project flume is being built and we have to cross it. How in the world we got high-centered, I can't explain. All four wheels are in the air, the entire load is resting on the reach. The team is down in the canal bottom, powerless to move the outfit. The foreman of a bridge project, whom I had met in Augusta as a patient, sees my plight and sends four horses and a man to help. They heave to and pull us out after several tries. But now the day is half gone and we have a tired team. We rest them a while and then go for the long hill out of the river bottom. We make some headway but they soon quit completely. Here it is six p.m. and only part way up this hill. The ditch camp was still in sight. The foreman must be watching because here comes a man with four more horses! Our tired beasts are unhooked and he hooks up his four. They start right off and don't stop till they reach the top. I come up behind leading Beauty and Beastie.

"How much do I owe you?"

"Well," he says, "cash is no good out here. Can't eat it or drink it. How about a quart of somethin'?"

"Mountain dew?" I offer.

"Sure thing, sounds good to me. And I'll be in to

see you. Got a feverish tooth needs yanking."

"Camping right here tonight," Bill chimes in.

We unharness the team, give them some oats, and put their hobbles on. Our water tank is full. There is an old deserted cabin here too. We cook up some bacon and biscuits brought from Augusta. Right then a couple of old prospectors, Jake and Jim, show up. They say they are on the way back from a British Columbia trip. They put down their bedrolls in the old shack after tying their horses to what was once a fence. Next morning, Jake and Jim decide to go along with us to Choteau. We head out across the benches, and each coulee is a real struggle for the team. On the third one, we are stuck. Wheels won't budge, and neither will the horses. Jake and Jim see no hope and tell us so.

"We'll go in to Choteau and send out a team and a man from the livery stable."

"We certainly won't be going any place," I reply.

Several hours pass. The team from Choteau Livery comes in sight. Our poor Beauty and Beastie get a load of help from the new team. Then, Choteau at last!

I ask at the hotel to set up camp nearby.

"Certainly, Dr. Kenck. We have been looking for you since reading your advance notice."

The clerk looks at us, trying to decide which of us is the dentist. Bill sets him straight right away, pointing a finger at me. "He's the dentist. I just drive the team."

"Besides parking my dental office by your hotel, we want to rent a room."

"Of course, sir. Glad to have you. The sign on your wagon tells everyone that a dentist is in town. I'm sure you will keep busy."

The hotel, called Choteau House, no sooner situated us than a redheaded, freckle-faced kid pokes his head in the door. He grins. "Are you really a dentist? My dad says you look like a kid." I can't help but grin.

"How old are you?" I ask him.

"I'm ten," he says, "and I'm Bing Hodgkiss. And, I'm also the homeliest kid in town. My dad says so."

"Do you believe it?"

"Well sorta. He should know 'cause he has to look at me enough. Every meal and in between."

"Where do you live?" I ask, thinking he was some friendly farm kid.

"I live right here. My folks run this hotel."

"So, what part is your job?"

"My job, I think," he scratches his red head, "is to do anything people ask me to do, when I'm not in school that is. And, I'll do anything you want me to do. I can run or I have a bicycle. Sometimes, or most times, it has a flat tire. I get stuff from the store or anywhere."

Sure enough, I give him a list of some things he could do for me and away he goes. Bing. Funny nickname. Where did it come from? I find out later. He explains at the hotel desk there is a bell and it does sound like that. This kid answers the bell, "I'm Bing. I heard you ring! I'll run get my mom for you." Bing Hodgkiss is a kid to watch.

I hear comments of the Choteau folk as they walk by. "So, this is the wagon dentist. He finally got here!"

My plan had been to be in Augusta only one week, not one month. Now I know I'll miss national elections. I've never voted in a national yet, and I really want to vote for Teddy Roosevelt. Sure enough, election comes and goes. Lots of talk about Teddy Roosevelt around here. I think he'll get the vote from Montana.

Cold weather makes me rent another room in the hotel for the chair and equipment in the car. Patients keep coming, three and four or more at a time. My car sitting outside advertises I'm still here. Bill is beginning to make talk about going back to Helena.

"Oakie, don't you think I should go back to Helena? It's going to be a downright mean winter here and everything will come to a stop."

"Maybe you're right," I tell him, while I'm polishing my new shotgun. "Stick around till we take the car back to Augusta. We'll leave it there for the winter. Impossible to get it to Helena now, maybe in the spring. Guess you know me, Bill. I'm not anxious to go. What with geese and ducks around here on all the ponds and sloughs, I can plainly see that towns like Choteau and Augusta are the best places to be. If you can help me get this rig to Augusta, I'll let you go. I know how much you'd like to be in Helena before Christmas."

"Okay, Oakie, sure thing. I'll help get the car to Augusta, and then I'll take the stage for Craig and catch the train for Helena. If you need and want me to, I'll come back in the spring."

Augusta people come over to Choteau. I tell them to spread the word I'll be back there for the winter. After just one month here, the chair, workbench, and cupboard are put back in the car. I buy some supplies at Hershberg's because I'm thinking how long it took to come from Augusta to here. Mid-November we hitch up to go. Frost is in the air. Beauty and Beastie breathe out white clouds. This time we go south and a bit east across the benches and finally to the big flume we'd gotten stuck in, but not this time. We jingle right along. The horses act as if they are going home. Nett's red livery stable with white trim is a good sight. Beauty calls "come home" sounds to the horses in Nett's corral. Mr. Nett looks up and waves a welcome. "Right happy to see you back. Lots of folks been askin' 'bout ya. They say, 'Is that tooth puller gonna be back this year?'"

We feel good to get a welcome like this. We rent two rooms at the hotel. It's too cold to do work in the car. We move the chair and furniture to one room. The car we pull alongside the hotel to let people know we are here, just like in Choteau. After all is settled in at the hotel, Bill says, "Oakie, I think you can get along without me now. I kinda want to go home." What can I say? I don't need a driver as long as we stay at the hotel. Bill packs his suitcase and "possible sack." Next day we are up by five and get our breakfast. The stage leaves at six for Craig where Bill will take the train for Helena.

Bill and I have been through a couple of years, so it's a bit sad to see him go. Dick Adams, the stage driver, cracks his whip and the horses lunge—they're off in a clatter.

My thoughts turn to hunting. Now that I'm in elk country, I will make time for it, thinking of this while I walk along Augusta's main street. It's early, but I hear the banging of a blacksmith hammer. I look inside. The big man, Joe Bush, is working on horseshoes. He looks up and says in broken English, "Ye be back. That's good."

"Yes, I'm back." He smiles and offers his grimy, blackened hand. Joe tells me several hunting parties have come through with elk and bear. I'm getting excited.

They pack out of the Charles Dorrance Ranch near Smith Creek. Joe says, "If ye want to talk to him when he comes in, I'll tell him. Ye be at hotel, ya? These are his horseshoes. Horses use lots of shoes in mountains."

"Yes, I'm at the hotel all winter, I think." Now I'm beginning to live!

I meet up with Charles Dorrance that very afternoon. He says a bunch is packing out tomorrow. He gives me some advice about what I will need for a hunting pack trip. Then he tells me what he does for hunting parties—like horses, for instance. One pack animal per person as well as one riding horse each. Plus a few extras just in case of a problem.

"Tell you what, Kenck. If you want to go on a short one next week, a week from tomorrow, I'm taking out a party for a few days. There's three and you'd make four. We can't be out very long—a couple of them have only the week to spend. We will go back to Patrick Basin. If the weather gets too bad, we'll come in. We really are after meat."

"Guess I could go. Haven't got any appointments set up. I'll just leave a note on my door—BE BACK IN A WEEK. Got a rifle, shells, and an outfit together. Being in the wagon has made me prepared to camp on the road."

Dorrance tells me, "I'll be going out with you. I furnish the horses, food, and camping gear. Also, I cook. You need a bed roll, warm clothes, and, of course, your personal stuff. Remember several pairs of warm socks."

The next Thursday night the guys arrive. The Great Falls fellows catch a ride on a freight wagon. The one from Helena comes in on the stage. We get acquainted at supper. One says, "I've hunted with Dorrance before." One like me is green.

Afterthoughts: It was a great experience. Charlie is an exceptional guide. He showed all of us an elk to shoot. We have no room to brag. One thing I've decided next time I go hunting, I'm going to write a journal. A bunch of guys in the mountains is a comedy worth writing. But I'm hooked for life. Is it the mountains or hunting? Both maybe. All I need to do now is round up a few fellows who want to go. No problem in that except it will probably not happen till next fall.

CHAPTER 4

AUGUSTA ON FIRE

The car gets a new parking place here in Augusta. It's directly across the main street from the hotel. I can see it from my north window on the second floor. I hardly think it would be stolen but I keep my eye on it. I'm kinda fond of it. It is the symbol of my escape from Helena.

Winter begins to close in on the country. The infernal wind beats us with no letup. Even so, the freight outfits keep coming through. The faithful stage driver, Dick Adams, leaves every morning at six. They tell me if the snow gets deep and packed Adams will use a bobsleigh. The freighters are talkative when they stop here at the hotel.

Will Barnard is one. He is a huge hunk of man with a beard flowing down his chest. Besides a freight business, his wife runs their store here. He tells me about himself:

"I rode into this here country in the 1870s pushin' a herd of XIT cattle. It was for Floweree. He hired me then too. I didn't see any future in that so I quit and went to work for the Warden outfit at Sun River. While I was there—it's a sheep outfit—I was on the shearing crew. One day we looked up and saw several guys on horseback comin' three quarter mile away, fast too. We dropped our shears and stood up with our guns at the ready. They had a sudden change of mind. All I can say—it was a sunny day and the glint off our guns was too much for their eyes."

He also says that he and Little Lottie—she's half his size—got married in 1881. "I'd been waitin' around for her to come west from Wisconsin, I guess." His belly shakes when he chuckles.

A man by the name of Clemons has a line into here from the Falls. He tells me Augusta is a booming town. Then there's Frank Key—hauls wool from the sheepmen around to the Falls and brings back supplies with his four-wagon, five-team outfit. He says it takes two weeks each way.

Christmas comes and goes, also New Year's. January 1901, I decide to take off for Helena myself. My plan is to crate up my office chair and furniture and have it shipped here. There is no problem with the stage so I put a note on my door, "Gone to Helena on business. Will be back in March." I'm thinking Frary could use me for awhile and Mama needs some repair work done around her home.

In Helena I get busy and make crates for my furniture. Also, Mama is too sad so I must cheer her. She still worries about my father—she keeps talking about how short the casket was when they buried it in the old Catholic cemetery—she keeps saying, "Charles was six feet tall." I tell her, "Mama, sometime in warmer weather I'll come up and get a Court permit to exhume the casket to answer your nagging question. Winter is no time to do that." That seems to satisfy her for the time being.

My brother Albert has a busy life. He writes documents for legal certificates—he won honors in handwriting at Gonzaga College. He plays violin in an orchestra. Once or twice a year they perform.

I'm anxious to get back to Augusta and Choteau. Then I have another idea: get a chair for the Choteau office too. My wheel for drilling and lab work I can take back and forth in a carriage. So, I order another chair shipped to Choteau. It is the county seat, and when Court is in session, dental business will be good.

That done, I feel the urge to get out of the city. George Hildebrandt, my long-time friend, wants me to stay. I say to him, "George, next time you get a vacation or get fired from Holter Hardware come over my way and you will see why I am leaving Helena."

By March 1, I'm on my way home, even if it's in a

hotel. It doesn't take long for the news to get around. The dentist fellow is back in business. This is better. I'll have decent looking dental chairs and more professional equipment. Also, I got information from Dr. Frary—the Montana Dental Society is having a meeting each year. That will be a source of new material and techniques for my practice.

Spring is around the corner. The Chinook wind—sometimes good, sometimes bad—has cleared the snow off the hills. March is here with promise.

Finally, the chairs get here. Now get them installed. Court will be in session in Choteau next month.

Four-thirty a.m., April 4, appointments are on my book. The cow, horse, and chicken noises don't faze me, but a terrific blast shatters the glass of my east window. I jump straight up. I see flames running along the edges of Adam's Store and shooting across the street. I grab shoes, pants, coat, and then a pillowcase to scoop up my medicines in. Drag them down the stairs and out. Then, dash across the street and stow it all in the car. If worse comes to worse, I'll get help and pull it away.

A bucket brigade is forming. I join, bringing water from the ditch on one side of town and the creek on the other. The word is SAVE THE HOTEL!

The flames make a roar and leap across the street, exploding every store. Within two hours every business in downtown Augusta is devoured and only then does the ravenous burning stop. We continue throwing water on the hotel. The heroic work of the brigade saves it. The collapse of the building next door relieves the immediate threat. We continue for a time to soak the siding to prevent flare-ups.

As the fire smolders in the remnants of all our stores and saloons, plus the regalia of lodges like Masons, Stars, and Oddfellows, we are in shock and exhausted. No one was burned or killed. We're thankful. The loss of the saloons was mourned, however.

The following weeks we go at it with fervor to get the town back in operation. Freight wagons bring lumber. Then, daylight to dark, hammering and sawing goes on. About May 1, I'm ready to take care of a few patients. Even then the banging of hammers and noise of saws is hard to work near. Mostly I put on work clothes and help with building anywhere I'm needed. Most of my office work is extractions.

Many evenings I head for the creek. The hammering and sawing noises go on till dark. Come September I'm ready for the hunting trip I'd planned. My friend from Helena, Lou Woods, has got his sights on it also.

The first frost and the first snow tell us fall and the hunting season are officially here.

CHAPTER 5

HUNTING PACK TRIP, 1901

The time is September 29, 1901. I'm standing, no, pacing, I realize, waiting for the stage. It will stop here at Augusta Hotel first. It comes from Craig and today will bring Lou. I keep looking up the road towards old Haystack Butte and, sure enough, here comes the stage rattling towards me. Yes, it is exactly six p.m. and Lou jumps down and says, "Oakie, I knew you'd be waiting for me. Are we ready?" All the while Lou is talking, he's taking gear down off the stage.

"You bet we are ready. I got a rig all spoken for. I'll pick it up at five a.m. tomorrow. We'll have supper in the hotel dining room and then go right to the room. Once more we'll go over all the gear and supplies. Like I promised, this trip will have a journal."

September 30: At five a.m. we don't need to be called. We cart our baggage down to the street. I go around to Nett's stables. He has the buggy and team ready. Art Nett says to me as he hands up the reins, "You fellows better bring home some meat."

"You bet we will," I answer. Soon we are loaded and reaching at full trot for the mountains. It is seventeen miles so we get a good view of those mountains as we continually urge the horses. At Dorrance's, Walt Williams, Hank Jones, and Joe Ralston are waiting. As we pull in, the horse language between our team and Charlie's full corral of pack and riding animals makes exciting music. Charlie goes right at it and cuts out riding horses, five plus a couple of spares. Then the important pack animals.

Big Jumbo, all black, the biggest packhorse I've ever seen, is first to be loaded. Charlie claims he's a good one. When we get him loaded and are bringing the rope up and over, some sound audible only to the horse turns him on. He is off bucking, ripping, and tearing across the place, getting rid of his whole pack in piles, and then he takes off at a dead run. Charlie is quick to his horse and after him. Packsaddle has to be repaired, all the stuff gathered and rearranged in the pack boxes. Now, after they've brought Jumbo back, he looks kind of sleepy, his head hanging down, but we don't buy that act. We still hang on to him at all times. All pack animals are loaded, and then riding horses saddled. It takes half the day, and by night we are on the way to Holmes Gulch—that is really Jackson's place, another packer. From there we head up the trail to the Springs, a hot pool. We barely get started and Jumbo pulls act two of the same scenario. Bucks off his load and runs off. The packsaddle is ruined this time. Walt goes after him. We had to go back to Jackson's to get a replacement packsaddle. While Walt is out getting Jumbo, he runs across an Indian medicine bag. Sorta like our "possible sack," only stranger items. What was the medicine bag doing there?

October 3: We make it to the Springs where we all take a leisurely dip. Extreme luxury for the mountains.

October 4: We move on to what has been an Indian camp, on the North Fork of the South Fork of the Sun River. All animals behaving, even Jumbo. Suddenly there is a commotion ahead. Here we find a packhorse, Jennie, caught between two logs, all four feet in the air and unable to move. She has rolled herself over a log. No way to get her right side up with that pack on her back. We lever around till we get that off and lift her up. She is okay so we repack her saddle. We finally make it to the Indian camp where we see a fresh hide and bones. We have to believe they were left by Indians but decided to camp there ourselves, tether the horses, and call it a night. Charlie says if we tether just one horse the rest will stay, but they don't.

October 5: Early up to find some horses gone. It's Kitten, Timberline, and Whitey. I see by tracks they are gone down the trail. I volunteer to go after them. I walk down four miles with my oat sack, and no more sign of them before I decide to go back to camp—and all this before breakfast! Then Walt decides to take one of the horses and go look. Walt finally returns at 1:30 with the horses. While Walt is out for the horses, Lou and I decide to go hunting. We come back toward evening empty handed and empty stomached. So goes the night.

October 6: Kitten again gets loose and we are late getting started toward Swamp Camp. Everything is going along until we get a couple miles from camp and something spooks Timberline. He decides to go back down the trail on a high lope. Since I'm last, I set out after him on foot. Walt says he'll go too. He takes off down the trail on his horse. Timberline put a lot of ground between him and Walt though. Finally caught up—even beyond our previous camp. All along the way he'd strewn the pack stuff. Sad to say his pack is our war bag—bedrolls and personal stuff rolled up in them. Besides the pack mess, Walt's horse fell with him over a log and kept him down for near an hour. Then he found Timberline with the lash cinch over a limb and around his hind feet. Three hours later he's coming in to camp. I meet him a ways down the trail. Hank Jones and Lou had supper ready when we got to camp. Food can restore lost spirits, that's for certain. Hank and Walt went hunting but found nothing. We decide the Indians had hunted this area about a week ago.

October 7: Up early and get buttoned up and move to Goat Camp on the summit. It's a hard trail, rocky and climbing upward all the way. Sure enough, as we stopped at a viewpoint, we count nine Indians leaving the Bench ahead, of course after driving all the elk out of the neighborhood. Walt sees this and gets a shot at a goat at about five hundred yards.

We never get him but Walt says, "I know I gave him a hit. You can always tell because they shake a foot at you."

We give him a bad time. "Walt, your eyelashes

blinked. That wasn't a goat's foot wiggle."

"Oh yeah it was. You guys just don't want to think I got a shot in when you didn't." We are setting up camp and settle down for the night. This is really high country and will be cold tonight.

October 8: Today we hunt goats. Walt and I walked our legs off. Finally we see one after we had climbed a considerable height. Walt says, "It's yours, Doc. If you can't hit him, I'll give it a try." Sure enough, my shot brought him down. We scramble down from our higher place and get him ready to pack down. Back to camp is twice as far as the way here. We hear about Hank and Lou riding north and finding the Jackson party camped right where we plan to camp next, but they have no game.

October 9: Kitten disappears during the night. I am appointed to find her. I ride all day and find no tracks or trace of her. Towards evening we move the whole camp to the other side of the summit. It's snowing now and colder than night before.

October 10: We wake up to find six inches of snow covering everything. We hunt all day with Jackson's five hunters. I got another goat! Jackson takes a shot at a kid goat, but it gets away from him.

October 11: Wonder of wonders, Hank appears in camp before breakfast with a front quarter of an elk. Now the puzzle is where did he get it? He's not telling and we do not see any more of it. It's a riddle we haven't solved yet. Lou and I take off to get the goat I killed yesterday. While we are skinning it, a billy appears within three hundred yards. We both grab our rifles and take a shot, and we both miss. Shame on us!

October 12: Hank and Walt go hunting but return with nothing. Lou and I stayed in camp. Today we see these birds that just stand still in the snow. We grab a few, dress them out, and decide they are edible so we roast a few on our fire. Also, we soak up some prunes. That night, strange as it seems, everyone decides to study astronomy. We all go out four or five times to study some new constellation.

October 13: After all the night's activities, we stay in the sack quite late, being in a weakened condition. Jackson's party of five left for Choteau this morning. Lou decides to go out for goats alone. He returns with meat but it isn't goat, just one lone grouse. Walt and I went out hunting but we return with only an appetite. Hank spends most all afternoon hunting for Buttons and Buck, our packhorses. He finds them about four hundred yards from camp. Also, very strangely, bear tracks appear, circling our camp within one hundred yards, and an elk cares so little for our marksmanship to bed down twice within three hundred yards of camp and then coolly walks away.

October 14 and 15: Today we move to Elk Camp on Moose Creek. The trail here is fair and the elk signs near the camp are numerous. Hank says, "Walt and I circumnavigated the earth today." Quite a walk, I must say. Lou and I start the opposite direction. We separate at Bear Creek. Lou has all the luck. He jumps a large silvertip, but he avers he lost no bear. So he gives him "ta-ta" as he disappears through the brush—by the quasi-cataleptic method of standing, standing, and shivering till even the noise of the bruin's departure ceases.

Later Lou again jumps game. This time it's four elk cows with calves. He gets two lightning shots at one cow and calf, but that's all he gets, excepting the excitement and foot race on the trail of the vanishing meat. But his race through downed timber and thick underbrush soon drowns his ardor and the reaction comes only too soon. Poor Lou drags himself down the trail with the awfulest dejected countenance ever seen on a tired, hungry, gameless hunter.

The good Lord don't do everything the way we think He should do or would, and this was one instance. For, just as Lou was walking in to camp primed to overflowing with excuses, he hears a suspicious noise coming from down the trail toward him. Deliberating, but with some misgivings, he squats on the trail, waiting for he knows not what, when striding along with a distracted air, oblivious to his danger, comes a big six-pronged elk. A shot from Lou's seven-foot cannon breaks the forest king's neck. With a tremendous plunge that tears up the earth and tree trunks for fifty feet, Lou lands a second shot at the base of the bull's brain, divorcing Herr Elk's spirit from its body without even a hearing. Man never worked with such energy, since the days of Hercules and Sampson, as does Lou in his dressing out of this giant of the forest. And yet he so far controlled his jubilant feelings that he comes to camp and meekly asks, "What luck did you fellows have?"

His premeditated coolness vanishes, however, like so much thin air when he discovers he had not performed the manual ablutions necessary to carry out his farce and he knows we have seen his gore-smeared hands, for rude we are, critically eyeing his digits. However, the hunter will out, and with breathless hassle Lou narrates the circumstances of the killing and of his day's experiences. Well, needless to say, the revival of spirits in that salt-meat camp rises at a marvelous rate, and to see how Lou is waited upon this particular evening leads one to believe he is a demigod having just arrived in camp.

October 16: Lou and Walt start out with two packhorses for the "first meat camp" while Hank and I are left ostensibly in search of bear. But having discovered some tracks of questionable recentness, we follow them till the conviction, already half upon us that the elk have gone back to the summit, causes us to turn back to camp empty handed. Reaching camp, we find Lou and Walt just returned from their task of bringing the elk to camp. It proved to be much larger than we had anticipated, for it dressed fully five hundred pounds, minus the head. But did not the first tenderloin from this elk fill a vacancy as nothing else on this earth can do! Juicy, delicious, but adjectives are inadequate to fully express the actual delight it produces among us four carnivorous mortals.

October 17: Decide to move because elk had left for the summit as snow has disappeared, and we may as well be at the mouth of the creek and wait for "the beautiful." Forthwith, we depart to the North Fork of the Sun River through a forest made up almost wholly of myriad small slender pines known to the occidental aborigines as lodgepoles. Three hours of wiggling through these pine poles, growing sometimes only six inches apart, with fat horses and packs protruding a foot and a half on either side, brings us to Sunstroke Camp, so named because of the sometimes oppressive heat at this late season of the year.

October 18: Sun comes out broiling hot for our hunting today and all hands irreverently applaud the suggestion that we follow the example of the Kansas farmer and pray for snow. As it is, successful hunting is difficult if not impossible, and furthermore t'would be sacrilegious to bring more meat into camp. In such warm weather, the four of us could never eat it up 'ere t'would spoil. But nevertheless all go hunting and fortunately all returned empty-handed.

Hank, Walt, and Doc [me] return early to camp and are soon honored by a visitor, Dickerson by name, who is in much the same plight as ourselves—empty-handed game-wise and wishing inordinately for snow. Strange-being we discover our guest to be—his tongue, being of those ceaseless undulating species, it soon introduces us to one of those incomparable hunters that this high, dry altitude always makes of hermits and sheepherders. Veritable egotists coupled with a morbid fear that the unappreciative world too bland to discover their true worth has turned en masse upon them. Yet with all this, hermit-hunter proves at least possibly interesting and uses one description that appeases strongly our visual faculties. In speaking of a certain Jumbo Wheeler, a man known for his extraordinary volubility and leaving you wondering what he had actually told you, he specifies him as "the man with stoppage in his speech." A contradiction of fact so apparent that one feels half inclined to dub Dickerson a wag.

Lou returns late with a large appetite but no game. Hank and I take a sundown stroll in hopes of seeing a vanishing white owl, but come back disappointed, and I especially so having left my gloves on top of the mountain.

October 19: Disorganization made its first appearance today. Walt has to leave for home, having his cattle to take care of. Hunting now seems practically impossible. He takes the head and horns of the elk with him. Hank, Lou and Doc [me] decided we may as well move farther up the creek, for we could at least spend time better that way than broiling all day in camp. Accordingly, we move to the surveyor's ex-camp on Biggs Creek, where we have good water, plenty of shade, and good pasture for the ponies.

October 20: Lou and Doc [me] tramp over several miles in a further quest for white tail or bear. We come upon two licks, natural ones, but find no fresh tracks. Homeward we plod our weary way. Hank had remained in camp all day and cooked up a mess of pork and beans. We all take a goodly portion. The heavens seem to have instilled in us another uncontrollable desire to go out intermittently during the night and early dawn and study well the stars.

October 21: This morning Hank starts for the river in hopes of white tail galore but discovers a deserted cabin. He explores and finds, to his glee, some ancient literature done up in the form of some tattered novel and prehistoric magazines. Perching himself on the doorstep, he is soon lost in the sporting news of the days of Washington. Lou happens along soon, unsuspecting, and discovers the pseudo-bookworm, mutually surprising himself and Hank. Both bring home a book and a magazine or two as the result of their day's meandering. Doc [me] stayed in camp all day doctoring my goat hides which sadly need my undivided attention. A big supper consists of elk steak and beans and we all retire. Oh what a night! Sleeping so little, sleep plays havoc upon the ambitions of the deer and bear hunters.

October 22: We spend the day in camp, all hands recovering while reading the antiquated magazines discovered in the cabin of yesterday's strolling.

October 23: Everyone is feeling better. Lou goes out again thinking of capturing a scalp of some description whether field mouse or elephant. Hank and I spend the afternoon in camp washing and doing various camp chores. In the afternoon we two had an ax to grind, and with it, a rifle, and a Kodak, start out for the lone shack where we had seen there an old grindstone. After taking some snaps and spoiling a couple of films by leaving the time shutter open, we begin our laborious task of grinding. We hadn't worked long when a snapping of a twig brings both to our feet, erectibus animus, in sudden crisis. Like the present, there is no time for prolonged observation, and action must of necessity be speedy or all is lost.

Hank, being more than equal to the occasion, owing to long experience in the mountains, springs for the rifle and all alertness. He stealthily treads toward the impending danger. I sit at the grindstone intently following every move, momentarily expecting to see a bear or lynx or at least a deer spring into view, when with cold deliberation Hank slowly raises his gun, takes careful aim and fires! With a bound, I was at his side with visions of several slaughtered menageries before him. Hank yelled at me to stay back. "I only stunned him!" Boy, did my heart beat with fear-begotten palpitations. But alas, before Hank could again hurl the deadly ball into the brute outside, it had vanished. Poor little chipmunk, how lucky you are!

Lou came home with visions of two little white tails vigorously bidding him a premature adieu through the gloom of the impenetrable forest some two-hundred-fifty yards beyond him.

October 24: This is a morning of high excitement owing to the number of participants in the event. Just as all hands are rolling out, someone, no one can decide who, first saw the fur-bearing quadruped. Needless to say, rifles were very much in order and after much maneuvering, vigorous chasing and rapid firing, Hank shoots off what he thinks is the animal's leg. And, horror of horrors, he escapes, despite the fact that Lou makes valiant dashes towards the escaping prey. Yeah, Lou even crawls on hands and knees through the netted underbrush in vain efforts to seize the meat, even as he says, if only by the tail.

A more dejected lot of doughty hunters never camped than these, but hot coffee and elk steak soon revive the morbid spirits. And then in hot arguments, they try to relegate the brute to its proper place in history. Alas! When the excitement of the chase and the subsequent argument subsides, all hands meekly acknowledge that 'tis but a chipmunk and we do not want him anyway. Consciences, oh yes. Well, they are readily placed in a quiescent state by the statement that the escaped villain had stolen well nigh half of our prunes together with the remnants of any dough gods we managed to leave undevoured. In the afternoon, Hank and I hunt white tail again with what luck—same old story. Lou appears in camp with the same story as well.

October 25: Hank and I explore the creek north of Moose Creek. On the same side of the river we find bushels of elk tracks, a beautiful park studded by a lake and two elk licks, all bisected by a creek with eight or nine hundred inches of water. Returning home we meet Lou who has been out in the opposite direction, watching for us with gun cocked and down on one knee, thinking we are elk or boisterous deer. Lou, on his return to camp, sees three deer, shoots three times

at their rapidly disappearing shadows and comes home blessing the vigilance and fleetness of species white tail.

October 26: Moving camp to Springs today. On the way down, ride over to Sunstroke Camp and climb the mountain, several hundred feet high, to get my gloves I'd left behind.

October 27: Lou rides up to Pretty Bottom, hunting deer, and returns at dark with his usual appetite. Hank and I spend the day exploring caves about the Springs, partaking of Major Patrick's hospitality and entertaining a visitor from the Falls, a Mr. Ward, who, like us, has hunted much but got only steak from an elk. One of his party had killed it the evening previous near our place at Swamp Camp!

October 28: Start this morning for Snow Camp in Patrick Basin. This move is due to glowing tales of uncounted, myriad elk heedlessly roaming thereabouts. Three hours of hard traveling over a hilly trail paved with fallen dead timber.

October 29: All hands start up canyon to surround and capture, dead of course, our legal allowance of bull elk. Hank and Sam on one side, Lou and me on the other. We have not left camp long before it has begun to snow. Lou and I act on the advice of both Hank and Sam to go back to camp rather than hunt in a storm, but Hank and Sam get on the trail of a bear. They get so far from camp that they have to stay out all night despite the fact that it is blowing a blizzard. Luckily they find a cave in which they are protected from the storm—assisted too by a cheerful fire. Lou and I spend the day and half the night preparing a good square meal for the belated hunters, and, at their non-appearance, eat it to prevent it from spoiling.

October 30: Lou and I spend this morning worrying about the fate of the still-absent hunters. What could have happened to them? We decide to wait here, no use to go out in this storm because we'd never be able to find tracks. All we could do to distract ourselves from worrying was read the old newspapers, when about two p.m. in come the two dirty-faced, ravenously hungry tramps! They have not eaten a bite since the previous morning. Everyone remains in camp after this. It's still snowing vigorously outside, and we rest for a hard hunt when the storm lets up.

October 31: Storm stops and all hands turn out in separate directions. I have not left camp long when I strike a fresh elk trail, and I'm off in hot pursuit. Lou follows me soon after, having followed a fresh deer track for about fifty yards—jumps his would-be victim and takes a shot through the thick brush at it's retreating form, but that's all he gets.

Sam strikes my elk trail too but farther down, and following it he hears the brush crackling just ahead of him. Instantly he levels his gun to fire—when it's not an elk, but me, on the trail ahead of him. He says nothing to me, but returns to camp in the evening, still nervous after this narrow escape from riddling one unsuspecting doctor with holes.

Hank meanders around for several hours, but

returns to camp with all his cartridges. I follow the trail up the mountainside and see Lou following below and wait for him. We two follow the trail for five hours without a stop, when to our glee appears a big bull elk! Both of us shoot almost simultaneously and both strike him in the neck. Either shot would have completed his course of existence. He has six prongs on one horn and eight on the other. We rapidly dress the game and, taking the head with us, start back to camp. Lou suggests a short cut, for now we are ten to twelve miles from camp and up a steep mountain at least a thousand feet high. We start down. It took two hours to descend, and to our disgust, discovered we cannot descend the "short cut" all the way down for it becomes a sheer rock wall. It is now rapidly growing dark so we have to run around and trudge back up the mountain almost to where we started. After two more hours trudging in dubious direction, we conclude we were both tired and hungry. Accordingly, we stop to build a fire and cook part of the head we've faithfully dragged along. No salt or pepper but 'tis awfully good. The moon rises soon after and gives enough light to let us begin marching campward. It's 1:30 when we arrive, and if you don't think we're tired, just ask us.

November 1: Snowing again but no grub left in camp except a little pepper and a can of jam. There is nothing for it but to go to the Springs again where we had left the bulk of our rations. After another tedious and rough trip, we finally get to Major Patrick's cabin, some four hundred yards from the Springs, where we set up camp. Lou and I decide to start for the elk today, but the storm and no grub changes our minds.

November 2: This leaves only Hank and me of the original party. These two, with Sam who is staying with the Major, spend the day gathering and chopping wood for our host who is getting a little advanced in years to do much of that kind of labor.

November 3: Sam and I take four horses and start out for my elk. Get about two miles up Wood Creek when we jump a silvertip bear. Of course the elk was forgotten. We tie our horses and take out on foot to track the bear. Snow is about four inches deep so tracking is easy. The tracks keep separating and coming together and coming together again so one will follow one track and the other will follow another. It so happens that I get on a back track and have left Sam but a moment when Sam sees all three bears.

Without letting me know of the find and with but six cartridges, he trudges after them, they being some two-hundred-fifty yards ahead of him and just going over a hill. I was some five or six minutes discovering my mistake, but then I hurriedly got back to the main track and followed Sam. I had just got to the summit of the hill where the bears crossed when I hear Sam shoot three times, near the top of the next one, some three-quarters of a mile away. Thus ends the story of Sam and the three bears that got away.

CHAPTER 6

BACK FROM HUNTING

Back from my hunting trip. I need to settle down and to be available for dental work here in Augusta. I've got a setup in Furman's Hotel upstairs, right in the middle of this more-than-busy town. That's right, Mr. Auchard told me about the different freighters coming and going—in fact, they all go right by his place crossing Elk Creek. I hear steps coming up the stairs and down the hall.

"I'm Tony Pings, Doc, and I'm suffering all night and for days with a toothache. Finally I gave in and come. Do you think you could do something for it?"

"Mr. Pings, I'm sure I can. Just step up and sit in this chair and I'll have a look."

I put on his towel and pump up the chair. With an explorer, I touch that tooth and he jumps.

"Oooh, that's it, Doc!" and he grabs his face.

"I see your jaw is swollen, which means the nerve is infected. Since it is a lower molar, I can extract it, and that's your only hope. If it were an upper molar, I would have had to wait until the abscess broke because I cannot put a needle into an infected upper gum—too much chance for the infection to spread."

"Go ahead, Doc. I can't stand this any longer."

While I get the needle ready, I ask many questions. Two reasons for this. I want to get to know the folks around here and I also want to distract him. First, I numb the gums at the crook of his jaw. In a few minutes it's ready and I slowly insert the needle. But Tony is losing color fast. Whoops, he's about to faint.

"Tony! Put your head down, way down between your knees. Quick, you are about to faint! Let's get some more blood to your head."

Down his head goes. I'm pushing it down too. "That's the way," I say and soon his color comes back. By that time the shot is working.

"Mr. Pings, what kind of work do you do in this town?"

"I'm a carpenter. Last year in April I was working on a house for Billy Lintzer, but because of the fire I'm side-tracked and am working on a hundred-foot store building. There's work here for fifty carpenters from daybreak till dark. I would like to find a wife but I don't see any ladies because I'm so busy."

"Tony, a hardworking man like you needs a partner. If I see any prospects, I'll let you know. I'm all for hunting and fishing in my spare time. That's not so good for a wife. Where have you built before you came here?"

"I was born in Wisconsin. When I first came west, my brother Frank and I landed in Helena and got jobs on the building of Fort Harrison. After a while we decided to get in on the homestead boom, so we homesteaded at Depuyer. Got us a small herd of cattle but we had to work to support them at first. We put up a tent—not a thing was there but it seemed a likely place. Next we built a bank and the very first stone building. Conrad just took off from that. It will be a good-sized town someday. Frank was the first mayor. He's still there. Me, I decided to look around some more. Came this way and find lots of work here. I'll stay awhile."

About this time the jaw was pretty numb so I pulled that aching tooth. Tony paid me and said, "I'll be back. My teeth need you." I think Tony is right about work in this town. Lots of building and the cold weather doesn't stop construction going on everyday, all day. This town is rising out of the ashes of the awful fire.

I hear steps coming my way again! The next person that finds the way up these stairs is that little Miss Rita Auchard with that soft New York accent.

"Miss Auchard, you found your way to my office."

"Yes, Doctor, but it's not my teeth this time. I'm here to ask for your presence at our family gathering on

Thanksgiving, if you don't mind meeting my huge family."

"I did not notice anyone except your brother Will when I stopped there last year."

"Truly, I have an unusual situation. My mother had a family and her husband died. My father had a family and his wife died. They were married and then I was born. So, that is how I got such a big family, but I am the only child of my parents. My mother has four, my father has four, together they have seven, though four plus four equals eight."

"Miss Auchard, I will be pleased to come to your Thanksgiving." I'm thinking it would be nice to be with a family at a time like that. "I have a question though. What could I bring to your feast?"

"Doctor, I think we will have plenty with all the cooks that will be coming, but perhaps if you have a musical instrument, we, you and I, might play a few pieces."

"How about a violin?"

"Wonderful. We could find something to play together. I will play the organ or the piano."

"Yes," I say, "but I'm so rusty. I haven't played since my Gonzaga College days."

"Well, good doctor, it is high time to get back with it." She chuckles softly in her New York way. "It will be Thursday next. Come early so we can practice a bit."

Wow! Now I gotta get the violin out and tune it up. Probably lost all my violin skills. What do you do when something like that is expected of you? Practice, I guess. It's like the fellow in Helena who asked, "Are you practicing dentistry?" I answered yes. He replies, "When you get practiced up, I'll be back and have you work on my teeth."

Come late afternoon I don't expect any more patients. I dig into the trunk for the thing I dread. Get it all tuned up and fiddle through a few scales. Wow, I'm rusty! See if I can tune it any better. I'll take it down to the piano and tune it. As I'm sitting here at the piano stool, Bud Tomlinson comes in. I met him at the store.

"Doctor, it's you! I heard this tuning up going on and had to see who was at it. Hey, we could have an orchestra or a band around here. Quite a few people play instruments. How about it?" He seems excited by his own idea. So, I tell him Rita Auchard asked me to bring it to the family dinner and we will play some.

"Let's get together on this band idea soon. We can get quite a group." Bud leaves me to my violin. I try a few pieces and then think of what Miss Rita and I could play at her family gathering.

Graduation from Gonzaga College (O. A. Kenck, center)

CHAPTER 7

THANKSGIVING AT THE AUCHARDS

The day finally arrives. It's cold but not storming, no blizzard as that would be an excuse. I have none. I get on my warm coat and knitted cap and trudge up the road past the willows along Eberle's ditch. The butte is dressed in white and stands alone and different. I know how you feel, old butte. We don't follow the herd. Now around the bend and across Elk Creek bridge to the Auchard pole gate. Miss Rita sees me coming and is at the door before I knock. Oh the wonderful smells that flow out when she opens it.

"You must be cooking great stuff. It smells most wonderful!"

"We've been cooking for several days," adding that low New York chuckle for punctuation. "Come right in, Doctor. I'll take your coat. We will have the front room to ourselves to practice a bit with the organ, or the piano, whichever works best."

"Really, this is the most pleasure I've had in quite a while. I studied music so seriously at Gonzaga that I was weary of it, but now I realize I really do miss it."

We go through my sheet music. Rita can play very well and by ear, I find. Before long, it really seems only minutes, but more like an hour, a buggy filled with folks arrives. The children look all scrubbed and excited with their pretty dresses and smart suits.

"This is Ida May, my half sister, and John Cottle, her husband." Miss Rita explains these are the nearest relatives, about four miles from here. Five girls and their younger brother, Henry, about six, curly haired, mischievous too. He slips around and pulls the sashes of the girls, running away with glee.

Miss Rita makes more introductions. "This is Etta, the eldest. This is Jessie, and this is Mae," as she gives each a pat on the shoulder. "And this is Doctor Kenck." Each girl offers her hand and says, "I am pleased to meet you." Miss Rita does the same with Minnie and Susie. The girls are shy except when talking to Miss Rita. "Auntie Rita, we are happy to come to your house." I can see Miss Rita is their idol. "These are my nieces," she explains to me. I'm thinking, wow, I'm surrounded by beautiful women. All my school life has been with boys and men. Suddenly I'm overcome with shyness. The size of Miss Rita's family amazes me. She explains, "And these aren't all. I've got two sisters in New York yet, Mina and Addie, and a half brother, Jay Nellis, near Ft. Shaw. Someday they will all come to visit."

Suddenly, I think about playing the violin in front of all these people. "Miss Rita, I wonder if I really ought to scare everyone with my fiddle. You mean we will play for all these people?"

"Why yes, Doctor, I often play for them. I also give them lessons."

"I'm still worried."

"Oh don't be," she reassures me. "We are all just learning, really." With a chuckle, she totally disarms my fear.

Richard Auchard, with his flowing white beard and dress shirt with suspenders, seems to have a proud chest today. He beams at all his beautiful women, grandchildren, and his daughter, Miss Rita. But, he catches little Henry on one of his sash tricks and sits him down on his knee. Little Henry squirms and leans away from the beard. Grandpa Richard's voice is so low and pleasant that it calms him, and he begins to listen instead of struggling. "Henry, where I come from we built boats because nearby there is a big canal like a giant ditch. I have here a small boat." He reaches for it on the shelf by his chair. "Here, Henry, you hold it. This is exactly like the ones I made in New York, but much smaller. Someday this one will be yours." Henry holds the boat. It fits perfectly in his two hands. He looks at it and then at Grandpa. Hardly anything more than his eyes visible behind that great flowing beard. Grandpa talks on. Henry runs his fingers around the beautifully hand-carved canal boat. Grandpa explains more. "All you need to do is come and see me and let me tell you about building boats and barns." Henry holds it tight while his grandfather talks. "But for now, we will put it back on the shelf." Henry lets go ever so slowly. "My name is Grandpa. You can call me that any time." Then he put Henry down, but now he acts like he would stay, if at all possible, curled up by his grandfather.

About this time the dog barks and another buggy arrives full of family folk. I'm surprised. The driver of this handsome tram is one of my patients, Darwin Ostrom, with his family. Miss Rita introduces them. "This is Emma, my half sister. Her girls are Edna, the oldest, and Maud."

I shake the hand of Darwin. "I certainly didn't expect to see you today."

"Nor did I expect to see my young dentist here. Nice to see you, Doctor." My thoughts: more people to hear my rusty violin playing. I know Miss Rita won't let me off.

The good smell of roasting meat must mean dinner is close. Tables are being set. The girls are counting the places—I hear at least seventeen. Tables are everywhere. The dinner is a feast to remember. Surely they gathered supplies for weeks and even thought of it as they canned their gardens. The goose, they roasted two, Miss Rita tells me. Also, there is roast of beef with Yorkshire pudding. Miss Rita explains, "Yorkshire pudding is an English accompaniment to roast beef, actually a bread baked in the browning juices of the roast. The potatoes, carrots, and squash are from our garden."

This good food makes me almost forget about the violin session coming up. My reasoning tells me if I can get this kind of food, I'll practice more. The dessert is a pudding called Son of a Gun in a Sack. It is made by making a sweet spicy dough with raisins and currants. This ball of dough is placed in the center of a large cloth, and the cloth is pulled together at the top and tied tightly with strong cord. Then this cloth ball of dough is suspended on a stick and lowered into a big kettle of boiling water for three hours. A sweet sauce is made of sugar, butter, and cream and poured over slices that have been warmed. This pudding takes time to make and was cooked up several days ahead of the event.

When we have utterly stuffed ourselves with stuffing and can eat no more, the men gather again in the easy chairs in the sitting room while the ladies chatter on as they take care of the dishes. Before I am ready (I'll never be ready!) they finish and bring their chairs around Miss Rita's piano. They chant like a chorus, "Music! Music! Music!" Miss Rita has a plan. We will not be the first. She plays songs for the girls to sing first. I can tell Grandpa Auchard likes to hear his girls sing and he has some favorite tunes. They gather around Miss Rita at the piano. The first one is *Row, Row, Row Your Boat* and then the popular *Clementine*. Etta Cottle plays a hymn, *Onward Christian Soldiers*, with the girls singing along.

I begin to think maybe they won't need or remember my violin, but Miss Rita finally announces, "I have a nice surprise for you. Dr. Kenck is going to play his violin." The girls scurry to their chairs and smooth their skirts and look excited while I get my violin from behind my chair. Miss Rita at the piano says, "I will accompany the doctor as he plays one of the pieces he played at a recital at Gonzaga College. It is called *Polonaise*." I played it okay. When I finished everyone applauds. "More, more!" they holler. Miss Rita says, "All right, one more then." I think she sees my brow is wet. This we practiced also—*Simple Melody*. I didn't realize that I'd ever be called upon to play those pieces again. I play that one all right. Of course, it could have been better with a little practice!

We finish playing, and after a while the older folks begin to make talk about getting on home. Both families had miles to go, and this time of year darkness comes early. Coats and bonnets are hauled back out of the bedrooms. Will, at the first mention of home, disappeared out the kitchen door heading for the barn to get the teams hitched to the buggies. They are now waiting for the bundled guests. The girls all call their goodbyes to Grandma and Grandpa Auchard. "Goodbye, Auntie Rita, and goodbye, Doctor Kenck."

And, outside, the nieces wave goodbye to their Uncle Will, and he waves back. Will is so quiet that it skips a person's mind he's here at all.

"Come sit down. We can talk awhile, and I'm curious about your life," Miss Rita says, heading for the sitting room. I explain I've had a life of study and work until I came here.

"Now that I'm here I've gone fishing many times and on two hunting trips with some fellows. I'm surprised I made it out of the mountains alive. We took so many chances, like going after silvertip bear. That was especially scary—hanging over snowy ledges and my friends having to grab my legs and pull me back." Mr. Auchard joins us and our conversation.

"Doctor, I overheard you say you have spent most of your short life studying. Seems to me you might be ready to join the men of the Masons and have some good times, because we do certainly enjoy ourselves. Besides, it's a good way to get acquainted."

"Papa," Rita chimes in, "that's a splendid idea." I hadn't thought of joining the Masons, but it did sound interesting. I remembered as a youngster in Helena watching the Masons going about their activities, and it seemed like they had a certain amount of fun.

"Well, it's time for me to go. It's not a long walk but darkness comes quickly. I thank you folks and especially Mrs. Auchard who cooked such a feast."

Mrs. Auchard answers back, "Doctor, we hope you will come again. It's been so nice to have you."

As I walk home through the cold November dusk reveling at such a wonderful Thanksgiving, I'm glad for my mother's knitted wool socks and gloves and also the soft wool scarf. It will soon be December and Christmas is not that far off. My thoughts turn to Mother. She would have liked me to be there for my birthday, but I'll go home for Christmas for sure.

I'm thinking Augusta will be my town. The folks here want me to stick around and are finding their way to my office more and more. Next morning at breakfast at the hotel dining room, Bing comes to my table. (This is the second Bing kid I've come across.) A scarf is tied around his head, and when he speaks his voice is muffled by it. He's the hotel chore boy.

"Mr. Doctor, I have a bad tooth. It hurt all night. Do

you think you could make it better?"

"Sure, Bing, I can make it better. That's my job."

"My job this morning was to milk the cows."

"Did you milk the cows this morning?"

"I did, but my face sure hurts."

"I'll finish the last bite and you come with me up the stairs to my office and we'll fix that tooth."

Bing follows me. I get the scarf off and sit him down in the chair with a towel and open his mouth ever so carefully. "Bing," I say gently, "this tooth is so bad it should be pulled. I can make it really numb and then it won't bother you anymore. You will get another in its place before long." He looks at me with scared eyes, so I hasten to explain it will be out in just a minute or less and will quit hurting. Bing looks sort of resigned, but still scared.

He says, "If we have to, we have to." I tell him I'll make it as numb as I can. Here goes then. He squeezes his eyes shut and grabs the arms of the chair. It's out and he doesn't realize it, so I tell him.

"Bing, you can open your eyes and take a look at that bad tooth."

All he can say is, "Is that it? Is that it?" I tell him he needs to have all his teeth looked at very soon so maybe I can help him from having so much misery. Bing goes on his way still wondering how I got that tooth out without him knowing it. Not long after Bing stumbles down the stairs, who should appear but Tony the carpenter.

"Howdy, Tony. I really thought you'd be too busy to come in. I hear you pounding and sawing from daylight to dark."

"Doc," he says, "I've got a break today, unplanned of course. My finishing lumber for Bill Cook's saloon hasn't got here. I think I'll have to hire a team just for my lumber only. Thought maybe you had a minute to work on this mess in my mouth. Gettin' so I can't chew my vittles very well."

"Of course," I say. "I've got a bit of time right now. I can start, but I'm going to be gone soon, that is until after Christmas. I plan to be at my mother's for the holidays. She hasn't had me home very often. At college, they didn't let us go home for Christmas, and when I was in Chicago at Dental College, it was just too far."

Tony explains, "I been so booked up. Many here want a house. I have enough to keep me busy for two or more years." I tell him we need to get his teeth in good shape so he can work steady. "Yeah, that's right, Doc, but I need a wife to help me, especially with food and my clothes. I'm getting older and I'd sure like a family."

I tell him, "I thought young women were scarce around here until I spent Thanksgiving at the Dave Auchard Ranch just out of town around the river bend. There were eight young ladies there, and the six older ones outnumbered me. Good looking ones too. Anyway, I think there's hope for you around here somewhere. Besides, there is a very nice one in the Manix family. She tells me she will graduate from St. Peters Mission School soon. Step up now and let's get into your mouth and get these teeth fixed. I can see a need for several bridges and crowns. But next Saturday I will be going to Helena and surprise my mother and then stay there until after Christmas. Today, let's pull one that's too far decayed to save. You will wind up with a toothache if I don't, and I might be gone. I'll make a bridge and fill the space."

Tony looks sick. "Gee, Doc. I didn't expect so much misery today."

I show Tony the anesthetic. "Well, I can really deaden it and you won't know the difference except you will be able to stick your tongue through that space."

"Okay, Doc. Let's have at it."

He hardly knows it happened but I tell him, "Tony, take that cotton wad out when you get home. The socket will heal if the blood clot stays in it, and don't rinse it out. I'll be back right after Christmas and we will make the bridge to fill the space."

"Okay, Doc!"

Tony's steps go down the stairs and now I can plan my trip home. First, a list of things to buy in Helena, a mental list of people I want to see—Doctor Frary and Bill Frank for certain. Before I get very far in my packing, I hear quick small steps outside. What a surprise. "Miss Rita! Nice to see you. I've thought about the wonderful feast at your house and I'm amazed there are so many young ladies in this area."

"Yes, Doctor, it does seem rather one-sided." I explain again that having gone to boys' schools and male colleges all my life, I like knowing there are a few pretty ladies around here. There it is again, that low-voiced chuckle.

"Doctor, if that is disguised flattery, I choose to ignore it. We ladies work hard to be pretty. What I came about is Mother. She needs new dentures and I would like to make an appointment for her."

"Miss Rita, I'm leaving for Helena. I thought my mother would like me to come and stay until after Christmas. I'll see my brother Albert and Uncles Chris and Jacob. Also, the new capitol building was just completed. I hear Charlie Russell painted a big picture of Lewis and Clark, and Paxton the artist is going to have something installed as well. After I come back we can set up an appointment."

"Doctor, I'll stop by when you get back. I hope the stage will have no trouble when you go and return. Have a good trip."

"Thanks, Miss Rita, and you folks have a nice Christmas. I know you will eat well, as your feast was delicious. Take care." My thoughts go back to the feast and all the folks I met at the Auchards.

Come Friday morning, I'm all packed for a short stay in Helena. Winter hasn't blitzed us yet, but I'll beware. Could be any time now. In less than ten minutes, Dick Adams will bring his coach by the hotel. Here it is!

CHAPTER 8

HOME FOR A KENCK FAMILY CHRISTMAS IN HELENA

"Hey, it's you, Kenck! Good, you got your horsehide on, 'cause it looks like snow." Dick cracks his whip over the teams and we're off. Dick yells down to me, "Gotta pick up a passenger just outta town." I wonder who, but realize at the pace the horses are running we would see whom right soon. We are up the road to the turn and then across the Auchard bridge. Why yes, there's a lantern swinging in the gray dawn. Someone from the Auchard place is taking the stage. To my surprise, as we pull to a stop, I see Miss Rita there bundled up in traveling clothes and luggage, standing next to Richard at the pole gate. I jump down to help with the bags and give her an arm to climb in.

"Miss Rita, you didn't say a word about your going to Helena yesterday."

She chuckles. "Doctor, I didn't really know myself until yesterday afternoon when Papa and I decided I should go shop for Christmas in town. He will come at the end of next week to help me home."

"Here, let me put this robe over you. It's going to be cold, much colder before we get to Craig. Here, put your feet on this hot brick foot warmer."

Almost before we are settled again, Dick does not spare the horses because away we fly. He knows he'll get fresh ones at the Half Way House. Snow begins falling but doesn't stick yet. By noon we are pulling in to the Half Way House. Dick and his helper are quick to get the horses unhooked and into the stable.

Another four-horse team is already harnessed and waiting. While that is going on, we are given a bowl of hot soup and coffee. We see the driver who is going from Half Way House to Craig actually has eight fresh horses hitched and ready to go in a very few minutes. We pile back into the coach and are off again. Miss Rita and I cover up with the buffalo robes again and put our feet near the refueled foot warmer. The hot soup and coffee give us warmth and we feel sleepy-headed. I think ahead about what else to do in Helena. I have a great idea.

"Miss Rita, do you go to the Opera House in Helena?"

"Do you mean the Ming Opera House? I certainly do, every chance I get. The opera folks in Helena put on some good plays and musicals."

I feel kind of brave. "Do you suppose we could go together some night this week?"

"Of course," she chuckles. "We certainly can."

"Are you staying at The Harvey?"

"Why yes, that's where I stay."

The rest of the journey to Craig we talk about bygone school days.

"At Gonzaga we did plays like Shakespeare's *King John.*"

"Did you play a part in *King John?*"

"Yes, I was Lord Pembroke. Can you imagine?"

"Of course. I bet you were a good Pembroke, although I am not familiar with that play."

"Learning the lines was a real job. The Old English is difficult. We did *Julius Caesar,* but in that I was just a conspirator, not many lines to learn. The part we men liked was when one of us had to dress up like a lady. It was hilarious. We could hardly keep from giggling."

"I know about boys and giggling," says Rita. "They have problems with that. When I'm teaching and the boys get started on that, I just about have to allow a recess."

Snow is piling up on our robes, but the steady running of the horses helps to get rid of some in the wind. Soon we reach the Craig Railway Station where we see our baggage piled on the express cart, and all we have to do to escape the swirling snow is step up on the conductor's stool and into the warm train coach. Before long, all the baggage and express freight is loaded and "All Aboard" is called. Now we appreciate the coming of the railroad. Only two comfortable hours to

Helena now. Our continuing conversation keeps us from getting sleepy and the time passes before we know it. There are the lights of Helena!

Carriages are waiting at the depot, and I promise to get in touch tomorrow. I buy a paper from the newsboy so I can see what's going on in town, especially what is showing at the Opera House. I know it will be a busy schedule for me. My list is so long, but I plan to go with Miss Rita to the opera at least one night this week. Before she leaves in a carriage, I discuss a possible schedule with her. "Miss Rita, may I stop by at the hotel around noon tomorrow?"

"Yes, Doctor, that would be fine. I will be ready around noon." She takes a carriage and leaves. The newspaper, *The Independent*, lists the current show at the Ming as a musical of Johann Strauss waltzes. It's getting late but Mama will be happy to see me.

I take a waiting carriage to my old house and find there are still lights on inside. I clamber inside with my bags calling out, "Mama? I'm here!" My German is more than a little rusty.

"Oh, Oscar! Is it really you? I've missed you so."

Many questions we fire back and forth. Albert is there and had gone to bed but comes out in his robe. "Oakie! At last you've decided to visit home."

"Yes, yes, I've got lots to tell you and we can talk in the morning."

In the morning, over Mama's good breakfast sausage we talk.

"Albert, what's my kid brother up to?"

"So good to see you, Oakie. Uncle Chris keeps me busy. The Kencks of Helena are doers. Hotels, saloons, and breweries, along with the houses that need attention. How long will you be staying, Oakie?"

"Until after Christmas. Maybe I can help Mama with her house. And I've got some ideas I want to talk with you about."

"Well, shoot. Sometimes your ideas are okay."

"You might be interested and you might not. I've been thinking I'd like a place, some land near the mountains, for fishponds and some cattle. But since I have the dental business started, I can't just up and become a rancher or a homesteader. Would you be interested in going at it with me? I will furnish the money and we can work this out together."

"Oakie, that sure sounds interesting since I'm not quite yet prepared for a profession. This could be a profitable way for me. Just what would I be doing in the beginning stages of this project?"

"The first thing is to find the right property. We could buy a homestead like so many are doing. When spring comes, you start looking around. Mike Reinig's folks I know have found places on the Dearborn River, and there's a canyon on that river that comes out of the mountains." I can tell Albert is game and the wheels are beginning to turn in his head.

"Sounds like something I'd like to do. Let's plan on it, Oakie." We laugh and give a handshake on the deal.

"Albert, I need to find Mike Reinig today. Know where he is now?"

"Yeah, he was here with groceries for Mama yesterday, and he's got a new house."

"Where?"

"Corner of Rodney and Breckenridge. He's got gas jets and a telephone. The fifty-first telephone in town, just three rings, according to Mike."

"Good, I'll find him this morning. I've got to meet a lady around noon."

"Wow, Oakie, a lady?!"

"Albert, don't you think it's about time? I'll not answer that. Anyway, I always find beautiful ladies."

All caught up on family business and time to get going. First I head for Mike Reinig's new house. I'm in luck. As I walk up to his door, he's coming out. He reaches for my hand.

"Oscar, the Kenck kid. You are in town again. When you left with that wagon contraption, I thought I'd never see you again." Good old Mike sure looks after my mother's needs. Brings her grocery orders and all the town news.

"I have come to spend the holidays with Mama and see what the government is doing."

"Great, great, and how is Augusta and your end of the county?"

"Augusta is vibrating with the sounds of saws and hammers, daylight to dark. All the buildings that burned in last April's fire are being rebuilt, Mr. Reinig." (We boys were taught to call all the Helena business men "Mr.," but even though I'm old enough and know him well, I can't call him "Mike.")

"I want to ask you about joining the Masons. I've gotten a suggestion from Richard Auchard in Augusta."

"Oscar, you've been raised a Catholic, but that makes no difference to the Masons. Their measure is your character, that you are an honorable man."

"The Catholic part is no problem for me, Mr. Reinig. I've made up my mind to separate somewhat from that. I can't tell you why exactly, but that's my position."

"Absolutely. It would be wise to join if you have the chance. We Masons do many good projects for our community. Besides, we have an active and interesting social life. You would get to know the most important people in your community."

"Mr. Reinig, I've known you ever since I was a little kid, and you always know what you are talking about. And all these years since my father was killed, you've been such a help to my mother with her groceries and advice in the business that Father left her." I shake his hand again. I see he's in a hurry, the pencil behind his ear comes down to write a note on his list pad, probably remembered the grocery order of some widow. Mike used to have a nicely trimmed black beard and hair, but I see the beard is gray and the hair is white at the temples.

"Before I go, I want to ask you about my brother Albert. I worry about him."

"I see him around town. I think his Uncles Chris and Jacob keep track of him."

"Yeah, I know, but saloons are not the best thing for him. I'm thinking of getting some land near the mountains, and maybe he will help me with that project. I see it's getting late. We'll talk again."

"Yes, Oscar, we'll talk again. I understand what you mean."

Next, I walk towards Main and get to Frary's office.

"Well, well! Welcome back! How's the traveling dentist business? I miss you, Oakie. There was always stuff going on when you were here. Besides that, I could go fishing once in a while when you took care of my patients. Do you get out to fish down Augusta way?"

"Fishing around there is pretty good, but I found out when I was back in the mountains last month on a hunting trip that there are no fish in the streams above the falls of Sun River."

"How come?"

"The falls are just too high for the fish to get up there. Somehow, fish should be planted back there, like crops. I keep thinking about how that could be done. Do you have any idea where I could find Bill Frank?"

"Yeah, I think I saw him working for Holter in the hardware store."

After I buy some supplies off of Frary, I head for Holter's Hardware. Sure thing, I find him there.

"Oakie! What are you doing in town? I thought you'd be so busy making false teeth and money that you'd never find time to come to town."

"Oh yes, I can find time when I need to take care of business. So, you got an inside job, eh?"

"Yeah, it's not bad at all, and I don't have to drive a couple nags across the roadless prairies. Ha!"

I have a pretty good visit with Bill, and I can see he needs an inside job for a while. That typhoid was hard on him. Next, on to the hotel to meet Miss Auchard and make plans to go to the theater tonight. I get to the hotel just as she is coming in. I'm thinking she looks so nice in her fur-trimmed hat and coat, just like a lady of the town.

"Miss Rita, did you see what's going on at Ming's?"

"Yes, yes I did. Johann Strauss' waltzes. How could we be so lucky? We'll love it."

"Did you shop already?"

"Yes, and I've got to do some more. I can imagine Papa will get anxious and maybe come sooner than he said, so I must get it all done today and tomorrow."

"We need to go a little early to the theater tonight. How about me coming by at seven so we can get a good seat?"

"Yes, yes, Doctor. I'll be ready."

So, I leave her to shopping and look at my lists and think about the treat in store for tonight. I am beginning to realize how much I've been missing music. The afternoon goes by quickly and in no time I am back at The Harvey, ready to take Miss Rita to the Opera House.

The music of Strauss is wonderful. We are spellbound. It ends too soon, and both of us are speechless for a while. We decide to walk around downtown. The gaslights are on. It is cold but we are warm in our coats, and the music is still vibrating through our heads. Finally, I say, "Miss Rita, we must plan to come to Helena again and go to another musical."

"Yes, Doctor, that is a good idea. In the spring, let's watch the Helena paper and plan another coincidence like this."

"Rita, call me Oscar, not Doctor. We are friends. We don't need to be so formal."

"All right," she giggles. "Oscar and Rita it shall be." We walk back to the hotel.

I say, "Let's have a cup of hot chocolate in the café." We talk about music. I tell her good night in the lobby and also that I'd stop by every day until she leaves for home.

"Good night, Oscar. Yes, stop by tomorrow."

The Christmas of 1901 with the Kencks in Helena is one to remember. Mama is smiling and laughing while she is busy in her kitchen. She greets me each morning with German phrases I had almost forgotten, while the aroma from her cooking is a hunger maker. She's on a baking spree using all the happy recipes she carries in her head. The fancy bread called *bobka* is Polish, but she claims they got it from Germany. She rolls out cookie dough to make triangles called *grebels* and gives them a twist before she fries them in the fat. All this baking goes on daytimes, after unforgettable breakfasts—like German sausage, *prutels*, browned and served with hot cakes and syrup. I would get as round as Uncle Jacob if I stayed long.

Yeah, and speaking of fat, you should see the goose. I find Mama with her coat on, sitting on a stool in the backyard. She has a big white goose in a pen close beside her.

I say, "Mama, what are you doing, keeping the goose company?"

"Na, na, Oscar, I feed the goose so it be fat for roasting for Christmas dinner."

"What do you mean? Won't the goose eat by itself?"

"No, no, no, Oscar. I stuff the food down its throat, and then I hold the beak together so he has to swallow. He gets fat and fatter. That's the way in the old country to make big goose for feasts. Then I keep him in pen so he not run off the fat."

The feast of our German Christmas is at Uncle Chris's house. The tree that Albert and I got up on the mountain stands in the big living room with little sparkling angels, bells, and figurines of shining glass from Germany. The organ, the piano, and the violins are at the ready. Tall, handsome Uncle Chris, in a suit, vest, and tie, welcomes all the Kenck folk and their friends. There's been no celebration like this since my father Charles was killed by Indians at Yellowstone Park twenty-four years ago. Uncle Jacob, the jolly brewer, not to be outdone, sports a new vest that actually buttons around his great circumference. With a twinkle in his deep-set eyes under bushy eyebrows, he moves about among the guests with witty remarks, offering the best of the Kenck brewery.

Now at the feast table, Uncle Chris makes the toast, in German, of course. "To the Kencks and our friends." Then, Uncle Jacob offers a toast to the goose. "Now, folks, here's to the goose that Leah stuffed and stuffed, and now we will stuff ourselves with the goose that was stuffed." I'm amazed at my Kenck family. I hadn't paid much attention to their qualities during my busy school years. Now I'm beginning to think of my father being one of them.

After the goose with oyster stuffing and at least seven vegetable courses, it's time for a music course. Uncle Jacob makes sure the steins are filled. He and Uncle Chris pick up their violins and Mama goes quickly to the organ. Now the singing of German-language carols vibrate through the house. This is wonderful. There's music in this family. It is no wonder I enjoy music so much. It's in my blood.

The singing goes on as long as anyone can name a song they know. The table is cleared of dinner plates and replaced with dessert plates. Now is served the two favorite desserts of this German family—*Black Forest Cherry Torte* and *Mumbe Teig*, a rich apple pie. And, the stories of the times before this family came to America are being told. This I do enjoy because the name of my father is often mentioned.

After days of visiting and feasting, I must get back to Augusta and take care of my patients. I tell Albert to come to Augusta when the weather breaks. He agrees. Mama keeps wiping at tears. "Mama, I'll be back in the spring for a visit to make sure Albert keeps his promise." Goodbyes are hard on mothers.

CHAPTER 9

THE FISHING DENTIST & THE FINGERLING PROJECT

Riding the train towards Craig, I listen to the clickety-clack of steel on rails. I am glad to be heading back to my own corner of the world. I begin to think of ways to solve the fish problem in the headwaters of Sun River. Just how could a person get fingerlings and get them back to Wood Lake and the South Fork of the North Fork of the Sun River?

A spell of sleep overtakes me, and I jump to attention as the conductor yells, "All those off-loading at Craig, please have your bags ready." Sure enough, Dick Adams is waiting at the station for the U.S. Mail, and I'm quick to stash my gear on his stage and stand ready for the "Let's go!" It's cold but Dick is prepared for that. There are three of us headed that way. Dick says,

"Kenck, I've been lookin' for you every time I meet this train, hopin' you'll get tired of foolin' around in Helena and get yourself back where you belong."

"Dick, I never gave that a thought. Didn't know anyone would miss me unless they had a toothache." We are off with the crack of a whip and a hoot and holler. He always gives a yell like that. He wants to excite the horses, I guess.

The fish project keeps nagging at my mind. Where to get fingerlings? How to get them back in those mountains? Looks difficult, if not impossible, but I keep talking to anyone who will listen. Some say it really is impossible. Yet I will not let it go. In my mind, I see those beautiful streams and lakes just waiting for fish.

One day, Judge Mayer comes in with a bad tooth. Sure thing I have to pull it. While I'm waiting for the anesthetic to work, I ask, "Are you a fisherman?"

"What? Am I a fisherman! That's really what I am, Doc. Being a judge and a rancher on the side just supports my fishing habit. Why do you ask?"

I explained, "When I was back at the place called the Benchmark area during my fall hunting trip, I looked at those streams and was stunned to find no fish. Not one."

"Yeah, I know," says the judge. "There's not a damn fish in all that back country and I suppose you also found out why?"

"Yeah, I did. Ranger Todd told me the situation. He also says he wished some ambitious guys would get a project going to put fingerlings in those streams."

"That's a pretty big order. Most of us fishermen have cattle to take care of and fences to mend." He feels his face getting numb now and tingly. We concentrate on getting the angry tooth out.

"One thing," I tell him. "Maybe it would be a good idea to get your teeth taken care of so you won't have to have them all pulled, or at the very least, avoid having a bad one when you want to go fishing."

"Kenck, okay, I'll come back. You give me a day and time and I'll get here. And yeah, we can talk more about this fish idea of yours. Maybe come up with something."

By the time Judge Mayer and I have some more talks and tell others, we find two more who are willing to work on this project. First thing is to find the fingerlings. Ranger Todd tells me he knows there's a hatchery in Bozeman that might supply them. I write to them. The answer is yes. They can sell us some fingerlings if we are ready to take them when they are ready to travel. Their reply letter also has some information on transportation of the small fry. It says they ship in barrels that are equipped with air pumps. They also ask how many we would like to handle. Judge Mayer and I go over this information carefully. Ranger Todd says the Forest Service can help with packhorses.

There is no road past the Ford Creek place. We will have to figure out how to put them on packhorses. I think of Jumbo, the giant bucking packhorse of our hunting trip last fall, and I shudder. Sherman, a rancher who lives in Flat Creek, is getting interested in helping. "I'll help if I can. It sounds impossible, but who knows. Lots of impossible things become possible."

Finally, after several ideas of how to contain and transport fish fry on packhorses, we order 50,000 fingerlings. Tony comes one day for his appointment. I tell him about the 50,000 fry we plan to receive off the train at Craig and get them up to the mountains alive. Tony says with wide eyes, "Kenck, what are you getting into? I'm really worried about you now." He keeps shaking his head.

"I happen to know. I'm thinking of all the times I expect to be going back in these mountains and how I'll take my rod and catch a few and cook them for my supper."

The weeks fly by and no message from the hatchery. They said they'd let us know about when to expect them. We go right to work and get twenty-four five-gallon oil cans, remove any residual oil, cut the bottoms out, and solder pairs together to make one long can. These cans, with screened openings at the top of each can, will allow the fry to be safely transported and let necessary air circulate as well. We think they will be just about right to pack two horizontally on each horse. The cans will be only partially filled and will slosh our babies around and circulate some air as we travel. The can openings will be on the topside with copper screens to cover them. These are all ready at Judge Mayer's place. We know from their information sheet it will be fall before they can ship.

The news of our fish project gets circulated around the country, so I'm getting a reputation as The Fishing Dentist. Yes, fishing I do this summer as the project is waiting, but it's making me more anxious.

It's late May 1902, and along comes a letter in the mail with that marvelous handwriting of Albert's. He writes, "I will come down next week if you still want me."

So, I fire back a note telling him, "That's just great, come on down." So, I'm watching every day as the stage comes rattling by. I know Dick Adams will let him off right here at the hotel. Also, I check my appointments and it appears good for spending a day looking for land.

Since my Helena visit, I've inquired of patients who live out toward the mountains about land. I hear there's a whole family of Beans who have settled near the Dearborn River. Might be a good idea to contact them somehow.

CHAPTER 10

DISCOVERING DEARBORN CANYON

Sure enough, in two days, as I'm listening to hear the six o'clock stage go by, I hear the sounds of a "stopping" stage. I quickly hurry down the steps and out. Sure enough, there is Albert grabbing his bags from Dick, so I yell, "Thanks, Dick, for bringing my kid brother!"

"Oakie," Albert says, "this place is sorta different from Helena, but I'm sure you've made it come alive."

"Come on, you're starved, and we can eat right here at the hotel." All evening we discuss all the news of Helena. I've really picked up on family activities since spending time there at Christmas. I rent a rig for tomorrow. We are going to look at the Dearborn River country near the mountains. I tell him, "There's a fam-ily by the name of Bean who have settled out that way, around a lake. Of course, now called 'Bean Lake.'"

In the morning, it's Saturday, we are up and full of breakfast with sandwiches packed by the cook. As we go west, I show Albert that spectacular mountain that guards this whole corner of land and calls all who have gone away to come back.

"What's it called?"

"Would you believe such an unusual mountain has a name that's utterly beneath its majestic stance? 'Haystack Butte.' But the Indians had a name that at least sounds mysterious, Shishequa. To them it means Big Head. See the profile there on the morning-sun side?"

"Yeah, I sure do. That's quite a landmark, and are

we going very close to that sunny side today?"

"Yes, that's just about right. We probably will be to the left of it today."

"Hey," I say, "before we get to the turn-off, we are going into Richard Auchard's place for a bit. I want to introduce you to him and Miss Rita. Remember my date you were curious about when I was in Helena last December? Richard Auchard is her father and that's her home. She teaches in that log school right there as we turn."

Mr. Auchard comes out as we drive up. Soon Miss Rita comes and stands like a little girl alongside of him.

"Miss Rita and Mr. Auchard, this is my brother Albert. We are out for an excursion up to the Dearborn Canyon area. I want to take a look to see if I'd like to put a cabin there. You notice how well I like to hunt and fish. So, today we will look. Also, Mr. Auchard, I've been considering that suggestion you made last fall about the lodge and I'm definitely interested. Perhaps we can get together and go over the procedure."

"Young man," he quickly grabbed my hand, "you will not be sorry, I assure you. Also, neither will the lodge. We need young men like you to carry on the good work."

I ask him for specific road directions, and then we are off and back on the road past the schoolhouse and headed toward the mountains once again.

Albert seems pleased with the sweep of the country. He exclaims, "Oakie, we can see the whole Rocky Mountain Front!" We meet a few wagons on the road, evidently on their way for Saturday errands. All give us a friendly wave. I'm thinking someday I hope to know everyone who lives along this country road.

We finally see the lake I've heard about. There's a house in a small meadow. As we get closer, we see a corral with horses. It appears the horses are moving. Someone is working with them. As we pass by, he waves so we stop. Yes, he is Ole Bean. I'd heard he is good with horses. Some say he can break the wildest kind to a dog-like nature. He comes over, and with a friendly handshake takes time to talk with us.

"I'm Kenck, the new dentist in Augusta. This is my brother Albert from Helena."

"Yeah, I've heard about you. One of my brothers,

Earnest, has been to see you. There's a whole kettle-full of us Beans. Five brothers and two sisters. Our dad moved from Massachusetts to Minnesota where he named a lake Bean Lake, and then to Montana, and now this lake is also Bean Lake. Our dad and us kids homesteaded some of our land and bought land alongside from the Bertch brothers. They still own land in the canyon up river." Ole points towards the gap in the mountains there. So, I'm quick to ask, "Do you know of land near the river for sale?"

Ole's ruddy, Scots-looking face breaks into a knowing kind of smile. "Well, if you could locate a Mr. Fisher, he has a claim along the river. Built a couple of cabins even, but I haven't seen him this year yet. Then there's the Bertch brothers, so very odd. They built several cabins and move from one to another. I think when one cabin gets full of newspapers and magazines, they move to another. Strange though. No one can figure them out. Maybe you could find out about the Fisher fellow at the land office in Helena. He might sell. The cabins look livable from the outside. His land runs along the river, or, anyway, it used to."

All this information is really grabbing my imagination.

"Does the wagon trail go up the canyon a ways? (I'm trying not to sound too eager.) I'd like to take a look."

"Oh yeah, the wagon tracks go along two or three miles after you cross that ditch over there," he points. "Every spring we put our cattle back up that way. Others put their cattle up on the Forest Reserve. Moshers put herders with sheep back on the Reserve. About once a month, their camp tenders make a trip in."

"Albert, I think we should take a look. It's still early. We'll get back to the road here in a few hours."

"I'm game, Oakie. We came to look, so let's 'git.'"

Ole tells us to watch out for mountain lions. He'd heard of one along the canyon. I think he is about to give us a story. I know we look like a couple of green horns.

My mind cannot believe what my eyes are seeing. The trail runs along the river, so we tie the horses and walk along the edge. I must be having a dream! I've never seen so many fish in a mountain stream. We both are speechless for a while. "Can this be true?" I finally say to Albert. I had packed my pole just in case we wanted to test the Dearborn River for fish. The instant the fly hit the water it was grabbed, and a good-sized grab too. We both held our breath and WOW. We've come to see just what is here so refrain from more fishing and go on up the river a ways, gawking at the surrounding hills.

Two buttes stand out, probably are called "twins." Then we look at the ranges and ranges of mountains. The nearer one looks like a giant steamboat. Back of that we see more and more. Close by we see a cabin, but no one around. This whole canyon with surrounding mountains is just the kind of country I dream about. I restrain myself as I think of the process to get title. Who owns it? Can we find them? Will they sell it? All these questions have to be resolved.

We walk back to our rig.

"Look, Albert, how the river has made other channels. I see ponds for raising fish."

"Oakie, you do dream. Go right ahead. It might come true."

"Ole and the Bean brothers have put fish in their lake. It might just happen."

By the time we thread our way along the riverbank and jump a few branches across the trail, we are sold in our minds on this location for our ranch. We hitch our team back to the rig and start back down the bumpy road. Soon we are past Ole Bean's and on towards town. I catch myself dreaming, and then I say to myself, you have a lot to find out about this land. There is legal work and negative possibilities.

As we go the sun is now showing up the other side of old Haystack Butte, so we urge the team to a faster pace.

"Albert, how about you going back to Helena to the land office to see who owns the property along the river besides Fisher and the Bertch Brothers?"

"Sure, I could do that. I'm kind of familiar with county offices. I've done manuscript work for several."

"Another thing we need to talk about and settle is, since we are both in this together, shall we use some of the money our father left us?"

"I don't see why not, Oakie. If we sell it between us,

we could agree that the original purchase price would stand. Also, on improvements we can keep records and divide the cost, or say if you build a house, hire me to help build it. For me, I'd just like a cabin."

"Okay, Albert, maybe we are crossing bridges or building houses ahead of time but no harm in having understandings. Main thing is finding suitable property. In this case, finding the owners and location of the acreage." A few days later we come to definite agreements as to what Albert should do and how. He heads back to Helena to do his part.

CHAPTER 11

THE VOTE AND A FINGERLING NOTE

Richard Auchard stops by my office with news. "Doctor, I've come by to tell you your petition to join is going to be voted on at our meeting tomorrow night. I'm sure you don't need to worry but all petitions are handled the same way." I'm thinking that's one way to know if I'm accepted in the community. The next day passes with patients. Tony comes in for his appointment. He tells me that he has met the young lady I told him of in the Manix family. "But," he says, "she is so young and pretty she may not even consider me."

"Tony, you are a good worker and can provide all the things she might need in life. Don't sell yourself short."

"Okay, Doc. I'll not give up before I'll let her turn me down."

Busy day and it's a good thing too. After supper, the idea comes to call on Rita to pass a long evening. As I approach, I can hear her and Mrs. Auchard in the kitchen. I knock and Rita comes to the door, with dishtowel in hand, smiles and says, "Somehow I knew it would be you. We all know this is the voting night. Come right in."

Mrs. Auchard looks up from her dishpan. "Dr. Kenck, you have no need to be anxious. Rita and I and Richard too are confident that you will be accepted." I'm thinking she has that low New York chuckle, just like Rita.

"I thank you, Mrs. Auchard, for your assurance." I turn and ask Rita, "Just what is this election business like? Do they just say, 'All in favor of admitting Oscar Kenck please raise your hand?'"

She chuckles at my elementary question. I must be naive.

"No, no, Doctor, it's not that open. The ballot is very secret. If the vote is not unanimous, no one will ever know who votes 'no.'"

"That sounds tough."

"Have they ever rejected a candidate?"

"Oh yes, they have, but even that is seldom discussed after the rejection vote. It is not at all wise." I do not press the subject further, for I can see they take this very seriously.

Mr. Auchard is back and gets out of the rig and comes in. Like always, Will takes the team and buggy to the barn. The verdict is written in the smile crinkles around Mr. Auchard's eyes as he comes in the door and he sees I'm here waiting. I kind of think he expected me to be here. He reaches for my hand and in that low voice, "Well, Doctor, I'm the first to welcome you as a fellow Mason." The smiles are all around.

Mrs. Auchard gives me a pat on the arm with, "Just like I thought. Now they have a good one in the lodge for sure!"

Rita is not saying much, just a contented smile. With this show of approval, I get the feeling this is my town, and these people are beginning to feel like family. I felt like the whole community had put the stamp of approval right on my forehead. With this good feeling I walk back down the road in the brightest moonlight I'd ever noticed.

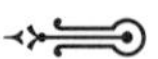

With membership in the Masons taken care of, I can turn my thoughts to my other big project. I should have heard from the hatchery as to when the fingerlings will be shipped.

Judge Mayer comes by the very next day. "Kenck, what do you hear about our fish? Do you think they really are going to send them?"

"Yeah, we should have heard something by now." I'll send off a note to the hatchery, asking for a report on the fingerlings we are waiting for.

A week goes by. At last a note! "Your fingerlings are hatching out nicely and should be just ready when the weather turns cold. By then they'll be a good size. Expect our note about the last week of October."

The Judge checks back. I show him the note. He says, "Yeah, I know it should be cool weather to ship them. Warm water will kill them."

I tell him about looking in the Dearborn Canyon and seeing fish in the river. He says, "You bet there is good fishing at Bean Lake. Those Beans stock their lake and every once in awhile a big one is caught there."

"Judge, I'll let you know the minute I get the message: Fingerlings are on the way."

My mind keeps going back to the Dearborn. It's July 1902. It's warm weather and I ought to take another drive up there. And oh, maybe Rita would like to come along. Also, a letter comes from Albert. He has found an address for the Fisher person and is tracing him. Besides he's also learning what properties are owned by others near the Canyon. He tells that David Auchard owns property along the lower Dearborn. Must be the brother of Richard Auchard.

Rita will know. It's Friday evening. I walk out to Auchards. As I open the pole gate, I see Rita in the glider swing.

"Hello, Oscar, nice to see you. Come sit with me."

"Rita, I have some questions as usual. Who is David Auchard?"

"He's my uncle, my father's brother. Yes, I see why you want to find out about him. His ranch is on the lower Dearborn, closer to the Missouri. I've been to his home."

"Just a minute, Rita, before you tell me any more about him. I want to see the Canyon and river again, and I've got an idea. Would you go with me, maybe tomorrow, up to Dearborn Canyon?"

"I don't see why not. I haven't been up there in a long time. I usually visit Uncle David's, but by way of the stage to Craig, and he meets me there. Shall we go early and take a lunch? I'll fix a basket for the two of us. I'll tell you about Uncle David tomorrow."

"Say, that's a great idea. I'll come by as soon after 8:30 as I can."

"I'll tell Papa and Mama tonight that we are going to take a buggy and look at the Canyon tomorrow."

I realize as I walk back to the hotel that going to the mountains is getting me excited. What is this that mountains do to me?

CHAPTER 12

RITA AND I LOOK AT DEARBORN CANYON

At 8:30 the next morning I walk down the lane from the pole gate. I see Will is bringing Rita's buggy up from the barn. Rita is ready with hat and interesting picnic basket. Mr. and Mrs. Auchard smile and tell us to be careful and stay on the traveled track.

Off we go. A turn to the left after the gate and then again at the crossroads. She points, "There is my school house. Many children at times, and many absent in stormy weather." We turn towards old Mt. Shishequa, the guardian of these hills, and that entire look must ponder that magnetic pull.

On the way, Rita tells of Uncle David Auchard and wife Agnes. "He came west first and then sent letters back. 'Good ranch land, thousands of acres of open grassland, and lots of water. Come on out, Richard.' It was plain to see Uncle David wanted help. Father came and they built an extraordinary and practical barn. Rock is the first story, and logs and lumber make up the second story with a huge loft above for hay and feed. Below is big enough to shelter calving cows. Their main house is large and full of fine furniture.

"They have no children. I've visited, but it is sorta lonely. No one my age and David is in his 60's, a very senior couple. He belongs to the Helena Masons and goes to their meetings. When he first came to the Dearborn about 1874, there were no fences, and he could run his horses and cattle anywhere. At that time the neighbors called him Kindly Uncle Dave, he told me. But, when homesteaders came and started fencing around him, he had to fence miles and miles to keep them off his 30,000-plus acres, and he became bitter, and of course, unpopular. I think now he is not very well. I haven't seen him for a while."

The Dearborn River is down from when Albert and I had seen it before. Rita tells me Ole has said before that they plant fish in their lake. We go up the wagon trail and over the ditch bridge. The Canyon where we see it looks better than ever. Rita and I tramp around and look at the cabins that had been built by Mr. Fisher. We also see the Bertch fellows working around one of their cabins. We are a little reluctant to talk with them, remembering what Ole Bean said.

We set out the lunch by the river. I say, "Where do you think we should build a house?" My face gets flushed when I realize what I've said. I think maybe— no, of course. We had never thought of such—we—a house? Rita sees my flush and giggles, but of course I change the subject.

"The river is full of fish. There very well could be a fish hatchery on this very place. I sure hope Albert is successful finding and making a deal to buy this property."

"Oscar, I'm thinking it will happen and you shall have this place for your hatchery."

"Rita, you encourage me. I feel so much like I belong to these mountains and that life is just beginning for me."

We gather our lunch basket and hitch up the horses, and, slowly at first, because I remember what Ole said about a mountain lion around here, make our way down the wagon track towards town. A perfect day, but there are probably plenty of obstacles just waiting to happen. But I can't worry about them right now.

CHAPTER 13

ORGANIZING A BAND

Monday, Bud Tomlinson stops by to make an appointment, but most of all to tell me he really means it about starting a band.

"Kenck, I need you for the bass section. Could you play a tuba?"

"I can learn. I did cornet in grade school."

"Kenck, that's it. You are counted. I've got a tuba that I brought over from our Massachusetts store. Also, what about Rita? She might be willing to play an alto sax or what?"

"Only way to find out is to ask her. Guess I could do that."

"Will you see her soon?"

"I could. No problem. I see her once in awhile."

"Thanks, I know you have several irons in the fire, as they say here in the West, like your fish project. Besides, you work every day here in your office. What's this I hear about you looking for land near the mountains?"

"Yeah, my brother Albert and I are looking. I want a place where I can have a fish hatchery."

"Have you got any possibilities?"

"Well, sorta. We, Albert and I, took a look at the Dearborn Canyon area. We talked to Ole Bean and he told us that a man named Fisher had taken out a claim and had built a cabin there, so now Albert went to the land office to see if we can find this fellow."

"Well, good luck. Gotta get back to the store. We

got a load off the freight wagon today. See ya later."

A band! I hadn't thought of that since we talked last fall. I guess he really means to organize a band. That evening I find myself walking towards Shishequa Mountain. The sun is setting and the mountain looks iridescent. At the corner, I turn towards the Auchard place. Seems I'm doing this pretty regular lately. This time I have an errand, the message from Bud. I walk down the lane from the gate and find Rita sitting out on the garden glider all alone.

"Rita, what are you doing sitting in the swing chair by yourself?"

"Come sit with me. I've been here learning my new ritual for the Star meeting next week."

"You are really serious about the ritual?"

"Yes. If a person takes an office in the lodge, he, or she in my case, should do the very best she can." I sit down opposite her and the motion moved the swing chair. "This is nice. Not to change the subject, but Bud was in the office today and asked me to see if you would consider playing an instrument in his band. Would you?"

"What instrument is he thinking of? I hope not a drum or trombone or trumpet."

"Oh, none of those. Maybe a reed. He didn't really say."

"I could learn to play an alto sax. He must be really serious about his band. And I know he has an extra alto sax from his store as well as other instruments."

"Yes, music means a lot to the whole Tomlinson family. When their new home is finished soon, he says, we will meet there as a group. A guy can get busy and busier—with fish coming from the hatchery this fall and Albert and I looking for land near the Dearborn. Of course, my practice is growing every day with new patients, and now the band! Since last fall when we practiced, I realize music is important, so I will be in Bud's band."

"I'm glad you feel that way. Life would be pretty drab without music."

"Where do you think we will practice? You know much more about places than I do, but I'll make a guess. Odd Fellows Hall that Tony Pings has just finished."

"Oscar, if I know Bud, we will be practicing for a

Christmas concert before long. Yes, we need a sheltered place to learn our parts." I wonder. Will Bud be able to get enough people for a band? I'm always looking for recruits.

Soon, Joe Bush, or rather Treffle Bergeron, comes in to my office. He's got a toothache.

"Hello, Mr. Constable. I see your badge. You are the law around here?"

"Doctor, I guess that is the word for the law. Between Gus Buckholz as Justice of the Peace and me, we are the law here. If it's a murder, I gotta take the guilty one to Helena, but otherwise we take care of it. We have a jail too, such as it is."

"Mr. Bergeron, come sit in my chair and let's have a look at this cause of your misery." I take my explorer, and every time I touch the tooth, he jumps.

"I tell you, Mr. Bergeron, this tooth is abscessed and we need to pull it out pronto." Poor Joe's color disappears. I tell him to put his head down, way down between his knees, so he won't faint on me.

"No, no, I won't faint on you, Doc," he says in a faraway voice.

"Just keep your head down. I'll get some spirits of ammonia and give you a whiff that'll raise you right up." And it did.

"Doc," Joe is saying very quietly, "do you have to give me a shot to pull it?"

"I usually do, but I'll consider your wishes. I can deaden that tooth easily because it's a lower molar and the anesthetic goes in way back in the corner of your jaw."

"Go right ahead, Doc. I can't put up much of a fight, with the shape I'm in."

I get the needle ready without showing it to him. Some of the biggest and toughest men faint dead away at the sight of a needle. I dare not let him see this one.

"Bring your head back up now and open your mouth wide."

I numb the spot well with oil of cloves and then, very slowly, get the anesthetic to numb his whole jaw. Here is where the real skill of conversation comes into play. The idea is to distract the patient as much as possible.

"Joe (yes it does fit better than Treffel), Bud is organizing a band. Would you consider playing an instrument?"

Joe revives a bit. "Well, Doc, I can remember when I was a kid in Canada, I played something for a while until Dad moved us to the U.S."

"What was it you played?"

"Some sort of horn. Made a big sound. I was big for my age and the teacher gave the big horn to me."

"Was it a tuba?"

"Maybe so. It was big, with a big booming sound."

"When Bud came in the other day, he says he is going to organize a band. He wants players. I think I will try the tuba after all. Bud's family owned a music store in Massachusetts. When they moved here they brought their stock of instruments with them."

"Doc, I'm not sure I can learn now. I'm so much older."

"What's that got to do with it? We all can learn, no matter how old. Does your face feel numb?"

He reaches up. "Yeah, I can't feel a thing."

I know this guy is squeamish. "Open wide," I tell him. I have the forceps on the shelf behind me. Quickly, I reach out for them while his eyes are shut, reach in and get a good grip on that bad molar, and out she comes! Easy pulling if the roots are straight. It's over in a couple seconds and the color comes back to Joe's face, but he can't talk much right now. I tell him how to take care of it.

"Don't rinse the blood out of the new socket, and if it gets to hurting too bad, come back and we will put painkiller in it. Anyway, come back tomorrow, Mr. Bergeron. I want to see how the socket looks then."

Joe mumbles, "Doc, just call me Joe. I'll be back tomorrow."

Now I can tell Bud there's another player for the band. But will he have enough? Everyone is so busy putting this town on the map after the fire. I find out Bud's list is gradually increasing: Ray Aldrich, Floyd Barrard, Coe Furman, Jack Lambert, and Ed Woods. Rita Auchard and Mathilda Tomlinson got busy and rounded up some ladies: Lulu Daniels and Zula White. Then someone found two Thomases, Dave and Hugh, along with Bingham and Homer Wellman. So, by now we had a beginning band recruited. "We will play for Christmas," Bud proclaims. Each is a victory for Bud. He makes us think people who play an instrument are a special breed. Maybe so. Our first practice session is the last Sunday in September. First we are learning John Philip Sousa's *Stars and Stripes Forever*. Even with our squeaks and snorts, it makes my blood run faster.

CHAPTER 14

LITTLE FISH . . . LET'S GO

I keep watching the mail. When will the message come from the hatchery? Of course, it's not quite cold enough. Soon, maybe. I have been out duck hunting. I come back to find:

Dear Doctor:

Papa and I have to go to Helena. Uncle David Auchard passed away. We must help Aunt Agnes with the funeral arrangements. He was a Mason. The Helena Lodge will carry out the burial ritual. Maybe we will be back in a week.

Rita

How strange. Just last week Rita told me about David Auchard. Now he's gone.

When I walk in with my hunting loot, the hotel cook throws up her hands and sings out, "Ooo la la, the goose hangs high."

"There's more than goose—plenty duck soup too, my dear cook lady."

"Oh, you are wonderful. Sometimes it's fish or elk, or bear, and now it's birds. You are the mighty hunter."

I tell her I'm waiting for our fingerlings to arrive so we can fill the mountain streams with trout.

At last the letter arrives. "Your fingerlings are being shipped today, October 28, and will arrive at Craig. Keep the air pumps going when the barrels are not in motion."

This is it! I quick put the note on my office door: "Kenck is out of town for one week." Then, quick to Nett's Livery Stable to pick up the spring wagon and fastest team. Then, I throw in a blanket. And then to Judge Mayer's. He's been expecting me any day, so we both climb aboard and hit the trail for Craig.

I say, "The fingerlings will arrive at eight p.m. at Craig. We can't go on the road till morning. We can pace the horses for now at a good clip, no load yet."

We stop at Half Way House for a bite and to water and feed the horses. After half an hour we are on the road again. We get into Craig just before that train. Then, there they are, the barrels of fingerlings. Five large barrels, five thousand precious fingerlings in each one. Each barrel has a foot bellows. We pull the spring wagon up alongside the car and roll them out on the edges. But we see what we have to do, work these foot bellows every so often. Judge and I decide to take turns, and we pump air into the barrels in twenty-minute intervals, all night long.

At daybreak we hit the trail. The motion of the wagon helps but still we put several pumps of air in for the fingerlings every half hour. We have to stop overnight at Ephraim Sherman's place. Finally, the second day we reach Judge Mayer's place where we had the special oil cans stored that we'll use when we get to Ford Creek. But one thing we know we must do, either slosh the little ones around or pump the bicycle pumps, which we do mostly. Now we get our big funnels out and start pouring fish from the barrels into the tin cans that will ride on the packsaddles.

Each can gets about two-thirds full, or about six gallons, and we pump in some fresh water and air. All five barrels are divided into six cans, two cans to a packhorse. This is plenty of work but we do get help from anyone standing around. The Judge and I are feeling the lack of sleep and food.

At last we are headed toward the mountains, to Ford Creek and the trailhead. Just a ways past there we have to winch the wagon up over the "Steps" at Ford Creek, and then we unload all cans. Todd meets us with the Forest Service packhorses. We load 'em up. I hope there's no Jumbo among them. I don't want to see my fingerlings flying through the air.

One better thing about packing these through the mountains is we follow Ford Creek and each night we unload the cans of fingerlings and lay them in the cold creek waters with the two screened openings in the direction of the current. New, cooler, and fresher water flows through each can, and we lie down on our bedrolls to sleep at last.

First, we off-load some fingerlings into Wood Lake, and find very few dead ones. Then we go on a few short miles to Benchmark. There we put the rest into the South Fork of the North Fork of Sun River. Now we know these fish will have little fish, and there will be fish here for years to come.

The last night here it begins to snow. What do we expect? It's November. This night several feet of snow falls, but the next day it rains. After the rain comes cold temperatures, and an icy crust forms on the snow, sharp enough to cut the horses' legs so they bleed.

One very dangerous thing happens. We run low on food and, of course, our fish babies are not edible yet. A hunk of cheese and a can of lard are the only food

we have left by the time we start back down the trail. The icy coating on everything makes hard traveling, so we leave the wagon and harness there. The horses are carrying the packsaddles plus the empty cans, which we might use again.

After getting home, I begin to worry about that harness, so I go back for it with a couple of horses and a supply of oats. Eph Sherman comes along too. Wouldn't I know, it's beginning to snow! We camp and wait a couple days, so to pass time while watching the white stuff come down, I make us snowshoes. They work fine and we finally make it out with the harness. The horses had to lunge ahead all the way down. We weren't able to get the wagon. These harnesses belong to Nett's Livery Stable.

There goes the old year. In comes 1903. What crazy things will it bring? In town there's a drift of snow, but I decide to see Rita. I've missed the whole Christmas season. Also, I'm still weary from the intense work of getting the fingerlings into the mountains. Seems like a lot of work that won't show for a long time, maybe even years.

Rita meets me at the door.

"Oscar, I've been worrying about you. What in the world have you been doing? You missed the practice session and the Christmas concert."

"Yeah, I know, but the fingerlings couldn't wait and then I got to worrying about that harness of Nett's we left at Wood Lake. Snow was about three feet deep."

"No wonder you look so tired. I hope that someday someone appreciates your good work. Most especially I hope it's you, Oscar."

"Rita, I'll be at the next band practice. I'll see Bud for the music. Right now though I've got to get some rest."

CHAPTER 15

THE MATCHMAKER

The lady who appears in my office is Norwegian, I can tell. "Vell, vell, you iss the new tooth doctor? Hans and I, vee notice your sign and say, 'Ya, vee need to see you.'"

"Come right in. You are Mrs. . . . ?"

"I am Miz Brusgard. Vee lif along the stage road. I would like you to look at my tooth. Iss hurting."

"Mrs. Brusgard, please take off your hat and be seated in my chair and I will look."

"Vell, Doctor, there is one and then there is more."

"Yes, Madam, I will look at all your teeth."

I look and see several that need fillings, so I explain.

"I'll take care of the ones that hurt first, and then another time we will take care of the others."

"Dat iss very fine, Doctor."

"Do you have a family, Mrs. Brusgard?"

"Vell, vee certainly do, vee haf four. Our eldest boy, Harold, then Olaf. Then vee haf two girls, Amelia and little Clara. Now Hans and me, vee say no more ven Amelia came along. I sleep downstairs and Hans he sleep upstairs, but von night I get so lonesome for Hans so I start up the stairs and vat do you know, Hans he has same idea. Dats ven Clara was result!"

I'm laughing inside, but hardly aloud.

"Well, Mrs. Brusgard, I think you are glad for Clara, yes?"

"Oh yes, very glad. Vee love her so much. Such a good child too."

"Your appointment now is for next week this same time. Is that a good time?"

"Yes, vee come to town vonse a week, easy."

My next patient is my good friend Tony Pings. "What are you up to now, Tony? I've been so busy with my fish project, I've lost track of what you are building."

"Doc, I've never stopped pounding nails and sawing lumber. Every house you see up the street I've gotten it started. My helpers have finished them. I'm building a good-sized house right now for Bud Tomlinson. He and his missus will carry on the music business, like piano lessons, and practice band in that house. But say, I do have a bit of news. Mabel, the girl you spoke of, and I are discussing matrimony."

"Hey, how about that? Just call me Mr. Matchmaker."

"Yes, Doc, and when we get married, I'm asking you to be the best man."

"Tony, of course I'll do that for you. Also, I hope it works out that way."

My next patient this day is a sheepherder. How do I know? Before he even speaks, I can smell him.

"Doctor, the only teeth I've got is what you can see. I'm wondering if you might be able to make me a set that I could chew my vittles with. Is that possible?"

"Yes, yes, of course I can. What is your name?"

"It's been so long that I don't right know, but everybody calls me Holy Smoke. But let me explain. I've got a band of sheep feeding along real nice out the south flat and I asked a young fellow to watch them for me. Of course, my dogs can do as good a job as anyone, but I'm on the move towards Canada and I can't stay around long."

"That's a problem but maybe we can work something out. Right now we could start and maybe two days I could have them ready."

"Two days is a long time to keep a band of sheep. When grass runs out, they gotta move. If you want to take chance, okay, Doc."

We get to work right away with the impressions.

"These front ones are bad. They gotta come out. But we can wait and pull them just before I put the plates in."

"You can?"

"Yes, I make them to fit the emptied spaces too."

"But Doc, remember my sheep might move and I'll have to go. If that happens, I'll not be back till fall."

"Holy Smoke, I'll try to get them done before the sheep eat all the grass out there. And I'll find you if you move."

"It's a deal."

I hurry and get the impressions made. I even tell Joe Bush to come back later this week so I can run my vulcanizer.

Finally, after three days, they're ready. Vulcanizing takes exactly four hours on each plate, upper and lower, and then I've got to trim and polish each one. I sent Bing, the hotel errand boy, out to find Holy Smoke. He comes back soon. "Holy Smoke's not in sight any-where." So, I hire a rig from Nett. I say to him, "I need the fastest horse—I gotta catch Holy Smoke." I load my foot engine, scraping tools, forceps and anesthetics. First I go east to the Sun River crossing. I know my patient would take his band of sheep up on what is called The Bench up north. I ask a fellow I pass at Sun River, "When did a band of sheep last cross?"

"Yesterday, about noon," he replies. At last, I find Holy Smoke with his sheep wagon, about ten miles from my office.

First, we pull those front teeth and then slip the dentures in to see how much to trim. I tell him, "It will take a few days to get used to them. Keep them in as long as possible." He pulls out a leather bag from his sack and pays me my thirty-five dollars plus five more for the horse and buggy rental.

CHAPTER 16

THE STORY OF DR. KENCK'S FATHER'S DEATH,

As Told by Old Chief Joseph of the Nez Percé

I'm not a real loner. The way I like to fish you might think so. After a day of emergencies: broken bones and warts on fingers and toes, and puncture wounds, not to mention fillings, bridges, crowns and dentures, I seek the rippling sounds of the creek. But I'm gregarious at times and hunt up humankind for talk. Lately I find myself hiking up the road toward Rita's. She is a good listener. Besides that, she laughs, I mean chuckles, at my jokes.

There she is sitting in the swing doing handwork.

"Oscar, there you are. Come sit here with me. I'm trying to finish this lace collar. We can talk. Oscar, tell me about your father. You never speak of him."

"I didn't know him. Everything I do know was told to me by Uncles Chris and Jake. My mother finds it too hard to speak of him."

"What happened?"

"He was killed by the Nez Percé Indians near Yellowstone Park. I was two and Albert just a few months old."

"How sad for your mother."

"Yes, and especially because she was a new bride from Germany and could speak no English."

"Does she speak English now?"

"Very little. She gets by because there are other Germans in Helena and especially Mike Reinig. He has a grocery store. Every week he comes by Mama's house on Jackson Street and takes her order and at the same time tells her the town news in German."

"Tell me. How did your father happen to be where the Nez Percé Indians could kill him?"

"He and nine other fellows made a pack trip from Helena to the Park. They wanted to see the strange geysers and wonders of the newly designated national park. Chief Joseph and his people at that time were trying to get away from the U.S. Army. They were supposed to have stayed in Idaho on the same reservation as the Cayuse. After several battles they decided to go across Montana to Canada where they would be out of the reach of the U.S. Army. After I finished college at Gonzaga in 1893, I decided to find Chief Joseph. He was being confined to the Colville Reservation, and he could not leave without a government escort."

Rita asks, "What is he like?"

"Joseph rose to my height, maybe more than six feet. He was dressed in white man's clothes. No beads or feathers. He held a Western-type felt hat. His dark hair was in two simple braids. His strong face was a statement of sadness. His mouth a straight line of no hope. When I found him, I wasn't sure he would talk to me.

He had, he said, tried and tried to tell Washington, the government, his message.

He told me, "They all say, yes, Chief Joseph, we hear you. We will do something for you. Nothing happens. What do I ask for? I want to go to my home in Wallowa Hills to die there and be buried there like my father."

I ask him, "Chief Joseph, I will ask you a question about my father. Will you tell me the answer?"

"Young man," he tells me, " I will answer if you will listen. Not many will listen anymore." I had to agree if I wanted to know what happened and why about the death of my father. It was good I found him in the morning.

I told him, "My father had nothing against you or your people, but your warriors killed him near the geysers and Yellowstone Falls."

Chief Joseph then told me the story:

I must begin at the treaty time of 1865. Old Joseph, my father, listens to the treaty commissioners. He said, "Take away your paper. I will not sign it. I will not sell my mother, the Earth." Old Joseph never again comes to the treaty ground. Commissioners got others to sign, but not Old

Joseph. He cut posts of timber and set them in fence fashion and said, "Wallowa Hills not for sale."

My father die, then I am chief. He ask me to never sell the Earth, our mother. White settlers keep coming in and try to claim land. Finally the Wallowa Hills are given to Nez Percé in 1873. The Government sends peace commissioners who say to me, "We will give you schools."

I say, "No want schools."

They ask, "Why don't you want schools?"

"If we take schools, you will send us churches. We don't want churches."

"Why don't you want churches?" they ask.

I tell them, "If you send us churches, you will teach us to quarrel about God. We no want to quarrel about God."

White settlers keep coming into our land that was set apart by the treaty commission. They decide we should be moved to the reservation in Idaho with the Cayuse. We not want to be with Cayuse. We have many horses and cattle, and Cayuse reservation too small. General Howard tells us in 1876 we must move in thirty days or else government soldiers will come and drive us onto reservation in Idaho. It is spring, Snake River is high. Why do we have to hurry?

While we get our people across the river, white man steal our best horses and cattle. My young warriors want revenge. I tell them: no killing white people. Nez Percé have never killed white people. But, in the night, young men sneak out and kill white men.

So, now General Howard will chase us to catch the killers. But we will first battle and go into Idaho and then over the mountains by Lolo Pass—all women, children, old folks too.

After the pass, Captain Rawn tries to stop us. We plan to go to Canada. We hold white soldiers busy at Captain Rawn's camp while our people slip through timber, and when all people are down the trail, warriors and chiefs make a big noise and we get out of sight, one by one. We get to the Big Hole where we feel safe, but General Gibbons' men kill many of us next morning. We thought General Howard was far behind us, so we camped at Big Hole. General Gibbons' men killed our women, children, and old people, but some of us get away.

When we get away, we decide we must get to Grandmother's land, Canada, quick. My warriors now collect supplies and horses from anyone who has them, sometimes kill, like your father was killed by our warriors. I am sorry.

"That's a sad story, both about your father and about the Nez Percé," says Rita.

"Joseph has tried many times to get permission to go back to Wallowa but someone who has some authority always objects. I've learned more about that war and the situation by looking into the records. I have no ill feeling towards the Nez Percé and especially Chief Joseph. It is the mishandling and the prejudice toward the Indians that is so cruel."

"Yes, Oscar, knowing the other side takes care of prejudice."

CHAPTER 17

THE PROPOSAL

After hearing about the death of my father at Yellowstone, Rita and I go into the house. The mosquitos are beginning to discover us.

Once inside, I see Mr. and Mrs. Auchard sitting in their favorite chairs. They greet me with their soft New York voices. Before I realize it, I'm overwhelmed with a tremendous thought and words come spilling out of my mouth.

"Mr. Auchard, would you and Mrs. Auchard consider letting Rita marry me?"

I look at Rita and she is in shock. Mr. Auchard is getting to his feet. I'm beginning to sweat. I'm amazed at myself. I hadn't planned on this, but here I am saying things that might totally change my future. How could I have thought he would approve of such? His low voice comes through in solemn tones. It doesn't match the twinkle in his eyes.

"Let me tell you, young man, I don't give my last daughter away easily. The man who gets her must meet certain standards. Are you prepared to hear them?"

"Mr. Auchard, all I can say right now is I'm sure I cannot measure up. I've heard that others have not passed the test. But I must hear them or I shall never know why I failed."

"These are my expectations: He must be able to support her, and he must have certain kindnesses women need. (I think he must be thinking about my hunting and fishing absences.) The husband must show her and tell her she is appreciated. Young man, do you think you can measure up?"

By now I'm bewildered. His stern voice doesn't match his smiling eyes. Mrs. Auchard looks like she is trying hard to look serious. Rita is turning her face away. What is this, the fifth degree?

"I don't really know, Mr. Auchard. I'm inexperienced at this marriage business."

"I certainly would hope so, but you can see what I expect." Then his voice begins to match his eyes as he chuckles and extends his hand. "I do think you can fulfill these requirements, but it is good I let you know what I expect."

Rita now says, "Oscar, you never asked me or told me."

"Yes, I know, Rita, I can't explain it either why I missed the obvious. Please, will you marry me?" As we walk toward the gate, Rita says, "Let's talk about it."

"I'm still discombobulated at what I have done." So, we walk down the lane to the gate. At the gate we can't find words yet. Finally, I reach for her hand.

"I'm six feet tall and strong, but I'm scared, Rita.

I'm not sure your father thinks I can measure up."

"Oscar, I'll tell you what's been going on at my house for weeks. Every day my Papa says, 'Has he asked you yet?' I answer him, 'Papa, he doesn't know anything about it.' Papa says, 'One of these days he's going to wake up.' It must be today."

"I guess you are right. How could I have been so sleepy? Now I'm stunned at my own misperception. I will go now, except, may I kiss you good night?"

"Oh yes, Oscar." We kiss and I am at once propelled out the gate by wonder and excitement. As I walk down the road, I'm saying to myself: What have I done? My life will be changed forever. Or will it?

Is it really a turning point? Maybe I've been going this direction for a long time and didn't know it. Not much sleep last night—my mind kept turning over. I stared into the dark trying to figure out what happened to me. This morning I look at the face in the mirror as I shave. He looks like a kid still, but now the kid must think like a man.

I talk to myself. Confucius says, "He who talks to self has captive audience." But to be a married man—

what about those times I'll want to go hunting and fishing? Now just a minute, Kenck. You've been hunting and fishing many times since you've arrived here with your wagon. Has Rita ever asked, "Why do you hunt and fish so much?" No. Why do I make a problem when there is none?

I hear my first patient's footsteps in the hall.

"Howdy, sir. I'm Dick Bean. I've got this tooth that's been botherin' me for a spell. Everything makes it hurt."

"Sit here in my chair and let's take a look. Yes, I can see your trouble. We might be able to save it. I'll clean it out and put a medicated filling in. It may settle down and then we can put a permanent filling in—silver. If it doesn't act up in the next few days, it may be okay." This takes about a half an hour. "Now, if this behaves, come in when you come to town again and we'll do the permanent filling. But if it starts hurting, we will have to pull it. About the middle of next month I'll be in Helena a week."

"That's good, Doc. I'd like to keep my teeth. Come in handy to chew. Ole told me you are looking to buy the Fisher homestead in the Canyon."

"Yeah, we have located him and he might sell. The cabins don't amount to much that are on it, but Albert, my brother, wants to build a cabin if we buy."

"Those Bertch brothers are odd but they don't give anyone any trouble. They talked of starting a store but know nothing about it."

"How long have you Beans been living near the Canyon?"

"Been here since the 1880s. Us boys were young. There are seven Bean boys and two girls. We were here in that awful winter of '86. Dad says the snow and winters were so bad in Minnesota he decided to move west where sometimes a warm wind breaks the cold. But we found out the winters here can be mighty tough."

"Seven brothers? How did your dad handle so many?"

"We had to work but we play hard too. We skate, have a punching bag we pull down in the kitchen, play shinny on the ice, and fish. Oh yeah, we fight good sometimes. Gotta go. Promised Carrie I'd be back before supper."

CHAPTER 18

TONY PINGS' WEDDING

Next one at my door is Tony. "Howdy, how's things with you?"

"Doc, the day is set. Wednesday, October 4, two p.m. Now I am depending on you to be my best man."

"I am looking at my calendar, Tony, and that happens to be okay with me. I'll mark it here as Wedding. Not my own yet."

"What are you saying, Doc, 'yet'?"

"Yeah, Tony, I guess I'm gonna be gettin' tied up someday before long."

"Nothing bad about that. I'm looking forward to it. Just think of it as getting a cook."

"Oh no, Tony, I got a different message. Anyway, we got to get you married since you got a date set. Where will it be?"

"It's gonna be at the Mission. Then there will be a dinner close by. Mabel's friend is doing that. Oh yes, bring your lady friend."

"I will, I will."

Tony goes on his way. I wonder if he even knows what house he's building at this point, and no doubt he'll build one for Mabel. I think Tony is getting married because he is anxious to have a home and wife. Me, I walk into it blind. Mr. Matchmaker, you fell in your own trap. Woe is me!

"Rita, I came to tell you I'm to be best man at Tony and Mabel's wedding October 4 at the Mission. And I'm to be sure to bring you."

"It's been on the grapevine for weeks. They've invited the whole town. All the buggies and carriages will be traveling there. We can take Papa's carriage."

"That's okay too. We can take another couple. I hope the weather holds well. But that's not all I've come to tell you. I plan to go to Helena on the sixth for a week. It's about the land on the Canyon. Maybe you can come up. We could go to a dance and the theater, plus we want to buy a ring for you."

"Oscar, I like that idea. You are so thoughtful."

"I'd better be too, after your father's mandate. I want to anyway."

I look at Rita and suddenly realize how special she is, so very calm and sure of herself. "I need you Rita. I'm just like the kid I look like."

Rita chuckles. "Oscar, I'm used to scared kids. When the little boys first come to school, they are both scared and in love with the teacher. You are not unusual. Of course, you have had men teachers most of your school days."

"That's right. I went to the Select Day School for Boys in Helena except for a short time in California."

"When in the world were you in California?"

"Guess I never told you about that. See these scars just above my eyebrows?"

"Yes, and what has that to do with California?"

"Mama decided it was about the time, Albert was four and I was five, that it would be good that she go live near her parents. They had emigrated from Germany about the same time she had. When they got to California, around the Horn, there were other German folk there, so they stayed. She put all our things into trunks ready to ship, and we went by stage to Salt Lake and then by train to California. That part was great. Going on the train was fine with me. Albert was scared until he got used to it.

"But the bad part of the whole thing was we, Albert and I, could speak only German. A kindly family friend persuaded Mama, and I question the kindly part, to put us in kindergarten. Strange language right away, and the other kids sometimes pointed at us and tittered. I don't know what they said, but I can imagine. We were two unhappy kids. But about these scars. The biggest Kenck kid in school had to do hand swings on the stair landing and, damn, he went face first into a glass door. Blood flowed all down his face. Result was we didn't go back to school. I don't remember much else except I kept saying, 'Let's go home, Mama!'

"After about a year she packed the things back in the trunks, and back to Helena we came. Albert and I were two happy travelers. Albert wasn't afraid of the train by then, and I felt right at home going up and down the aisles."

"That's really interesting. So, you started your education in California and you have the scars to prove it. What day do you plan to go to Helena?"

"First, we—you—will come with me to Tony and Mabel's wedding on the fourth of October, and then on Friday, October 6, we will go to Helena."

"Of course I will go with you to Mabel and Tony's wedding. Many others will go. It will take us about three hours to get to the Mission. We better hope for good weather."

Sure enough, the first snow hit us on September 21. Richard Auchard said it's the storm of the equinox. The *Almanac* says it will be light and melt. The frost will be on the squash and pumpkins and the garden will freeze. Then we will have Indian summer. Time to dig the potatoes and gather the squash and put all in the cellar. Rita and Mrs. Auchard are busy with sauerkraut and pickles.

Mrs. Auchard says, "Oscar, if you get some meat hunting, we can use some for mincemeat. I have an old recipe from New York. We've made it every year out of some sort of wild meat."

"Now I'm hearing why women don't complain about the time a man spends hunting. Rita, let's see if our friends Dick Adams and Victoria Terry will go with us to the wedding. Only thing, I gotta get there early to find out what the best man will do."

Rita chuckles and says, "That will be fun to go with them, or I mean, if they will come with us."

"Yeah, Dick Adams and I can fix up some surprise trick to give them a bad time, like a chivaree deal. I think we better be careful about tricks on Tony. We might want him to build something for us soon. I already have an idea though—like using a couple five-gallon cans filled with rocks or such, and as soon as the wheels start rolling they will fall down and be dragged, making an awful racket. Vic and I can make crepe paper streamers to decorate their buggy."

"Oscar, don't do any mean tricks because we might get paid back. You watch it."

It is finally Wednesday, October 4. The weather is Indian summer so we set out for St. Peter's Mission early, like eight a.m. Dick gets someone else to drive the stage that day. There is a procession going across to the Mission. Mabel's mother, Etta, has a big family. Phil Manix died in 1898 and left a young family. Mabel is the oldest.

Dick Adams takes one of the stagecoaches to carry guests to the wedding, as well as the bride and groom. We go on the road to Great Falls but take the cutoff after reaching Ft. Shaw. It is a merry procession—actually we are strung out for about a mile.

The Ursuline sisters are on hand to welcome all the guests and direct them to the chapel. I do believe we filled this chapel. Being best man and in charge of the wedding ring, Tony gets me by the elbow and makes sure I'm beside him.

"Kenck," he whispers, "you be sure and keep this ring for me till we need it in the ceremony."

"I'll put it in my vest pocket here. No, I'll put it in my jacket pocket."

"Yeah, you'd better remember which pocket, Kenck, 'cause I'm not for standing there a half hour while you go through all your pockets."

"No, no, Tony, don't worry. I'll hold it with my teeth if necessary."

I can see he's getting worried about some trick I might play on him. All is getting ready. Probably the ladies are in the back room fussing over Mabel's veil and gown while we are across in another room. I guess this is a confessional. I say to Tony, "You got anything to confess? Now is the time."

"Kenck, shut up. You are getting me rattled. I've learned what to say and if you keep buggin' me I'll forgit!"

"If you forget, I'll whisper in your ear."

"Kenck, you have no idea what I'm s'posed to say. You've never been married. Now be still. I'm forgetting already and it's your fault."

So, I did quit, because my problem now is how Dick Adams and I are going to get the cans tied to Tony's buggy without him knowing it. Dick has agreed to do it.

All is ready. Someone plays the organ and Tony and I come out and stand at the altar. Tony has started to sweat and shake a little. I reach in my pocket to get my extra handkerchief and wouldn't you know, the ring flips right out with it onto the floor and rolls a little ways away. Tony lets out a groan, and I jump for the ring. Yeah, I got it, but he will now forget everything he memorized.

I quickly put the ring into my vest pocket where it should have been in the first place.

The Father says, "Anthony, will you repeat your vows to Mabel before God and these witnesses?"

Tony opens his mouth but not a sound comes forth. This is all my fault. Tony will be mad at me for life. I really didn't mean to scare the words right out of his head. The Father realizes Tony is in trouble and says, "Anthony, will you repeat after me . . . " and he goes through the ceremony. Of course, Mabel has no problem and gives all the answers without hesitation. I hand over the ring as though it never had a chance to escape.

After Tony and Mabel had knelt on the beautiful tapestry-covered cushion and received the extra long Latin blessing of the Father, he pronounced them man and wife, i.e., Mr. and Mrs. Anthony Pings. All the pianos, along with the organ, resound with the wedding recessional. The Father then waves his hand to speak and invites all to the lunch and wedding cake provided by Mabel's family. I see where Rita is and make my way there.

She whispers to me, "What did you do to make Tony forget all his vows?"

"It was totally accidental. I saw Tony was sweating so I reached for my handkerchief and the ring flipped out and rolled along the floor and I had to make a grab for it."

"Oh no!" she suppresses a chuckle.

"But I got it right away and made sure it was in my vest pocket."

"What else are you and Dick up to?"

"Yeah, something, but I'm worried now."

"What?" she whispers.

"We've got some big cans tied to Tony's buggy. Now I'm worried, but Dick says he is going to stand by ready to grab the bridles just in case."

"Oscar, people who play tricks get tricks played on them."

"That's true, Rita. We will remember 'aye what' as you English say."

"Oscar, I'm a lot other than English."

After lunch and the newlywed's initiation of the beautiful cake, Mabel changes to her going-away outfit. Now Tony is helping her into the buggy. Just like he said, Dick is right there holding the team. Tony tucks her into the seat beside him. He calls to Dick, "Never mind, this is my gentlest team, no need to hold them."

"Okay, Tony," Dick calls but he doesn't move away. Tony grabs his reins and lets out his 'Go Ahead' yell. The team moves out but all the tin cans fall and make a wild clatter. The horses leap ahead as though they are struck by lightning. Dick uses all his force to pull their heads down to a walk. They are shuddering, ready for a run, no matter how gentle they are supposed to be. Tony climbs down and comes up front to calm them. Dick hollers, "Kenck, come over and help me, some foolish person's fastened a bunch of cans to Tony's buggy."

(Strange that Dick and I get them untied so easily.) The crowd is standing by and they start to snicker. Then when Tony starts out again the crowd shouts goodbyes.

CHAPTER 19

SERIOUS PLANS—A TRIP TO HELENA FOR THE RINGS

After making our own goodbye sounds, we lose no time getting across country to the well-traveled road from Great Falls to Augusta. The horses know they are homeward bound and need no urging. After we go by the turnoff to Gilman, the lights in farm windows guide us even though the horses need no lights. After we let off Dick and Victoria (Terry), I move closer to Rita and put my arm around her.

"Rita, I've got special plans for us."

"Tell me, tell me, Oscar," she begs.

"First, I have no appointments for the sixth through the fifteenth, this Friday and next week."

"Do you plan to go hunting?"

"No, no. I'm not interested in that this year. It's something far more important and exciting."

"You better tell me. I can't imagine anything that will excite you more than hunting."

I hug her even closer. "Rita, you marrying me is more exciting than anything else in the world."

"Oscar, I'm speechless!"

If the horses would have stopped, we would have savored our ecstasy, but they were determined to get to the barn. We just hugged each other tightly. Before we got to the gate, I said, "My plan is for us to go to Helena day after tomorrow. Will you go?"

"Oscar, of course I will go, but I know that Papa plans for him and Mama to go to Helena on Friday also."

"Wow. Looks like the whole family is going. That will be fine, but I want you to be free to go with me to meet my mother and my uncles. Also, we will go to the jewelry store to buy a ring."

"Oscar, I will love meeting your family, and of course we can pick out a ring."

"Rita, shall we see what is going on at the Opera House?"

"Yes, yes. I'll never forget the beautiful Johann Strauss musical we went to last year. Oscar, you do plan such exciting things for us."

"Yes, my good lady, there are many things to see and do in Helena. We will get around to some of them this time, and go again another time."

Now we are at the gate and soon here comes Will ready to take the horses and buggy. I say to him, "Thank you, Will. Your horses are the very best. They found their way home even in the dark."

Will replies in his almost whisper voice, "This team is the best and fastest," as he climbs in to drive them to the barn. Rita and I go in. We find Papa Richard and Mama Helen still up, sitting by the cozy fire.

"Well, how was the big wedding?"

"Papa, it was a very nice wedding. Many people were there, even though it was a three-hour drive from Augusta."

"Well, it was good that the weather stayed nice for their wedding. Did anybody give the newlyweds a bad time?"

"Papa, I'm not sure, but Tony forgot completely what he was supposed to say, so the priest had to tell him every word. Then during the wedding, someone tied tin cans to Tony's carriage. His lively horses would have run away if Dick Adams hadn't grabbed the horses' bridles. But they calmed down. Tony was kind of shook up, but Mabel was totally calm." Papa said, "Well, who would do those tricks, I wonder?" At this, Rita changed the subject.

"Papa, Oscar wants me to go to Helena Friday. I told him you and Mama plan to go that very day. He wants me to go to Helena and meet his mother and uncles. This will be good for all of us to journey together on the stage and the train."

"Yes, that will be fine. You and Oscar can plan your own things. Mama and I are going to take one whole day for a trip to Silver City to see my sister Jane and her boy David at their ranch. She is lonely since her husband got killed in that bad fall off the barn. I've not decided if we'll do the fifteen miles to their place on the train or rent a carriage."

"Papa, how nice of you. I've been to Jane's a few times and she really appreciates family coming since losing Bartholomew. She's such a tiny, plucky, little lady."

"Rita, *my birdie*, you are a tiny plucky lady, and we will make the most of these days before you are off and married."

I can see how this man adores his daughter. I'll never forget his admonition speech.

Rita tells her father, "Papa, I'm twenty-nine—too old to be called by that little girl name, *Birdie*."

Richard sighs. "Ah yes, I gotta let you grow up and be a married woman pretty soon."

Mrs. Auchard makes a little laugh as she keeps knitting and purling on a pair of socks.

"Good night, I must go. I have several appointments for tomorrow. If all goes as we plan, we will meet Friday on the stage."

Rita steps out the door with me. I hold her face to mine. "Rita, my darling, I love you. We'll meet on Friday. You are my good lady. Good night. It's too cold to tarry outside." Walking down the road, I dream of life with this wonderful girl who has been listening to me for several years already.

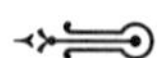

'Tis early Friday morning and there is a winter chill in the air. Dick comes swinging by the hotel with his stage and the eager team. "Hi, Dick! We are to pick up Rita, also her mother and father. We are all headed for Helena."

"Okay, sounds like an important family affair." He cracks his whip and gives a holler that really livens his team and we clatter up the road. Not long and we stop at the Auchard gate. There they are, all three bundled up with suitcases. Will has brought them with their bags in his buggy. "Goodbye, Will," they say as they climb aboard the stage. His soft goodbye is barely heard over the clatter of the horses. We tuck the ladies in, cover ourselves with buffalo robes, and put our feet near the foot warmer. There is a cold wind so we keep our faces covered. Before long we reach the Half Way House and climb down for a hot bowl of soup inside. The team is changed and we climb back aboard. We're off again for Craig, where finally we step on the train. The warm train brings us to Helena in only two hours.

Richard, Mrs. Auchard, and Rita catch a carriage to the hotel. I catch one to Mama's house on Jackson Street.

"Mutter, I am here to see you!"

"Oh, Oscar!" In German, she tells me I'm a surprise. She chatters on. "You are hungry? I fix you warm supper."

"Where is Albert?"

"He will come home soon." She stirs the fire in her kitchen stove and cooks a few sausages and eggs, all the while telling me in German about other Germans and also about Mike Reinig.

Albert finally comes home. "Albert, good to see you. What's new about the property hunt?"

"It's close to a done deal, Oakie. We will have the papers and signatures soon and then we will turn over the money."

"Albert, that's great because I'm getting married in a few months and I want that project to be on the way sooner."

"It sure will be! When spring comes I'll be there building a cabin."

"When you get the papers, bring them down to me and we'll get the money to the sellers right away."

"I'll take care of it as fast as I can, Oakie. Now, just when are you getting married?"

"We are not exactly sure, but it will be early next year."

The week in Helena went by so fast. We did some things I'd planned but not near all of them. Of course, I took Rita to meet Mama. I had to interpret, as Mama still is not good in English and Rita's German is not good either. But Uncles Chris and Jacob do all right. Next, we went to several jewelry stores. Actually all are located on Main Street. At Mettlers we found a band and diamond set that seemed just right.

A few years before I was thinking I was stuck in Helena after college, and it didn't seem a bit interesting. But with Rita it was much different. We had a good time as I showed her some places I had known as a kid. Up on the hill I showed her where, one extra cold morning, I had taken a wild sled ride when I was about thirteen. I related the story to Rita while we looked down the steep street.

"The night before, one of the older boys had opened a fire plug and let water run all the way to the bottom cross-street. Somehow I knew about it. I got my sled up to the top of the hill early in the morning. Down I went, lickety-split, faster and faster, by block after block of houses. I had not thought of the new horse-drawn streetcar crossing. I was concentrating on guiding my sled. Suddenly, I remembered about the streetcars. I was getting close to the crossing. I heard the bells of the streetcar and the clatter of the horse's hooves.

Whoops! I was getting too close. I dragged my toes as hard as I could, but it was no use as the ice was too hard. Oh, too close. I'm going to smash! The horses went past. I'll hit the wheels, I thought. I laid my head down and somehow missed the front wheels, and under I went and out the other side, the back wheels missing me too! How I ever missed being crushed, I'll never know. Some kids standing by let out a wild cheer. I never let on how scared I was but it did one thing. It made me watch for the street car before I started down every time after that."

Rita listened, then exclaimed, "That's one of the reasons you got called 'One of the crazy Kenck Kids.'"

We walk up and down Main Street. There are still two old Chinese laundries. (Often I helped Mama deliver her clothes to one of these.) In the four years I've been in Augusta this town sure has changed.

The next day we climbed Mt. Helena. I showed Rita the trails we made as kids. I told how many townspeople climbed the mountain every day in 1883 to watch the progress of the first train's rails being laid. We saw the old water flume that brings water from the mountain springs to the town, and I told Rita about the time I was caught playing in the rushing water.

Another day we walk out to the new capitol. It is just two years old now, but already seems busy. Rita and I read the newspapers where it said the design is neoclassical. Well, parts of it look like pictures of ancient Greek and Roman buildings. We were able to go inside. The rooms and ceiling were immense. They do need some large paintings to adorn the plain white marble walls. Someone said Edgar Paxson was commissioned to do giant murals for the House of Representatives and other buildings. We also heard that Charlie Russell was hired to do another giant-sized painting, but he hadn't got around to the actual painting of it yet.

The folks come back from their visit to Jane (Auchard) Gehring and son David. Richard was always glad to see his sister Jane. He was worried though because Jane had broken her hip in a fall and was in a wheel chair.

Richard then went to attend a Masonic meeting, mainly to tell them of the property endowment that his brother Dave had left to the Masons. The Masons were having a dance party Friday, so we all decided to go. The folks don't dance anymore, but they love hearing the music and watching the dancers. Rita and I practiced some of the waltz steps we had learned in our dance sessions at the Augusta Hotel.

Bill Franks is still at Holter Hardware. I tell him about my plans to get married soon. "Good for you, Oakie. You need a wife!" Then surprise—I find my long-time friend, George Hildebrandt, working there too. As friends, George and I go back a long way, to 1884. He came that year as a little four-year-old German boy. Those years I was like his big brother. I helped him learn English and watched out for him till I left to attend Gonzaga. He is just starting at Holter in the shipping department. It was a busy week doing all I had to do plus all I wanted to do. Of course, we left some more fun things to do next time.

We all take the morning train back to Craig on Saturday. The weather is some colder. Of course, Dick is there with his stage. We waste no time getting aboard. The foot warmer is there to keep our feet comfy. We snuggle down under the heavy robes to keep the cold wind off our faces. The stage ride, sitting close to Rita, doesn't seem as long as it used to. I don't wonder why.

Rita and her folks get off at the Auchard pole gate. Will is waiting there with the buggy to take them and their suitcases to the house. I tell Rita, "I'll walk out tomorrow afternoon. Good night, my lady." Rita makes sure I hear her "Oscar, in time for dinner" before I'm past the gate.

CHAPTER 20

FINDING A HOUSE TO RENT

Back at my own door, I find notes from several people. Mrs. Wellman, Bud Tomlinson, Mrs. Brusgard (no message), and Mrs. Grand Christian. Looks like I'll be busy next week. I reflect about our Helena trip. The days were busy or full, I'll say. I used to think Helena was dull. Not anymore!

The next day I arrive a short time before the usual Sunday dinnertime. My mind is bursting with all we need to talk about.

"Rita, I found notes from four people and probably some came who didn't leave a note. So, I'll be busy this next week. Of course, you know most everyone in this country. Do you know Mrs. Brusgard?"

"I certainly do, and I know exactly how she talks. Very Norwegian."

"Yes, I won't forget the first time she came to my office. Has she told you about how Clara happened to be born?"

Rita grins. "Isn't that some story? She tells it like it is."

"Has she told you other stories like that?"

"She always has something to say to us women, like, 'Vell, Vell, vat a pretty dress you haff. Vere did you get it and how much did you pay vor it?' I say 'I made it.' Then she says, 'You made it! Vould you loan me the pattern?' I answer, 'I don't have a pattern, I just made it up.' She replies, 'Vat a smart girl you are.' On and on she goes, just likes to talk."

After we sit down at the dinner table, Mr. Auchard brings up a subject. "Oscar, I've been thinking. Have you found a house in Augusta for you and Rita to live in after you are married?"

"Not yet. I thought about the Bud Tomlinsons' moving soon to their new house. It's about finished. Maybe the house they move out of will be available."

"Well, I want to assure you, if nothing turns up, you can live here awhile. We have plenty of room."

"That's generous of you folks to offer that. I think it will be best for us to be responsible for getting a house. People call for me in the middle of the night. That would not be good for you folks to have your sleep interrupted. My office can still be in the hotel for awhile, and we should have a home nearby."

After dinner, Rita and I have a long planning session. Rita knows everyone who lives in Augusta and on the outskirts. We talk about house possibilities. She is confident that something will turn up and says, "People move around a lot. I'm not discouraged."

Monday starts with Bud Tomlinson at my office door.

"Howdy, Doc. Several people were anxious to see you last week, even me. Did you two sneak off and get married?"

"No, not yet, Bud. I introduced Rita to my mother and uncles in Helena, and we bought a ring."

"Well, I'll say you are serious, if that's possible with you."

"Well, Bud, we are serious this time, and there's one thing you can tell me. Are you going to move into your new house? We are looking for a house when we do decide when to get married."

"The new house is about finished and, yes, we will move right away because we need the room for our music sessions."

"Will your old house, the one you're moving out of, be for rent?"

"I'm not sure. It belongs to Tony now. I gave it to him for part payment, and he has already built one for his new bride."

"If you see him, tell him I want to talk to him right away."

Wow, I think about the ring fumble and the cans

tied to his buggy. Maybe he'll not know about my part in the can-tying job.

I do one filling for Bud today. He hurries back to his job.

Next day early he's back for the other filling.

"Did you see Tony?" I ask him.

"Yes, late yesterday. I told him you wanted to see him. He mumbled something like 'He better be sorry.' I pretended not to hear."

"I'll probably have to confess. Dick and I tied a bunch of cans to his buggy just before the wedding. Also, unintentionally, I dropped the wedding ring. Not actually dropped, I had put it into my pocket, the one with the handkerchief, and I saw him start to sweat so I pulled out my handkerchief to hand him and the ring flipped out with it and rolled away on the floor. Tony forgot all the words he was supposed to say."

"I thought that was normal. Most grooms can't remember a thing at such a time. Before I leave, I want to tell you the band is starting to practice next Sunday for the Christmas concert we'll play in December. We practice here at the hotel about 2:30 p.m."

"Okay, Bud. Rita and I will be coming."

Tony doesn't come. It's been days. I begin to think he doesn't want to talk to me. Now I am worried. I get busy with the people who had left notes last week. Here's a lady at my door now.

"Hello, Dr. Kenck, how have you been? I left you a note last week."

"Pleased to see you again, Mrs. Wellman. I'm doing well. What can I do for you?"

"I have a tooth that needs attention."

"Put your hat on that table and hang your coat on that hook above. Now step up into my chair and we shall see the problem."

I take a look with the explorer, and sure enough, the left molar needs attention. I tell Mrs. Wellman she will need a filling.

"Doctor, I think there might be others. I would like you to look at all of them. I want to keep my teeth as long as I can."

I do a complete exam. "There is a small decay in the

left lower bicuspid, and in the lower right first molar, a small decay as well. I can fix the one that's bothering you today, and you may come back another time for the other."

After I finish drilling and put an amalgam in the molar, if possible, I like to get acquainted with everyone. "Your son, Bingham, is a hardworking boy."

"Yes, that's my boy. Also, he saves his money."

"How many children do you have?"

As she puts on her hat and coat, she explains. "Bingham is the oldest. He's eleven. Alma is next at nine. Homer, my music child who also wants to be in Mr. Tomlinson's band, is seven. Naida, my other girl, is five, and Percy, the baby boy, is three. That's all and enough, I'd say. We live right near the newlywed Pingses. She is watching my two little ones now."

"A good-sized family. When will you come again to get the other tooth fixed?"

"Will this day and time next week be all right?"

"I'm writing it down, yes, about 10:30 in the morning."

"Thank you and goodbye, Dr. Kenck."

Not long after, another lady comes in. "Doctor, I am Mrs. McGraw. We live up Elk Creek a ways. I was happy to hear a young dentist had moved to our town. Helena is such a long way to go to get our teeth cared for."

"Pleased to meet you, Mrs. McGraw. What is it about your teeth that brings you in today?"

"I have several that I'm worried about and they all need cleaning."

"Please, Mrs. McGraw, put your hat on the table there and hang your coat on the rack. Step up and sit in the chair when you're ready. I will have a look and see what needs to be done."

When she is settled in the chair, I look around and see this molar (I tap it with the explorer) that needs some care. The decay is small but if it is fixed now the tooth will certainly be saved. I tell this to Mrs. McGraw.

"I see you have a bridge where you lost a molar below."

"Yes, I had that done in Helena a few years ago. I hope it is still in good shape."

"Yes, I see no problem with it. I can do the filling

today and the cleaning, but if you come to town every week, we could wait on the cleaning until next week."

"Fine, do the filling today and the cleaning next week."

After the filling is done, there is no one waiting and Mrs. McGraw wants to talk. "Doctor, I heard you recently took care of a lady having a baby, there being no doctor in town."

"Yes, it seems like babies decide to be born when no doctor is here. Also, they pick night time."

Mrs. McGraw nods her head in agreement. "For several years I've been helping women here have their babies."

"Have you kept track of how many?"

"I've lost count, but many. I never was blessed with children of my own, but I do love seeing the children I've delivered grow up. Let me tell you again, I'm grateful you have decided to settle in our community. We need you badly! I will be back next week unless it storms early."

As Mrs. McGraw is leaving, she is met by Mrs. Brusgard who has been in before. I listen, and there goes the dress story, like Rita told. I chuckle to myself as I'm getting ready for her. I am getting to know the folks who live in the country and in the town. I hope Tony comes in soon.

At the end of the week, here he comes. "Kenck, I have something to say to you. First, I want to thank you for being my best man. Also, I've decided to forget about the ring and the cans tied to my buggy. But I'll tell you one thing. I heard from Bud that you're hunting for a house and that sure tells me you are going to get married and maybe <u>you'll</u> get some crazy treatment like that." He sticks out his hand to shake mine and I'm relieved of a guilty load.

"Tony, the ring thing was just an accident, and I got to worrying about the can trick after it was too late to change it. Yes, you guessed right too. Rita and I are getting married before long. We don't have a date set yet. It will serve me right if somebody pulls a chivaree trick on us. But what can I do for you today, Tony?"

"I would have been here sooner but the work piled up on me. Getting set up in a new house and also getting married takes time. Take a look at what still needs to be done." Tony climbs up into the chair and opens his mouth.

"Yes, we are going to bridge that place where I pulled the molar. Today I'll make an impression." After that I get up the nerve to ask him about the house Tomlinson is vacating.

"Yes, Doc, I'll rent you that house. Bud will be moving in February. His new one will be done about the fifteenth, I'm pretty sure."

"That will be just right. I'll tell Rita tonight. Thank you. Come back Friday and I'll have the bridge ready."

I'm excited about getting to the house after Bud's family moves to their new one. After I get some work done on the impressions, I lock my door and head for the Auchard place. Rita sees me come through the gate and opens the door before I can knock.

"Oscar, you look like good news."

"I do? Well, you see right." I grab both her hands. "Yes, my little wife-to-be, I've been worrying several days. Tony finally came in. He even forgave me for the ring and cans at his wedding. I did explain the ring thing was an accident and the cans got me to worrying too late to do anything about them. Best of all he said he'd rent the house to us."

"When will the house be available?"

"The Tomlinsons' new home will be ready about February fifteenth, and we can have it after that. So, that sets our time schedule. But, he also remarked that maybe we'd get a chivaree trick played on us." Rita laughs and we automatically reach for each other in a hug.

"We will plan well and make sure we don't let anyone know where or when we will get married," she tells me.

Bud is planning a Christmas concert and we are supposed to practice this Sunday afternoon about two-thirty."

"I've been in Tomlinsons' so I know what furniture we can start quietly collecting." Rita makes a list of what we have to find. This must be on the "q.t."

We tell Mr. and Mrs. Auchard. We also explain why we can't tell anyone when or where. We just don't know yet.

Mrs. Auchard says, "Oscar, I know you've had no supper, right?"

"I forgot all about that. I thought only to tell Rita about the house."

"Come, sit down with us. I've set a place for you. Things will turn out right for you two, I know. Good things happen to those who expect them."

After supper, Rita gets out her pen and paper and we work on a list. After a while she puts it away and sits down at her piano. She got out some Christmas songs. This is a wonderful sound. Christmas music sounds lovelier to me than ever before in my life. Sooner than I expect, it's time for me to go. I've got to work on Tony's bridge. I did the impressions. Now to pour the models, and then the crowns and the porcelain fill-ins tomorrow. On my walk home, I'm thinking how wonderful life can be. A fiancée like Rita, work like I have, all in a wonderful country. Next thing we will have our own land to live on, in these majestic mountains so very near to that guardian butte, Shishequa.

CHAPTER 21

A LOVE LETTER & THE AUGUSTA COMMUNITY BAND

November 1, 1904—I find a little letter in my post office box at Will Barnard's. A year ago Will got the appointment. It's a better job for him than freighting. The writing on the letter looks familiar, of course. It's Rita's. A birthday note, kind of like a poem. I'm sure she made it up. My first love letter!

Dear Oscar:

My one and only.
On this occasion I will try to let you know
Exactly how my life has taken on a future
So exciting, with you.
It is because we plan together

To meet the future with love for each other.
May you have a happy, happy birthday.

With my love,
Rita

Nothing can keep me from walking out to see her this evening. She is at the door before I can knock. "I got a birthday letter in my mailbox today." With fake pretense, her reply is, "Who in the world knows it's your birthday?"

"Rita, my good lady, you deserve a kiss for that first love letter." With a happy smile, she looks up to me. I hold her face with both my hands. Our eyes meet, magnetized, and then our lips. Ecstasy races through us. Soon (or is it?) Mama Auchard rattles the kettles on the stove and brings us to our senses. Mrs. Auchard talks through the door. "Oscar, you must be hungry and, of course, we planned for you to come. Rita has baked a cake."

All my days are full of patients. Some nights too are stolen or begged by people in trouble and women having babies. Early November I get another letter. This from Lou Woods, my Helena hunting friend. He wants to know if I could arrange a several-day trip in December to go hunting with him. Now, this is a problem. I remember very well telling Rita I would not go hunting this year. This begins to gnaw on me. What can I tell him? I've got to answer soon. I want to go hunting and I also want to keep my promise to Rita. What can I tell her, or him?

When the last patient leaves my office, I keep thinking, and I find myself heading out to her house. Rita, of course, is expecting me, but she is so perceptive.

"Oscar, you are worried? You are so quiet."

"How can you read me so easily?"

"Just the way you do or don't talk." Wow, women can really pick things up!

"Well, I might as well spill it. I got a letter form Lou Woods today."

"And he told you something, maybe not so good?"

"Yes, remember I told you I certainly wasn't going hunting this year?"

"I remember," she puts her hands on her hips and looks me right in the eye, "I never made you promise any such thing, did I?"

"That's right, you didn't. Well, Lou wants me to arrange a four-or-five-day hunting trip next month, December. I have to let him know I can't this year."

"Oh yes, you can. I have no intentions of asking you to refrain from doing the things you really like to do."

I am totally flabbergasted. "Rita, what an understanding wife you'll be. I'm the luckiest man alive." I grab her with a hug, and since no one is watching, a kiss. "Rita, how I do love thee!"

We spend the evening going over our to-get list: table and chairs, bed and mattress, wash stand, bowl and pitcher, teakettle, coffeepot. . . . The list gets long.

"Oscar, I've been collecting for quite a while. I have three blankets, all wool, and Mother and I have a comforter on the stretcher with a wool bat in it. The pieces we sewed together make a pattern called *The Barn Door*. We saved feathers from the year's chicken killings for the two pillows too."

"I sure don't have much, especially for a household. I'm glad you know what we will need."

December is not far off. I must talk to Charlie Dorrance to get the go-ahead for the pack trip. What a coincidence! Next day, Charlie comes right into my office. "Doc, I've got this bad tooth. It aches a while, then quits, then starts again."

I look. "Yes, it's too far gone, about to abscess. It needs to come out."

"I figured as much. Can you give me a little painkiller? I'm tough about most pain, except for my teeth."

"I sure can, because it's a lower, and I can put the pain killer back farther, not in the infected area."

While the shot is taking effect, I ask him if there is a possibility that Lou Woods and I can get out and hunt for a few days, maybe even get an elk.

"Sure thing, Doc. There's a couple other guys who want to spend a few days out. How about the fifteenth through the twenty-second?"

"That will be just right. I'll be through with Bud Tomlinson's Christmas Concert and that hunt will end before Christmas. Tomorrow I'll send a note to Lou. He'll be happy to hear we can go."

The band concert on the eleventh is a success. Bud is pleased with the audience turnout. Many came in their sleighs so Mr. Nett took the teams to the stable. It was just right for a picture, with sunshine, little wind, even if a little cold.

The photographer made the trip from Helena pay off. He was able to get several families to have pictures taken at the hotel. Our youngest band member, Homer Wellman, was pleased to be in the pictures. He has just started trumpet lessons with Bud. Pictures will be sent next week.

1904 Augusta Community Band—Walter Woods of Great Falls sent a copy of the above photo, suggesting The Sun *not identify the musicians for a week to test the old-timers' recall. However, since a small version of it was in* The Shadow of the Rockies, *the newspaper will identify everyone, hoping the photo reproduction turns out well.* FRONT ROW FROM LEFT—*Hugh Thomas, Riley Smith, Henry Lempert, Bingham Wellman, Stanley Milan. Second row—Lou Aldrich, Miss Carter, Rita (Auchard) Kenck, Bud Tomlinson, Mayte Tomlinson, Zilla Gardner, Joseph Daniels, John Thomas. Back row—Ray Aldrich, Floyd Barnard, Emery Beach, Dr. O. A. Kenck, Judge Mayer, Jack Lambert, Arthur H. Woods.*

December 1904—January 1905

Lou arrives on the evening stage, so on the fifteenth we are lucky the snow is not deep and we make it easily to Charlie Dorrance's. We waste no time getting packed into Patrick Basin, and the next day go out to hunt. It seems our world is far away as we concentrate on looking for and following elk tracks. We are ready to shoot if we see that rack of horns. My thoughts go back to my first hunting trip in these parts. The everyday world of business is remote. Even so, the end of our week comes too soon and we must return to reality. A successful hunt and we have meat to bring in.

Rita and I dance the old year out and the New Year in with the steps we've learned at our dance class: fox trot, two-step, minuet, and of course, the waltz. How I do like those Johann Strauss waltzes. The dance lessons pay off; my big feet know where and when they should go.

CHAPTER 22

THE WEDDING

January blizzards make the Adam's stage use a bobsled, which follows the tall marker poles set earlier in the fall for just such times as this. Rita and I keep watch of the weather patterns. When the weather breaks and the snows thaw a bit, we'll be ready. We agree that we'll marry in Helena or Butte. Butte is just a quick trip by train from Helena. We want to be by ourselves for a few days.

Tony comes to my office and interrupts my constant thinking of the near future.

"Kenck, this tooth," and he points to it, "is just too achy. I'm thinking that sometime soon you just might be gone a few days too many and this bugger will really be achin'."

"You could be right. You have ways of knowing what a man about to get married might do. Let's take care of it right now."

He tells me as the painkiller works, "Kenck, this being married surely beats being a lonely bachelor. My Mabel sure knows how to cook and take care of a house."

"To get a good wife is important. I'm glad you are satisfied with Mabel. I thought she would be just the kind of a girl you should have."

"Yeah, Kenck, don't waste any more time. You will be glad you've decided to end this bachelor existence."

"Don't worry, Tony, we have plans. It won't be long now."

February 1905. Rita and I decided that sometime in the spring we will get married. I have come out to supper. Afterward we are talking by the organ where she has been playing.

"Rita, I think we should wait no longer to get married."

"Oscar, I agree. Why wait?"

"There is no good reason. Here we are both almost thirty. It is high time. What do you think about going to Helena tomorrow—maybe get married there or we could go to Butte."

"Oscar, that's a good idea. What about your patients?"

"Strange thing. I've made no appointments for all next week."

"Let's tell Mama and Papa we'll go on the stage tomorrow."

We go to the sitting room. Papa is dozing in his chair. Mama is knitting by lamplight. (She really doesn't need much light to knit socks).

Rita announces, "Mama and Papa, we've decided to go to Helena tomorrow and be married."

Papa really comes to attention in his easy chair. In his low New England voice, "It's about time. I've been wondering what was taking you so long."

Mama is all smiles and drops the knitting on the floor as she stands up and claps her hands. "We have been waiting for this announcement. This is wonderful!"

I say to Rita, "Let's right now get our suitcases packed and be ready. I'll go right to my hotel room now."

I bid the folks goodnight and make a quick exit. Walking down the road is altogether different. The moon is bright and the stars brighter than ever. Life is different. I'll soon be a married man. I decide to shave this night so I'll be ready at quarter to six in the morning.

As I look at that man in the mirror, I say: "Hey, you will be a married man soon. Yeah! I agree with Papa Auchard—it's about time."

I sleep just a few minutes and then wake up. The

hours go by. I hear my clock ring the quarter hours all night long.

At five, I'm up getting ready. Finally, at quarter to six, I put my overcoat and fur cap on and grab my suitcase, make my way down, and stand in front of the hotel. Along comes Dick with his snorting and blowing horses—stops for his hotel passenger.

He sees it's me and shouts above the clatter, "It's you, Doc! What's going on? I didn't know you'd be here waiting."

"Yep, it's me, Dick." I climb aboard into his stage. Right away I say, "We gotta stop and pick up Rita at the Auchard gate."

Dick says, "Oh, oh. What's up, Doc?"

"Dick, you can make your own guess. Right now I'm not talking much."

March, 1905—Being gone ten days serves to make the dental business pile up. Several notes left at my office door made me realize I'm working steady. The first person to greet me was George White.

"Doc, I've been waitin' days for you to get back. It

Wedding picture of Dr. O. A. Kenck and Miss Rita Auchard, February 23, 1905

shouldn't take ten days for a man to marry. Boy, I sure didn't take that long. I married Tillie and I'd only known her ten days, but she was willing to marry me right away."

"When was that, George, that you could get a gal to marry you so easily?"

"It was in the fall of '92. I had taken a carload of horses to Grand Forks, North Dakota. I was invited to a dance. Tillie was there. Cutest doll in the place. We danced and danced. By the end of the dance I knew she was the one, so I really rushed her for a solid week. There was a local fellow that kept giving me dirty looks and trying to talk to Tillie. Finally he tried to get me to fight him. I said, 'No, I don't want to fight you. I just want Tillie. If she decides for you instead of me, I'll be on the next train west.' Tillie said, 'I don't want him. He's a real dud.' That settled it, so we made plans and got hitched right away. We were here in Augusta before Christmas."

"George, I think you are a fast worker. What brings you to my office?"

"Oh, Doc, it's this pain in my mouth—a bad tooth. I mean, two bad teeth."

"Open wide and let me see. You are right, George. They are both badly decayed. Too bad to save. Do you want them out right now?"

"Well, Doc, that'd be the best. An achin' mouth is the worst thing."

That evening at home I tell Rita about George White and Tillie getting married on such short notice. "Yes, George and Tillie live up Elk Creek. But there is another family of Whites who live near there. They first started on Smith Creek with a sawmill business. They are the children of Joe and Jennie White. There are many Whites and easy to get them all confused. George and Tillie's girl is little Charlotte—the one you took a picture of, by the Adams' house on the corner."

The middle of March and word comes from Albert that the property deal is done. Now I must go to Helena and take care of the money and deeds. That really doesn't take much time, and right now I'm not anxious to spend time in Helena, away from Rita, but Rita will spend the day and night I am away with Mama and Papa.

Albert comes with me to set up camp on the property. He is dead set on felling and peeling logs for his cabin, so that is what he does. In Augusta he gets Clemons Freight to take out a load of nails and finish lumber for windows, door frames, and flooring. Albert seems happy to finally start building a cabin.

By June of 1905 I've come up with an idea. I keep hearing that Choteau is a populous town, especially when the Court there is in session. "Rita, what do you think of us staying in Choteau when the Court is in session? I keep hearing it's a busy place at that time."

"Oscar, where would we live?"

"That's really no problem if you wouldn't mind living in a hotel during that time."

"A hotel would be fine. Certainly not much housework for me. I could be your office assistant."

"Rita, you really wouldn't have to work for me but I wouldn't mind your being there."

CHAPTER 23

BROTHER VAN

During the second week of June, Rita comes from the post office and stops at my office. "I saw Papa at the post office. He shows me a letter he got from Brother Van."

"Let me guess."

Rita pulls her lips together like they are sealed. "He is coming to preach in Augusta?"

"Exactly. Tomorrow he expects to preach at our community church."

"The one across from Barnards?"

"Yes, and of course he stays all day and preaches in the evening too. He will stay at Papa and Mama's house. We have almost always had him. Dinner after church and then supper after the evening Service. He stays the night and has a good breakfast before he goes on his way. And, as usual, I will play the organ for both Services. This time it will be different, however. Maybe you will agree to my plan?"

"Rita, whatever your plan is, I agree."

"After the morning Service, I will go home with Papa and Mama to help with the dinner and you will have made arrangements to have a buggy waiting at Nett's to bring Brother Van out after he has finished talking with any new converts. What do you think?"

"Sure, I'll do that for you and for Brother Van. Since he is a tireless worker for the church, I'll be glad to do it."

Rita goes on her way to our house. I finish my appointments and all the drop-ins. Several are telling me Brother Van is coming to town for Services. They all say his name with a sort of reverence. I must ask Rita to tell me about him. Everyone is talking about him like he is someone extraordinary.

She says, "I can tell you some things about him. We first heard of him when Mama and I, along with our family, came to Montana on the Missouri River steamship *Rosebud*. People would say 'Wait till Brother Van comes to our town. Many folks will make a special effort to come to the Service he will hold.'

"Finally, when I was about twelve, he held meetings in this town. The thing that impressed me most when I was young was how he does love to sing. He sang songs we children especially understood. He'd break into song in the middle of his sermon. His voice boomed and we could understand every word. If I were getting sleepy, his song would surely wake me. After I learned to play the organ, I would play and he would sing—just to be singing. He might change key in the middle of the song. I learned to listen carefully and change key too.

"What was best about his coming was he often stayed at our house. Mama and Papa always insisted he stay with us. This parish was so large that the need for establishing new churches kept him busy in all the newly settled areas."

"I've heard of him but never sat through a sermon, so this will be interesting for me. Do you suppose I will like his preaching?"

"Oscar, knowing you, and also what kind of a message he gives, of course you will. He never criticizes people of other beliefs. He just talks about the Lord Jesus Christ and God. He never tries to make anyone feel uncomfortable. Nor does he brag about how much he is doing. He's established many churches and got many parsonages started. Also, a project like a Christian college and a hospital. He's getting older now. I think someone said in 1900 that he was 52 years old."

"Most Protestant preachers have a wife. Why doesn't he?"

"He doesn't speak about it much, but I heard he was engaged once to a Montana girl. She died of TB before they could marry, and he just decided he would meet her in heaven."

"So, he doesn't have a home or a home place?"

"No, he constantly travels. He has come here with one of the bishops or other preachers of the Methodists. One thing you, of all people, will notice about him is his teeth."

"Why so? Are they bad or crooked or what?"

"No, I don't think so, but he has had all that show covered with gold crowns."

"Wow, that's unusual. I wonder which dentist or dentists did his work?"

"That I don't know. Oh yes, he has good table manners except when he eats soup. For some reason he slurps soup very loudly. I guess he thinks if soup is to be enjoyed it must make noise."

We clear our dishes away and make sure we are ready to be at church tomorrow.

I make breakfast on Sundays, as it's good practice. (I'll know exactly how when I will go camping or on hunting trips.) After breakfast, I go to make sure the buggy will be ready to take Brother Van out to Auchards after church.

After that we go early to make the church ready for the Service. Rita opens the doors to air out the room and then sits down at the organ and runs through a few pieces that she is almost certain Brother Van will sing, or have us all sing to. Brother Van arrives with Mr. and Mrs. George Christian. He made it as far as their place yesterday. He's come from the Falls. Their ranch is right close to the main road. Rita quickly greets him and introduces me.

"Brother Van, I want you to meet my husband, Doctor Oscar Kenck."

Brother Van is surprised. "Miss Rita! Oh no, that's not right any more. You're Mrs. Kenck now. I'm glad to meet your husband." He reaches for my hand. "Dr. Kenck, congratulations. You have a wonderful lady. She always has accompanied the church services when I've come here. She started when she was a very young lady and gets better every year."

Rita changes the subject. "My father and mother are expecting you for dinner after the Service and for supper this evening. And, of course, overnight, like you have always done."

"Your folks are so gracious when I come. I do appreciate their kindness."

"Mama and Papa will be here soon for the Service. I've asked my new husband if he will bring you out afterwards. I will go home first with Mama and Papa and help with the dinner. That way you can visit a bit with your old friends."

Several minutes later I hear the organ playing so I go in with those who have just arrived. Rita is playing the organ to get the people to come in and sit down. After all find a place in the wooden pews, a hush falls over the crowd. (This is new to me. I've not been to Services other than Mass.) Brother Van comes up to the pulpit. He gives a glad welcome to all who have come. He has a happy countenance, not terribly solemn. He then gives a simple prayer, definitely <u>not</u> in Latin. The well-worn Methodist songbooks are pulled out and opened. With Rita playing, Brother Van's booming voice leads the whole congregation gustily singing several songs. They all seem to already know the words and tune.

After about four songs, Brother Van announces that the usual church officers will take up a collection "for the Lord's work." He then opens his Bible and begins to read the story of the prodigal son. After he finishes the story as written, he says, "Let us pray." It certainly seems like he's having an actual talk with God.

He launches into the Bible story about the son who got his inheritance and went to a different country where he spent it all and then had to eat with the animals that he was hired to feed. The father constantly looked for the son to come home. This story Brother Van uses to remind us all that our folks would like to see us or to hear we have been converted from a life of sin to a life of believing and obeying God.

At the end he invites people to repent and come forward to accept Christ as their Savior. He then breaks into a song, something about a mother's son. As he closes, he promises at the evening Service that he will tell of his buffalo hunt with the Blackfoot tribe.

Leaving church is a slow process. Many want a few words with Brother Van. He knows many by name and is interested in how each is getting along. People show they really like him. When most have gone, I go quickly to Nett's and get the buggy and team that I hired earlier. After the last talker has gone, Brother Van picks up his satchel, comes quickly to my waiting buggy, and climbs in beside me.

I'm sure he's hungry after his sermon and hearty singing. Even so, he starts a conversation as we head toward the mountain. He says, "That old mountain there (he's pointing at Haystack Butte) calls me back just as though he's been waiting for centuries for a preacher to come with the word of God. Young man, this town is blessed with you coming and being their dentist. Where did you come from?"

"I came from Helena where I had my first dental practice. My first dental office here was a box made and set on a wagon frame. I worked my way to Wolf Creek, to Augusta, and then to Choteau. Since Rita and I have married, we will be in Augusta, with maybe short stays in Choteau."

"Where in the East did you come from?"

"I didn't come from the East at all. I was born in Helena in 1875."

Brother Van explains where he came from too. "In 1872 I came up the river from St. Louis. I was born in Pennsylvania. Helena was a village of saloons in Last Chance Gulch when I first saw it. It was a one-street mining town. During the 1870s the county was really wild, and in 1877 the people were all worried about the Indian wars."

"I know a bit about them even though I was very young. My father was killed near Yellowstone by the Nez Percé warriors."

Brother Van turns toward me, his eyes wider and he says, "Your father!? I remember there were two killed and others who escaped narrowly. Why yes, I do remember one of those killed was a Charles Kenck from Helena. You are his son? How strange that I should meet you now. That was so long ago."

"Yes, it's been 28 years. The only way I know is that my mother and uncles told me."

"I was around Bannock and Argenta. The message raced around the country telling people the Nez Percé were on the warpath. It was frightening."

"What did you and the people do when you heard

this news?"

"General Howard was trying to catch up with the Nez Percé but they were always ahead. The Bannock folks got ready for the Indian war parties. They were sure the Indians were coming. No one came to church services then. It would be risky taking family across the prairies where they could be attacked and killed. The Nez Percé used to be peaceful, but when they were forced off their promised homeland and some of their horses and cattle stolen, they were angry and ready to fight. After the battle of Big Hole, where General Gibbon caught them by surprise early one morning, killing many of their women, children, and old people, they <u>really</u> went on the warpath."

"Brother Van, you have the right picture. After I finished college in Spokane, I made a trip up to the Spokane Reservation where Chief Joseph was held in confinement. I talked with him. He told the Indian's side—the United States Government's policy of breaking treaties and the crowding of several tribes together on smaller reservations. The Nez Percé had large herds of beautiful Appaloosa horses and large herds of cattle.

When the animals were stolen by the whites, the young warriors became angry and wanted revenge."

"Dr. Kenck, I'm surprised you know the facts about that war and understand the Indian attitude, even though you lost your father. I've come to know many Indians, but mostly Blackfoot. They receive me any time I hold Services at Browning now."

We are turning in at the pole gate at Auchards. Will is waiting. He knows Brother Van and greets him and then takes the team to the barn. Mr. Auchard comes out. "Brother Van, you are just in time for dinner."

Rita appears on the porch too. "You must be hungry and dinner is ready. Come right in. There is a basin of warm water for you to wash up in."

"Miss Rita, no, Mrs. Kenck, I mean, you folks are so gracious and thoughtful. Your husband and I have been talking of the Nez Percé Indian War. Later we will talk some more. I'm sure he knows more than I do."

Yes, Brother Van is hungry and eats with great relish. Talk is set aside while the delicious food is stowed to empty stomachs. Visiting preachers were often served fried chicken, but Brother Van didn't look like he was tired of *anything*. Mrs. Auchard also knew his favorite pie was custard, and he exclaimed over it. After dinner we give him time to rest. It seems to me that traveling and preaching is enough to tire any person.

After half an hour on the sofa, Brother Van raises up and brightly says, "Dr. Kenck, we have a bit more to talk about—Chief Joseph. You said you have been to see him on the Spokane Reservation. Tell me what was he like? Especially, what did he say?"

"When I got there, he was pacing back and forth from one teepee to another. The Agency had built him a house but he did not want to live in it. He stored his things from his pre-war life in that house: guns (but no ammunition), his medicine bundle, and his ceremonial dress articles. He was dressed in white man's drab clothing. His hair was braided and hanging down the sides of his face. He looked at me for a while, saying not a word. Then he turned his face away and kept looking off to the south. I was actually north of him. His once broad shoulders were sagged hopelessly and matched his sad countenance. Another time of silence, maybe ten minutes, but it seemed like an hour."

"Did he finally talk?"

"Yes." I related the whole story about my talk with Chief Joseph.

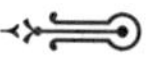

Back at the church, the conversation moved on to Brother Van's projects, and we heard about the progress of the Methodists in Montana, especially about Wesleyan College, which Rita had attended, the Deaconess Hospital in Great Falls, and the Deaconess Home for Children in Helena. Where funds for these great institutions came from, only Brother Van knew. He goes on during the rest of the evening about his buffalo-hunting story. Unusual for a preacher, especially a green young man from the East.

The events that led up to the hunt were not ordinary. Brother Van was invited by the Indian agent on the Teton to hold a Service. (The Blackfoot had earlier run the Catholic brothers off.) For this Service, he had an interpreter. The largest tent was used. All went well and they were listening quietly when a young brave stuck his head in the flap and made a short excited speech. Then all the Indians filed out.

The interpreter told Brother Van, "All their horses have been stolen." He and Brother Van right away offered their horses to two braves to go look for the herd of horses. Two hours later the two braves came back with all their horses and filed back in to listen to the rest of the sermon.

Little Plume, the young chief, showed his appreciation and invited Brother Van to go on a buffalo hunt the next day. They left very early and rode about eight miles before they found a herd. The hunters stayed out of sight in ravines and any low places we could find. The herd was resting and feeding quietly several hundred yards away. (When alarmed, the herd will stampede blindly. Indians often incited a stampede and ran them off a cliff, called a *buffalo jump*, where many would fall to their death.)

This time there was no cliff but the buffalo were spooked to run down the ravine past the hunters. "I was to shoot the *king buffalo*, the herd leader out in front. The old king was thought to have the best leather and it would be a great honor if I could bring him down. I

didn't want the Indians to know I was scared and quaking in my boots. I'd never hunted before. I waited, trembling, until the Chief yelled, 'You shoot,' as he pointed to the king buffalo. I'm praying, and kicking my good running horse, Jonathan, in the flanks and getting the gun up. We raced the animal and caught up. I cocked my gun, aimed, and pulled the trigger. The great bull went limp before he hit the ground. I never claimed my hunting skill got that buffalo. He was killed by prayer." The audience breaks into applause.

After the Service, Mama and Papa Auchard are ready to take Brother Van home with them. Before they pull out, Brother Van says, "Tell Mr. Adams I will be ready at the gate tomorrow morning. I'm on the way to the Methodist headquarters in Helena."

We do just that. Dick says, "I've had this preacher on my stage before. He's a good traveler." 'Tis good we've taken care of Brother Van's Augusta visit.

We go through with our special plans. "Rita, my good lady, we can think about Choteau. I've got reliable information from Joe Bush that the Court will be in session there after the Fourth of July. So, pack your suitcase and we'll go soon."

"Mama asked me today, 'When will you and Oscar be going to Choteau?'"

"What did you tell her?"

Rita smiled, almost laughing, "Oscar is sometimes unpredictable, so even though I don't know exactly, I must be ready."

"That's a nice way of saying I don't know what I'm doing."

"My good man, I've been watching you for several years already."

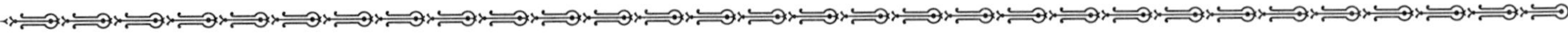

CHAPTER 24

CHOTEAU NEEDS ME

July 6, 1905—Now I get my instruments and supplies packed. Oh yes, a thought: "Rita, be sure and put in your dress-up clothes. The ladies there are friendly and will invite you to their doings. We also will go to a lodge meeting and some dances."

"Sounds like we'll enjoy Choteau. I've got an idea too. Let's take the buggy and team that Papa gave me a few years ago. Then we can always be ready to come home to see the folks."

"Sure, if that's all right with your father."

"Of course, that's all right with him. When he gives something, it's for keeps."

"It's settled then. Prince and Queenie go to Choteau with us. I appreciate your father's generosity."

July 7, 1905—the buggy is loaded—bulging, in fact. We leave the dental car in Augusta. I've got an office in the hotel, Choteau House. This is quite a different trip from my first one in this direction, across the hills and coulees. 'Tis more than a bit better to have a bridge over the big irrigation flumes.

"Is this the place you and Bill got stuck?"

"Yes, one of the places. My wagon high-centered on its reach and we couldn't move an inch. The foreman of the building outfit sent a four-horse team to pull us out and on up the hill that time."

Choteau House gives us a hearty welcome. The Court in session creates a busy county seat. My first caller after I've posted my sign in the hotel's big front window is Doctor Brooks, MD.

"I'm mighty happy you've come here. But I must warn you that this town gives no rest to either doctor or dentist. I hear that you have done more than just dentistry in Augusta."

"Yes, every few days—or nights too, I should say—I'm called to a medical emergency. Doctor Albright is overwhelmed at times. He'd like to sell his practice and leave. I'll get a rest now since you are the doctor in this town."

"Don't count on it. Calls are so many, sometimes, that I cannot get to all of them before it's too late. Got to go now. Mrs. Cook, up the Teton, is in labor and is waiting. Well, I hope she's still waiting. Often babies can't wait for a doctor. I'll be back though—I've got a couple of teeth needing your services."

"Come by any time you get a chance. Hope you make it in time."

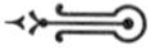

Soon a familiar young face shows at my door. "I'm Bing. Do you remember the ugliest kid in town—warts, freckles and all?"

"Why, howdy, Bing. Long time, no see. You look five years taller and must be in high school, of course."

"Yes, sir, I'm in high school this fall. My mom says my teeth need you."

"Okay, Bing. Take the chair and I'll take a look. Your mom is right. My explorer finds several cavities. If you can start now, the sooner the better."

"Is this going to hurt?"

"I'll go real easy, a little at a time. A toothache later will hurt far worse." I take care of those. One needs a medicated pad on top first. I put a temporary filling in to make sure it can be saved. The other two take silver amalgam. "That's enough for today. Can you come back tomorrow? Don't chew on hard things today."

Bing is glad to close his mouth. He rubs his jaw.

"That wasn't so bad, was it?"

"No, but I'll get busy and brush every night. See if I can keep them from . . . what's the word?"

"*Decay*. Yes, twice a day for brushing is better. To-morrow I'll show you how to brush."

"All right, tomorrow 'bout this same time I can be

back. I'm working for Dad. He's building a house. I carry lumber right to where he needs it. He builds all the time."

The day passes quickly. Several people—some businessmen—welcome me back, remembering my wagon-box office. Also, one nameless fellow (maybe *transient* is a good name) needs to get a bad one pulled.

Rita and I have our supper in the hotel dining room. She likes this "non-cooking" life. I tell her about the Bing here in Choteau, same age as the other Bing in Augusta, both ambitious kids.

The next day Bing is back and on a talking streak. He tells me his past and his future, as he sees it. So, when Rita that night at supper asks, "Did Bing come back?", I have a continuous story to tell.

"He'll be a freshman this fall and expects to play football and everything else they have for the boys. There is no limit to his plans. A dentist is the only one who can keep him from nonstop talk."

Rita has a knowing smile and goes on. "His past, what about it?"

"He claims to be the first white child born in this town. Others must think so too. He was given a tract of land of about two acres because of this honor. He says, 'Someday I'll build a house for my family. But first I'm going to have a ranch—that is, after I finish college.' He takes high school very seriously. A Mr. Guthrie is the principal, severe and strict. If a kid gets called into his office, he'll feel as high as a fly on the floor when he leaves."

At the finish of today's work on his teeth, I give him the tooth-brushing lesson. "Bing, are you sure you want to hear it?"

"Of course I do. No one's ever shown me how to brush my teeth."

"If you get weary of it, then stop me."

"I won't stop you. If there is a better way to do it, I want to know." Bing listens attentively.

"I'll use this plaster model of a mouth with teeth, uppers and lowers. Now, with a toothbrush, I lay it inside the back lower molars with bristles pointing down. Then I twist the brush so the bristles sweep the gums first and then all the way up to the chewing edge. This action exercises the gums and sweeps all food particles from between the teeth. Place the brush like-wise, a little towards the front, and repeat the action to the center. Do this again on the opposite side. Reverse this action and do the uppers until you have exercised all your gums and all the tooth surfaces have been swept clean and polished. Lastly, give several brush strokes to the roof of the mouth as well as to the tongue as far back as you can without gagging."

"That is quite some lesson. Do you suppose he will do it?" Rita asks.

"I hope so. It will help save him from gum disease and some cavities. I tell him to use tooth powder once a day and a good pinch of salt in a glass of water at the end of the day."

"That certainly is a different and more thorough way to clean the teeth and the mouth. I have to admit I have not been using that method, but I will certainly do better now that I've had the same lesson as Bing."

After our supper and the brush lesson, we take a stroll about the main street of Choteau. A poster catches our eyes. The Old Timers Dance will be Saturday night. "Oscar, that is a good idea. Now I can use my dress-up clothes you reminded me to bring."

"Yes, let's go. We haven't danced in months."

Saturday night arrives. We get dressed up and make our appearance. The crowd there are all ages—lots of kids, old folks, and middle-aged like ourselves. A square dance goes on first. The caller is a striking look-ing fellow: tall, broad-shouldered, but with long white hair and contrasting black mustache. A happy counte-nance with a booming voice. When the one o'clock break is for refreshments, Rita and I come home. This is the first dance since we got married. We did dance a few times, but without knowing many people, it was unlike Augusta back home.

A few days later Brooks is back to get work done as he promised. "I have a report to make, Brooks. My wife and I went to the pioneer dance."

"Oh, I bet you saw my rancher partner."

"If I did, I didn't know who he was. There were so many there. A few I knew—the people who have been in to get some work done—but the rest I didn't know."

"Oh, he's the square dance caller. You can't miss him. A huge fellow with a booming voice."

"You mean the big man with white hair and black mustache?"

"That's him, Bill Cook. He's unusual in more ways than looks."

"How do you mean?"

Brooks is easing himself into my dental chair and acts like he's glad to sit down. Seems like he wants to talk a while just to have an excuse to rest.

"Bill was a bachelor until just a few years ago. A girl named Millie Meyer came to this country from Europe somewhere. She was searching for her brother who had come west earlier. She found out he had been killed, but she liked this Choteau area and decided to stay here. She happened to take out a homestead claim up near my ranch on the Teton, and when Bill laid eyes on her, he made up his mind he wanted her as a wife. They've had a child every year since they got married. Just had one about a month ago."

"Maybe Bill is smart but doesn't know how to keep from having babies every year."

"Funny thing. I told him there are ways. But he says, 'What's wrong with having a big family?' Then he springs one of his smart answers, like, 'Millie is a bit hard of hearing, so when we go to bed I say, 'Shall we go to bed or what?' She says, 'What?'" We both have a chuckle over that remark.

"Brooks, I think being a doctor here is hard work and more so because some nights you get little sleep."

"How true. Sometimes I'm at the point of exhaustion. That is why I have a cabin up at my ranch where I can go and regroup."

"I'm beginning to feel like that. Doctor Albright is practicing in Augusta, but at times he can't be found, so I'm pressed into medical service. Hope it's better here."

"I wouldn't guarantee you'll see that. Guess we'd better get on with my teeth before someone discovers where I am."

CHAPTER 25

LIFE IN THE BIG TOWN OF CHOTEAU

The ladies have a get-together today. Dr. Brooks tells me his wife is having what's called a *Tea*. Its purpose is to make Rita feel welcome in town.

"How was your day?" I casually ask as we are at supper.

"My good husband, seems to me you must have let the word out that I might be lonely here."

I stop, put down my fork, and look right into her brown eyes. "Rita, I didn't really instigate anything. Brooks himself brought up the subject the other day. He asked me if you would enjoy coming to the ladies' little tea parties. So, I told him you are a friendly lady and would be pleased to get acquainted. How was it?"

"Doctor and Mrs. Brooks are thoughtful. I met Mrs.

Julian Burd, Mrs. Guthrie, and of course, Mrs. Hodgkiss and Mrs. Brooks when they came here to invite me. We had a lively time as we did handwork. Mrs. Brooks suggested I bring my crocheting or knitting. She explained that our fancywork makes good conversation. She said it is fun to see what other ladies are doing."

"What did you take?"

"When I know I'm going to be talking, I usually take crocheting. I can see the design pattern and don't need to count very often. Mrs. Burd's husband has a store here on Main Street."

"Yeah, I know that store, and Mr. Burd too."

"She said the group gets together like that about once a month, at one of their homes. Strange though—

they all talked of where their husbands came from. They were amazed when I explained you were a native. I had fun with that for a bit. Mrs. Guthrie said, 'A person would never know it. What tribe is he from?' I smiled at that. All faces in the room were on me, waiting for more. 'I mean, he was born in Helena.' They all sighed in relief."

"Is that Mrs. Guthrie the principal's wife?"

"Yes, she's June Guthrie. She spoke of her children too. She has several alive and more than one who didn't live long after birth. Mrs. Brooks' name is Margaret, same name as Mrs. Hodgkiss. The doctor's wife is a pleasant hostess. Even though she has no children, she is interested in others' children, I guess because her doctor husband has brought so many into the world."

"I was worried that you would get too lonely here, but now it looks like you will be occupied and have all manner of social life."

"I had no idea you were worried about me. You are so sweet to care about me like that, Oscar."

"My good lady, I care so very much. Even though I sound like I am joking, I'm not, when it comes to your

Sheriff Joe Bush

place in my life. I've been thinking lately maybe we'll find a house and settle down here. I could go to Augusta once every three months and live here. Just a thought though. We'll see."

July of 1905 is a busy month. August looks like it will be the same.

Joe Bergeron ("Bush") comes into my office. "Howdy, Doc. Had to come over today, something about the trial that's going on now. But I've got a special message for you."

"Good to see you, Joe. Can a sheriff deliver a good message?"

"More than one person said, 'Tell Kenck to come back to Augusta. We miss him and our teeth need him.' Let's see now. It was Mrs. Todd, Dr. Albright, Claude White, Mary Thomas, and a bunch more. Can't remember all of them."

That evening I tell Rita, "Joe Bush came in today."

"What did he have to say?"

"He said he had a message from some people in Augusta and named off several." I repeated the list Joe reeled off.

"My, my! All those people sending a message. What about?"

"The message is, 'Come back to Augusta. We need you!'"

"What do you plan to do?"

"I'm thinking we could go back. The Court session is going to end maybe next week. We can tell the folks here we will be coming back as soon as we take care of the people who've been begging for us to come."

"I'm having a good time getting acquainted with the Choteau folks, but I miss Mama and Papa. They would be so happy to have us back, even if it is just for a while."

"I'll put up a sign saying when we are going to be out of town in Augusta but that we'll return here. I had thought of a divided practice but it does wreck our housekeeping, or, I mean, your housekeeping."

"My good husband, never fear about spoiling my housekeeping. I've enjoyed being here and don't mind going back and forth."

That settles it. I let it be known I'll be gone a month or so after August 17. A few come on in who have been putting off coming in. Frank Pings is one. He's Tony's brother and lives in Conrad. He's practically building the whole town himself. "I'm sure glad to catch you. I heard you are going back to Augusta."

"That's true but it's not permanent. After I get all the urgent ones taken care of, I'll be back here."

"Glad to hear that. I could come to Augusta and see my brother Tony, but I'm building the town. Got a couple of stone buildings in progress. But my teeth are giving me fits so I'm glad you are still here." I get Frank settled in the chair.

"Yes, I see, Frank, you have a couple of molars still fixable by putting crowns on them."

CHAPTER 26

BACK TO AUGUSTA

September 15, 1905—We load our clothes, dental equipment, and supplies into the buggy, get our team from the stable, and we are off.

Todd, the forest ranger, was the first one in when we got back and settled in once again in Augusta. "Kenck, I've been checking on the fish stocking project. I stopped at Wood Lake last month, and sure enough, your babies lived. There are fish in that lake and all the other places we planted. In the years to come, will those who fish those waters above the falls know, or even think of, how they happened to be there?"

"Probably not. Just you and I and a few who were in on the job will know and then it's forgotten. What's your problem today?"

"These dentures you made for me in 1901 are loose, and I heard about this business of relining."

"Sure thing. They can be relined, and these two broken teeth can be replaced."

"Go ahead, Doc. I've got this week in town getting supplies and my horse some new shoes."

No sooner do I have the impression compound set in Todd's mouth but I've got another patient waiting at the door.

"Howdy, Ole. Have a seat there. I'm just about through with Todd's impression."

"Doc, I got a message from Albert. He stops at my place when he goes to Clemons Post Office for his mail. He asked me to give you a message. He wants to talk about buying a few head of cattle."

"Ole, if you see him before Sunday, tell him I'll try to come up on Sunday."

"Okay. He tells me you plan to build a house and live there in the Canyon."

"Yep, that's right. I do dream about it. Especially when I go up and look at the place. It's so beautiful. The mountains are the best place to live."

"If you and Rita decide to make a home there, all us Beans will like you as a neighbor."

"Good neighbors are important to have and it's important to be a good neighbor." We stop talking about the ranch and get going on the tooth he wants fixed.

As Ole leaves, Dr. Albright shows up. "Howdy, Albright. How are things with you?"

"I'm busy enough. Too much, most of the time. I'd really like to move away. I badly need a rest. I figure the only way a doctor can get a rest is to move to some territory where no one knows he's a doctor."

"Yes, that's really the only way."

"A young fellow from Minnesota, just graduated from Iowa Medical School, has written me about coming west to practice. Name is Bateman. He heard I might sell and wants to know my price."

"What price did you give him?"

"I don't have a way to value my practice, so I just said $500."

"That's a good amount but probably too much for a young fellow just getting out of college."

"You're right. He wrote back saying he doesn't have anything like $500 but would I hold on for a few months so he can search around for a loan? I'll let him try awhile. I'm glad you're back in Augusta. I need some cavities taken care of."

"I'll be going back to Choteau, so spread the word. I'll be back here again in maybe a month or two. Hop right into the chair. Let's have a look at those cavities." I start the examination and find them right away. "There are two, all right. One upper left bicuspid and one lower left bicuspid. You also really need a cleaning."

"Can you start now? I want to stay out of sight unless there's an emergency."

"I sure can. I know of a couple who plan to come in today, but we may as well use every minute."

As I am working on Albright a young fellow comes in. "Howdy, sir. Do I know you?"

"You may not know me, but you know my mother, Mrs. Manix, and my sisters, especially the older one married to Tony Pings."

"I sure do know your sister and your mother. What can I do for you?"

"Mother insists that I get my teeth fixed before I go away to school. I've been working on a ranch since I got out of school at the Mission."

"Well, I'll be finished with Dr. Albright in half an hour. You can wait or come back."

"I'll be back, thank you."

Doctor Albright's cleaning job is about finished when young Manix comes back. Before Doc leaves I ask, "If that young Bateman comes, will you be leaving right away?"

"Faster than I got here. I need some time off. Babies coming keep me up nights. Emergencies and sickness take all my days. Especially Sundays it seems."

"This town and the country around will surely miss you, but I understand, since I get calls for emergencies when no MD can be found." Albright and I say goodbye, and young Manix is ready.

"Clarence, first I'll examine all your teeth. Please get up in my chair." Using my mirror and explorer, I tap two likely looking teeth gently. "Yes, I find two cavities."

"Yes sir, that last one sorta hurts when I eat ice cream."

"First I'll take care of the cavities. Then ice cream won't bother you. Last I will clean all of them and give you my special lesson on brushing." I go right to work cleaning the decay from the two molars. One is a bit deep so I put a medicated floor in it. After these fillings, I let him rest his mouth while I prepare the cleaning paste. With a brush in my chuck, I polish every surface of every tooth. That done, I say, "Run your tongue around and feel how clean."

"That does feel better. Wow!"

"Now the brush lesson. I call it my 'Bing' lesson because he was the first person I taught this lesson to here. I learned it at the first meeting of the Montana State Dental Society. Bing is a young fellow in Choteau. He told me his dad said he was the ugliest kid in town. He wasn't, really. He just laughed." Clarence listened attentively. After the lesson, he said, "If brushing like you say keeps my teeth clean as they are now, I'll sure give that a try." After this we have time for a talk.

"So, you are going away to college. Where will that be?"

"The Father at the Mission persuaded my mother to send me to Gonzaga. It's over by Spokane."

"Clarence! Gonzaga is my alma mater! I graduated in 1895, ten years ago."

"Whew! Ten years ago. What is the college like? I mean, do you think I will like to go there? Were they strict like at the Mission? What kind of teachers?"

"Wait a minute, Clarence. I can't tell you everything at once. How soon will you be going?"

"I'll be going by train next week. I'm a few days late, but the letter from the college said it will be all right because I must be fully prepared to stay. Means getting all my things together and getting my teeth fixed. The list is long. I'll be wearing suits to classes and work duds to wear while helping around the grounds."

"That's right. They expect the boys to do their share of work in the dairy, the cleaning of the buildings, the gardens. They'll keep you busy. No time to be lonesome or wonder what to do with yourself."

"Will they let us come home for Christmas?"

"Don't plan on it. The boys just get over their homesickness and going home will make them homesick all over again. Father Rodmann is especially kind to the boys. Very dedicated and certainly helps them get used to the school routines. At first I felt like I was in prison, but before long I got so busy I didn't have time to think of life before Gonzaga. Actually, I claim we were working so steadily we didn't even have time for a good fight with another student."

"Where did you live when you were a boy?"

"I lived in Helena. I was born there. My father was killed by the Indians near Yellowstone Park in 1877. I grew up without a father and pretty much was my own boss, so I understand how your life has been. Your mother, I know, is a widow. When did you lose your father?"

"In 1898, when I was just ten years old. I'm the oldest boy. My sister, Mabel, is the oldest girl, and I have five sisters and one brother. We all go to school at the Mission."

Another patient, Mrs. Sam Larkin, comes in.

"Well, Clarence, if you want to ask some more questions about Gonzaga, come back. I wish you success at the college."

Mrs. Larkin is happy to see me. "I'm so glad you have come back from Choteau. We do need you here."

"It's good to hear the Augusta folk want me to stay here, but Choteau says the same. Now I'm torn between the two towns. But Augusta might win out as Rita's folks are close here. Also, I'm acquiring Dearborn Canyon property for a ranch operation. Mrs. Larkin, what brings you to see me today?"

"It seems there are a couple of cavities in my molars and I really need them so I can chew my vittles. I want to save them if possible."

"You are so right about saving your teeth. Please put your hat on the table there, and I will have a look." After I put the dental towel around her and get my sterilized mirror and explorer in hand, I see what the trouble is. "Yes, Mrs. Larkin, you are right. The decay is in two molars on your lower left side. I can start now if you have time."

"Oh yes, Doctor, no matter. I will take time if you can save them."

Before long, the cavities are prepared and filled.

The fillings are silver and will last many years. I like to put gold in any that show when you talk or smile. These won't show.

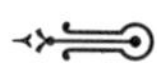

It's evening now. Rita wants to hear who all has come in every day. We have been able, with Mama Auchard's help, to have enough food at our house for suppers so we can be by ourselves some evenings. Dick Adams and Bud Tomlinson are happy we are back in town for a few weeks. I tell her this evening about young J.C. Manix going to Gonzaga, how his attitude changed when I told him I had gone there. "Rita, we need to go up to see Albert Sunday. He sends word by Ole Bean that he wants to see me."

"Is he having a problem?"

"I don't think so, but he must have the fences in place. He wants to buy some cattle."

"Do you suppose, since it's such nice weather, that the folks would like to go on a picnic with us up there Sunday?"

"That's a good idea. Let's go out and see if they would like to go up with us. It could be a lovely picnic."

We find the Auchards sitting on their porch. The evening is warm. I tell them about Ole Bean's message from Albert. Mr. Auchard pipes up, "Yes, I keep wondering how your brother is making out up there in the Canyon."

"As far as I know, he's going right along with the homestead proving up. Ole sees him often as he goes by and often stops on his way to the Clemons Post Office. He wants to talk with me about getting a few head of cattle, so we need to go over. Rita and I are wondering if you folks would like to go with us tomorrow. Rita says she will fix a picnic box." Right away Mama Auchard speaks up. "Oscar, that is a very good idea. We haven't been on a picnic since you folks moved to Choteau." Rita and Mama go into the kitchen to make food plans. Mr. Auchard and I talk.

"How's the dentist business in Choteau?"

"It's a busy town. Many freight outfits come and go each day, so that brings people who need dental work. There's another dentist there, but still there's plenty for two. He's Dr. Beaupre, and he wants to retire. Besides freight wagons coming and going, the Court is in session every so often. Dr. Brooks is the medical doctor. He is overworked. He tells me he has a ranch up the Teton River and hides out there to get a rest."

"Do you help him with his emergency calls?"

"Yes. If they can't find him, they often try to get me. I had to go on a baby delivery just the other night for the absent Dr. Brooks."

"What about the Masons and Stars there?"

"They are a friendly bunch. Invited us to their meetings and parties. Also, the ladies don't let Rita get lonely."

"Do you plan to live there for good?"

"I'm thinking strongly of doing it. Rita should have her own house, so we need to decide which town. For a while we'll rent in each town though. In the days to come, we'll have to decide on our main home. Every trip to the Canyon makes me want to live there, especially summers and falls. Albert and I are working on expanding the acreage. The original parcel we bought from Fisher has been increased by Albert's claim. I plan to make a claim to add to that. Sounds like our picnic plans are working out in the kitchen."

"They can really cook up a good meal, working like that together. Rita cooks well. I know you are right—she should have a house and, of course, a kitchen wherever you locate."

Rita and Mama Auchard come out from the kitchen. "Mama and I have gotten all the food for tomorrow ready and put in the spring cooler. We won't tell you what—just surprise you tomorrow."

"I like that kind of surprise. You do it quite often, and sometimes with something I've never tasted before. Mother Auchard, you have taught her well."

Mama looks pleased.

"She's a better cook than I am."

"No, no, Mama, that's not possible."

"Rita, let's go home now. We need to be up early and get here at eight o'clock."

Papa Auchard looks at Will dozing in his rocker. "Take note of that, Will."

He's not really asleep. He opens his eyes and says in his whisper voice, "Don't worry. It'll be ready right when you want it, with Onyx and Shadow hitched to the surrey."

On our way home, Rita talks. "Papa just loves to get out the surrey and drive around with his black trotters and several of his pretty granddaughters in their best dresses and stylish hats. He dresses up too and puts on his New York hat."

"Your father is a remarkable gentleman. He does just like he instructed me that time, follows his own advice." I put my arm around my good lady and give her a hug and tell her, "I do so appreciate a wife who has been taught by her mother to cook good stuff."

Sunday morning we are up early after a good night's

sleep, thankful that I didn't get called out on an emergency delivery case. Of course, Dr. Wright is still here. I've not asked him where he hides when he needs a rest. Maybe I shouldn't. I might be tempted to tell when someone comes to *me* for medical help.

CHAPTER 27

A PICNIC IN THE CANYON

We take our own buggy and go out to the ranch. We need to hurry this time, and we'll need it when we come back at the end of the day. Just as he said, Will is standing by his beautiful black team hitched to the surrey. Papa Auchard helps Mama into the back seat, then Rita beside her. The food box was already stowed under the seat. Will whispers, "Good morning. I'll take your team and buggy, and it'll be ready when you get back tonight."

"Thank you, Will. Seems you are always ready to take care of horses and buggies when we need them."

His soft voice is so unusual. If a person asks, "Did you lose your voice, Will?" Every time he answers with something witty, like, "Yes, and it never came back like my horses do. They come down when they are headed this way."

"You have a way with horses, Will. Your soft talk must make them feel safe, so they cooperate."

"Yep, soft talk tames any horse. Don't nobody yell at my horses or they go off down the road."

All's ready to go. We head out towards that magic mountain. It must have guided the Indians as they traveled the Old North Trail to their hunting grounds or to their berry-picking patches. Now as we go by the different ranches along Elk Creek, which becomes the South Fork of Sun River, I see I've come to know many of these people—the Converses, the Cottles, McGraws, the Chisholms, and of course, the Ole Beans that I met first. That is my wish fulfilled.

Before long we are close to the Canyon and the Dearborn River. Now I'm seeing Indian camps. I've learned that these are out of Canada, descendants of the French Indian families of pioneer French trappers with Indian wives. Ole says they move up and down the Canyon according to the time of year. Just a few build permanent cabin homes. They certainly don't want to go back to Canada after they escaped punish-ment for the Riel Rebellion. Mostly they were fearful of being found by Canadian forces and driven back to be penned up by that country.

At last we arrive by the river where Albert has built his cabin. He sees us and is standing in his doorway.

"Hello, Albert! Long time no see."

"Yeah, Oakie, been long time wanting to see you!"

"Your cabin looks good. Who did you get to help with raising the logs?"

"His name is Garvais. Funny thing. He has no cabin himself but he knows how and has helped others to build them. Right now I'm putting tarpaper on my roof, just in case winter comes before I can get shingles at the sawmill. Gotta use tar paper under the shingles anyway." We walk around the cabin. He has window holes but no windows yet, also needs more lumber for a door. I whip out my tape measure and take down the dimensions in my pocket notebook. "Tony Pings' freight team can bring them to Augusta. It'll be winter soon. What kind of furnishings do you have?"

"A few boxes for my stuff but no real furniture. I made a bed out of some hay I got from Ole."

"I see you sure do need stuff, like a real bed and mattress, a table with a few chairs, a few dishes and more than one small kettle."

"Oakie, it's like this: I've been so busy getting a cabin built and trying to get some fencing done, my head is ahead of my hands and feet, but since you mention all these things, I can't object. Yeah, I need all that and a lot more."

"I've been mighty busy too, and now that I've seen what's really needed I'll get busy and see that you get more to make a comfortable place here. You need a decent stove that will keep you warm."

"If you see a better stove than this tin thing, I'd like

one with a cast-iron, two-hole-top, with a side oven. That would be a great improvement since I have to cook everything from biscuits to fried meat or fish. A flat-top stove would be perfect."

"Speaking of food, Albert, Mama Auchard and Rita fixed a lunch for today. They said something was a surprise too, probably a pie, because yesterday was baking day."

"Just hearing the words makes me hungry."

"They are spreading a blanket right there close, and Richard has made the fire by the pond for his coffee pot."

"Out here alone, I sure miss Mama Kenck's cooking so much. I didn't appreciate it like I should have."

"Let's help spread the food."

Mrs. Auchard looks at Albert. "You do look hungry, Albert. We thought of you 'batching' in your cabin so we brought plenty for today and more to leave with you."

"Mrs. Auchard, you are so thoughtful to consider my lack of cooked food. I didn't realize how much I'd miss a cook."

"A man does need a wife to help in situations like this. A decent meal every day is a real help."

"Mrs. Auchard, if you see a lady running 'round loose, who doesn't know where she belongs, I'd like to meet her."

"Albert, just because I was lucky and found a wonderful cook, you should know there are very few to be had for just mentioning the need to eat."

"Here's a plate for you, Albert. I'll serve you first because I know you are starved. My husband, Richard, is very lucky he doesn't have to eat bachelor food."

After the lunch Rita and Mama Auchard put all leftover potato salad, ham, and a big piece of mincemeat pie on Albert's tin plates and spreads a kitchen towel to keep off the flies.

"Albert, Mama wants you to have all the food that is left, so put it in your cabin on your wooden shelf. Put any you don't eat today in a can with a tight lid. The pack rats are hungry too."

"I do thank you ladies for today. It's like being home again."

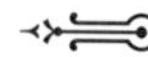

Albert and I take a walk to the river's edge. I say, "What's on your mind that you sent Ole to tell me to come up and talk about with you?"

"I've been talking to him about getting some cattle. Yes, I know there's a lot to be done, like finishing the fencing and a barn for my team and saddle horse."

"You are right, Albert. Of course that's our goal—to run cattle on our place as soon as we make it ready."

"Ole says he will sell us a few steer calves as soon as we can handle them. Steers are easiest. We run them about two years before selling. It's not like having cows with calves."

"With livestock we need to plan for the winter. An extremely long winter with deep snow like '86 and '87 can wipe us out. I'd rather wait till we can put up hay. That's good you are listening to Ole and the others. Make notes of what we need to get in order to be successful in the cattle business."

"You are probably right, but I'd sure like to get started in cattle now."

"In the meantime, let's think also about making some fishponds and selling fish to the restaurants. We can ditch the river into these low places," I point to a couple, "and we'll look at Ole's lake to see what we need to put into them to make them happy and grow. I know we can get more fingerlings up from the Bozeman hatchery, and there's another hatchery by Avon, just across the mountains from here."

"You are the one who knows about fish. Sounds very possible. I'm the one who's been listening to the cattlemen. I've been working with the Bean boys to learn the cattle business. Just next week I'm helping with their roundup. They'll be branding and castrating. I got those three horses from Ole. He's good with horses. The saddle I have used to belong to old man Bean. It's had a lot of use but will do me for a while."

"You are learning the best way, by helping the cattle ranchers who know what they are doing. I've started a list of supplies to send up to you. I've got down windows and a stove. One thing for sure: I want you to stay warm. Also, I don't want you to be without food, so I'll add floor lumber and basic food supplies to my list. The food will all be put in cans. How long will you be helping the Beans?"

"Ole says it will take a full week, maybe eight days. So, don't send stuff for two weeks."

"That will be fine. It gives me time to round up the stuff. Albert, you listen and learn all you can from the Bean fellows. They are savvy from years in the business. Make notes of what we need to go that route. If there's anything else you can think of, send a list over to me. I'll be in Augusta for awhile and will come back again from Choteau around November 1."

"I'll remember that. I have a hunch you'll go back there to go hunting in November, right?"

"Right. I told Rita I wouldn't go hunting this year, but she wouldn't hear of it."

"Lucky you. A wife like Rita is hard to find, and besides being good natured and a great cook, she even laughs at your jokes."

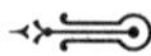

The lunch things are packed. We hitch up the surrey and head back. The sun is on the other side of our magic mountain and the horses do not need urging. In fact, at times we have to slow them. Now we know about Albert's needs and what we need to do and get to help him. He's also getting lonesome. I don't doubt but what he will spend some time in Helena this winter. His three horses can spend that time with their old buddies at Ole's place.

Next day, I listen to where the sawing and hammering sounds are coming from in town. Sure enough, Tony is the one making all that racket. He tells me Aurora Clemons is the freighter who will haul anywhere, so I go look for him.

"You bet I'll haul up there. I'm busy but I'd like to make a trip up that way. Got an uncle there that I can drop in on for a spell. He's got the post office at his house." Clemons went into a long story about his uncle's travels before he settled down near the Dearborn. So, we decided on the approximate time, and I tell him, "About two or three weeks from now." That gives me a deadline to get all the things on my list ready.

Back to my office. Mrs. Manix comes in mostly, I

think, to tell me about Clarence's letter from Gonzaga. "He writes me," she says, "'Dr. Kenck is sure right about this place. We students are so busy we can't even think of having a fight with another kid.' So far he likes it, and the teachers are good to the students."

By the end of September, all of Albert's needs have been sent up on Clemons' freight wagon. He says, "I don't know what he will do with all that stuff, but he seemed most happy about the grub and the stove."

CHAPTER 28

AUCHARD FAMILY MINCEMEAT

It's October 1905. We journey back to Choteau for a stay at the hotel again. First patient to call is Jay Nellis of Fort Shaw. He comes to both Augusta and Choteau. Of course, when in Augusta he visits his mother, Mrs. Auchard, which makes him a half-brother-in-law to me since he is Rita's half-brother. Jay is trying to build up a sheep operation. After I take care of his tooth troubles—a filling—he talks a blue streak.

"Oscar, you are a lucky man to get a wife. Batching is lonely. I need a wife, but I'm getting along in age and it doesn't look hopeful that I will find one."

"Jay, if I hear of a lady who you might be interested in, I will let you know. Fact is, I've been known to be a matchmaker as I meet many women in this type of business. Many ladies take care of their teeth. One man I met in Augusta, he was afraid he was getting too old, I pointed out a certain lady to him and now they are happily married and even starting a family."

"Oscar, if you do see one that might be interested in a sheep rancher, I would be very happy to meet her."

"Well, whatever. I hope you find someone. I'll be remembering your plight. I didn't realize how lonely I was till Rita and I got married. When you think you can stand more drilling, you do need some more work on your teeth."

I tell Rita tonight about her brother coming in and wishing for a wife. "Yes, Mama worries about him, wishing he had a wife, but always ends her talk with

'He's so quiet he would never get up the nerve to ask a woman to marry him, and at least they have to be asked.'"

"Is that the problem? When he comes in next time I'll kid him a little and tell him, 'You gotta ask them, Jay. The ladies can't read your mind.' I see single ladies, sometimes several a day, in my office for dental work. I told Jay I had experience as a matchmaker too."

Rita is laughing, "Yes, Oscar, but it took me almost five years to get the right words out of *your* mouth." This calls for a bit of smooching and hugging. We are happy.

October slips by. We are busy with patients, and sometimes at night a run with Dr. Brooks to save a life or bring a life into the world. "Rita, next Wednesday let's go back to Augusta and be there for November and December."

"Yes, my good man," she giggles, copying my expression. "Let's spend the winter holiday months near Mama and Papa."

"That means we will leave for Augusta next Wednesday, November 1."

"I'll be ready. I hope the weather is agreeable."

"The good old wind will blow us the whole distance. That way the horses don't mind."

November 1, we are ready. Everything is stowed in the buggy, but I had to take care of a last-minute patient, a crown I had ready for Mrs. Guthrie. I had told her to come in as early as she could after she got her kids off to school, which she did. We closed up the office, and then we were off for the crossing at Sun River. We stop at the stage station there and get warmed up with some hot soup, and then off again toward the west. A bit into the winter wind we are going, but the horses know they are going home.

When we get to the ranch it's late afternoon, and darkness comes early. Mama Auchard and Richard are happy to see us. Mama says, "Oscar, I didn't forget your birthday, so even though it's not baking day, I baked an applesauce cake for you." It makes me feel good to know I have family now and all the good things a cook can do. I told Mama about her son's visit and

Jay telling me he would like to have a wife.

It's hunting time. I keep having that old longing to get out in the backcountry. The mountains in the fall always call to me, and even Rita is talking about hunting season. Finally she says, "Oscar, hasn't someone suggested you go hunting with them?"

"No, not yet. Why?"

"If you want to go, I think you should. You have hunted for four years now. I think you are missing it and besides, you need some time away from work and the emergency night calls." Whoops! With that urging, I go into action and send off a note to Lou, telling him the time is perfect. His fast answer says he's been hoping I would suggest a hunt as he's afraid to be the beggar every time, and with my recent wedding and all, well, he just didn't feel right suggesting it so soon. He plans to arrive November 9 for the proposed hunt dates of November 10 through 22.

That's how it is. Charlie Dorrance takes us out with four others. Rita decides to spend that time with her folks. She and Mama Auchard plan to do some of the cooking for the family get-together on Thanksgiving.

The mountains are actually hot during the day for four days, with cool nights. The quaking aspen are brilliant yellow, fluttering continually in the slightest air movement. Huckleberry bushes are blood red. The crickets are playing their swan songs because soon they will go the way of all crickets before them. Ptarmigan are busy fattening on grasshoppers, but we leave them alone. We are a wee bit smarter now. We fish the creeks and find some of the results of our hard labor getting fingerlings up in the creeks. It's so satisfying to lay a few eight-inchers in our frying pan. A couple of the fellows refuse to believe the story of the planting of these beautiful trout. Oh, well, there are believers and there are unbelievers.

November 15: We wake up to a silent world. The soft falling snow has sneaked up on us in the night. It continues till noon and then the clouds separate. Three inches of snow have ushered in a silence all through

these high elevations. We can walk softly. An elk still makes branches crackle when he moves. It is near the end of the rutting season, and we hope the elk will give a few more bugle calls. We walk and then stand a bit, listening. Suddenly, I hear him, a bugler, and then see that rack of horns as it comes through the trees. I take a shot! Lou is twenty-five feet to my right and decides to help. A shot from Lou and the elk comes crashing down about fifty feet from us. It's a huge *Lord of the Mountains*. He'll weigh out to a good load. We get a couple of horses and get him back to camp where there are poles set just for such luck. Lou and I decide to share this one after there are more days of hunting. Half an elk as big as this makes a good number of steaks and roasts, with enough from neck and bony places for a big batch of mincemeat.

Back home, I ask Rita about this mysterious stuff. "Rita, what goes into mincemeat besides the mincemeat?"

"Our recipe calls for quite a few things. I have it from memory, but I think it should be written down sometime." She recites then the long recipe.

AUCHARD FAMILY MINCEMEAT

10 lbs. beef and elk meat, chopped and minced
2 lbs. suet, chopped fine
10 lbs. apples, chopped
5 lbs. raisins, seeded and chopped
3 lbs. carrots
4 tbs. each of cinnamon and mace
2 tbs. allspice
5 lbs. sugar
1½ gal. cider
1 tbs. salt

Mix all together in large kettle. Bring to a boil and simmer 4 hours. Seal in jars.

CHAPTER 29

MORNING SICKNESS AND A MOVE TO CHOTEAU

After Thanksgiving, when we are alone, Rita and I get back to the subject that seems to be on our minds: a family.

"Rita, my idea is that the best place to raise kids is on a ranch. They need to grow up where they learn to work and make do with what they have. Besides that, they, the boys anyway, need to learn to hunt and fish. I say this because I always longed to do that."

"Yes, I can see our boys, when we have them, grousing about doing chores. But chores are good for them. I don't know how things will work out, considering the way we have gotten our ranch started, but I must not worry about the future. It often works out better than our plans."

"Good thought, Rita. We'll leave the far-off till it gets here. The doctors I know seem to handle their ranches, like Dr. Brooks has a hardworking couple taking care of his outfit on the Teton."

"This is strange. We are getting ahead of ourselves. We must have the kids before we can raise them. If we love a lot, maybe it will happen." She then gives out her low laugh. For that I give her a hug and a long kiss that gives me a charge as I look deep into her eyes. "Rita, I do love you. With you I'm living the good life."

We're staying in Augusta this December. The band concert is a busy deal. We're practicing on Sundays.

161

Christmas is a Monday this year so that leaves Fridays and Saturdays for community parties and programs. Bud decides our concert should be on Saturday, December 23.

Saturday morning, big concert day. I'm rolling out. It's time to build the fire and start the oatmeal. I do it most mornings we're living in our own house in Augusta.

"Oscar, I'm sorta sick. I feel like I'm going to throw up. I think it's something I ate at our party last night."

"Oh, oh!" I'm thinking it may not be that at all. It might be morning sickness because I ate the same foods Rita did, and I feel just fine.

"Rita, you just stay in bed. Maybe you'll feel better later. I sure hope you are able to play in the concert."

It's time for me to go to the office, so I look in on Rita to see if I can bring some breakfast to her but she is asleep. I quietly go off. I'll come back at noon.

A Frank Palmer is coming back for more work. Last week I pulled a tooth that was abscessed so he decided to get the rest of those cavities fixed, and he's waiting outside my door. He's going to look for homesteading property out north of Choteau.

"Mr. Palmer, if you go to Choteau, please tell them I'm coming back after New Year's. I have an office all set up in the Choteau Hotel."

"Doctor, I'll be glad to tell them, and also I'm glad for myself you will be in Choteau. The country I'm thinking of looking at for homesteading is near what is called Power."

Shortly after Christmas we realize that Rita is having that thing called "morning sickness" for certain. Mama Auchard tells her, "Rita, my dear, you are going to be a mother. Every morning, before even lifting your head, eat a few dry crackers that you put by your bed the night before because they might help. Don't drink water or anything for a little while."

Rita tells me then, "When you go back to Choteau, I will stay with the folks. I know staying at the hotel will not help me feel any better. I would like to have a house there, I think, and not have to stay in the hotel."

"That settles it, my good wife. I'll find a house for

us in Choteau. Mr. Hodgkiss might know of one, or he is a fast builder and will build us one."

Back in Choteau I have to explain to Mrs. Hodgkiss that Rita isn't feeling very well. I can tell by her reply she suspects something quite different. "Is it serious?" she asks.

"No, I think she will soon be all right." She seems satisfied and asks no more questions.

Soon, my friend, young Bing, comes in and wants me to look over his teeth. They do have a tendency to decay a lot.

I say, "Bing, Mrs. Kenck doesn't feel well, so she didn't come this time. But she plans to come if I can find a house."

"I'll talk to Dad. He knows every house in town, almost. If he can't find one, he'll build you one for sure!" After I finish cleaning his teeth, he goes to find his dad.

Dr. Brooks appears at my office the next day. "Kenck, I hear you are here for a spell."

"Yes, but Rita's not feeling so well, especially mornings, which usually means pregnancy. I wish there were something to help this morning sickness misery."

"The best thing I know is keep some soda crackers by the bed and nibble on them a while before even getting up. Don't drink anything for a half hour or so either."

"Her mother told her about the crackers, so that must be an old remedy."

"Usually after the third month the nausea stops. When did she know she might be expecting?"

"About Christmas. In fact, two days before. We want to find a house here for several reasons but especially so she can be near you when it's time to deliver. How are your Teton Ranch people getting along?"

"I was up one night just after Christmas and delivered number three. I have to get back to the office. I see a couple of rigs tied up at my place."

A bit later, Bing comes dashing in. "Dad says the big, two-story, log house that Shuler Carson built down the main road is going to be empty soon. That family just built another one on their homestead."

That noon I go there and catch them before they get moved. He is glad to rent it even before he's out of it. I tell him who I am and that my wife is still in Augusta but doesn't want to come just yet until I find a house. The rooms are nice and big and there are bedrooms upstairs. We don't need them, but if we have a family we might need them after all.

So, a note goes right off to my little lady to tell her the good news. The days are flying by for me even if not for Rita. Dr. Brooks had me go with him out to a lady on a ranch. Yes, she was in trouble. She had been having hard labor pains for a couple of days. He gave her a shot to relax her, had her lie down, and soon she was asleep. He used some chloroform so he could then use his instruments. It was a very hard birth. The baby was too big to deliver easily. At last he is able to get the head and shoulders out, and the rest is no problem. I can't help but think of Rita. I sure hope ours isn't that big because Rita is a small lady.

Brooks says, "If I'm not available, they will call on you, so the more experience you get, the better."

"When the time gets close for Rita to deliver, I hope fervently you will be available. I didn't think about this until it comes my turn to see my wife deliver."

"I'll watch carefully that I don't take that risk when it's close. Don't worry so much. I've been through it personally with my first wife." Brooks tries to get my mind off it with questions.

"Didn't you say you are getting a ranch started?"

"Right. It's the Dearborn Canyon area. Actually, my brother Albert has built his cabin there. We first bought out a couple of previous homestead properties. We plan to buy additional land. He and I have an agreement. If he ever wants to return to Helena, where we grew up, I will buy his homestead and his share of the rest."

"You are lucky to have a brother to work and live on the project."

"He talks of going back to work in Helena, but so far he stays."

It's June 1906. Rita is still with her folks. She is finally getting over her nausea, she writes. "Oscar, I'm finally getting better every day. Now that you have found a house, I feel good enough to go back with you."

That's all it takes! I close up, hastily making a sign for my front door with a small paintbrush. "WILL BE BACK IN 10 DAYS OR LESS." Sort of indefinite, but I can't judge exactly. I've never moved a pregnant wife before. It's noon. If I can get going, I should be there by dark. My team is in good shape. I urge them with a few taps and shouts like I've heard Dick Adams use. In times like this a fast team is essential. I just give a passing wave to those I meet or even pass on the road.

We come down the slope to the river at the usual crossing. It's wider than usual. The snows are melting with the warmth of the lengthening summer days. I'm dismayed. I hold the team back for awhile. I see a couple of outfits on the other side hesitating to cross. One is a frail-looking buggy. Oh how can I get across? I want to see my dear good lady! I watch the freight wagons begin their crossing, and then the ferryman comes out of his cabin. Never have I had to use the ferry. It takes a precious hour to watch the procedure.

If he makes it to this side with the freight wagons, I'll get a passage back to the other side. A bigger rig than mine is coming across when he docks against the wharf. I'm right there waiting. Whatever he charges, I'll pay it! This is urgent, of course.

"Hey, Mister. I've got to get across. It's urgent."

"Well," he switches his pipe from one side of his mustache to the other. He acts like he's not too sure I'll buy passage.

"Young fella, you know the season is damn short here. For me to be here when a ferry is needed takes up my time from my pigs and chickens and garden work."

"Yes sir, I realize a ferry is first needed at strange times but I'm willing to pay whatever you ask—that is, if I have it."

"Well," he pushes his dirty cap back off his shaggy eyebrows and scratches his uncombed head. "How about twenty? I'm a needy man to live at the whim of the river."

"That's more than I make in a week sometimes, but right now I need to get to Augusta so badly that I'll pay it. So, I hand him the money and he poles his ferry raft over into the shallows so I can board my rig. I talk the team into getting on. The old guy knows how to guide that ferry and we steadily make our way across. When we reach the shore, I don't have to urge the team to walk off. Away we go! Somehow they sense they're going home. We lose no time. It is just dark when I turn in the gate at Auchards. We grab each other, Rita and I. If I ever come close to crying for joy, it's now. I don't think I fully realized the love bond between us until now.

"Yes, I can tell you are feeling better. I've missed you terribly, even though I'm busy at the office. There's the loneliness that falls on me about five o'clock every evening with no wife to go home to."

The next day I go to my Augusta office and work the rest of June, until July 11. Business is very good. Going back and forth between Choteau and Augusta does make people come in right away because they never know when I will stay around for them to make up their minds.

It's July 1906, and I'm thinking soon Rita will have this baby. She doesn't show much but that doesn't mean it's a long way off.

Friday, July 7, I'm really busy. Today I had ten patients. Brooks figures the baby will come sometime between the last week of July and the first of August. We plan to leave July 11 because the river is down some, and Rita and I want to be together when the baby is born.

The freight wagons have already shipped the household goods: furniture, Rita's pretty dishes—a gift from the Auchards—packed tightly in the bedding and linens. Each dish is packed separately. We have all the rest stowed in the buggy box, with our lunch for along the way. We are up early. Her brother Will has beaten the sun by an hour. His haying teams are already in the big pole corral. He doesn't have to wrangle, as they are eager to come in for their treat of oats. The cow too wants her special attention and gets milked.

Mama and Papa Auchard get breakfast while we finish packing our bags. Papa sets the table while Mama stirs the overnight oatmeal in the top of the double boiler. She then boils some eggs in the bottom part. She sprinkles freshly ground coffee into the boiling water in the big enamel coffeepot where it gradually settles to the bottom, creating the wonderful aroma of the stuff we love to drink.

Will comes from the barns after he has harnessed our team, bringing a bucket of fresh milk. He pours it through the strainer cloth that Mama has made ready in the springhouse. He comes in and tells us in his abbreviated low voice, "Team's ready when you are."

We have a delicious breakfast at the big table. Everyone seems a little anxious, but we don't talk much.

I send a note for Bing Hodgkiss at the Choteau House. I ask him to show the freighter at which house to unload. He is to watch the house with the furniture and trunks in it. He's a real help and likes to do special kinds of jobs like that.

Mrs. Auchard is crying some. She is such a worry person. Rita says, "Don't call her 'worrywart' to her face; she can't help it." Rita tells me she worries about the stage driver during winter storms. If he doesn't come by before six o'clock, she is glued to the window where she can see and hear the stage when it arrives.

Mama stands by as I help Rita into the buggy. Her apron goes to her eyes a lot. Papa keeps clearing his throat to be strong, to bid us goodbye. He finally manages a few words to lighten the sorrow of parting. "Oscar, you'll soon know what it's like to be a father."

Off we go. Will is holding the pole gate at the end of the lane for us to go through. We call out, "Thank you, Will!" He smiles and waves us through. Sometimes life is too full of goodbyes tearing at the heartstrings. Hellos are usually better.

Before we get to Augusta we meet the stage. Dick gives us a wild wave as we pass. It seems the whole town has heard and is standing at their gates and walking the streets this early morning. All are waving as we pass. There are the Wellmans, the Adamses, Tony and Mabel, and the Manixes, Clarence, John, and the girls. The Bud Tomlinsons in front of their new home. Joe Bush and his wife, Mrs. Bergeron. Something tells me, "This is my hometown." Another feeling is strong: We'll come here to live someday. Maybe it is the magic mountain, the beautiful butte pulling at my back.

The sun is overhead when we reach the crossing. No need of a ferry this time. The water reaches the horses knees. We circumspectly ease our way, avoiding the flood-washed boulders. Our team has to ripple muscle to get up the north slope. Soon we are going by the duck sloughs, and then after another hill we go by Freeze-out Flat's cabin.

In late afternoon we pull into Choteau's cottonwood-tree-lined main street. The seed fluff is already beginning to fly on the constant summer wind. "Rita, first I'm going to take you by our log home. I want to take a look-see about our freight we sent."

"It should be there. I'm anxious to see if it's the same house I remember being on that street."

As we pull up, we see the freight is there, and I can see Bing has carefully unpacked the big stuff. We go on to the hotel. Mrs. Hodgkiss insisted Rita lie down while she fixes a supper for us.

The next morning, Bing helps us get our bags over to the house, and we manage to move in. After only a couple of hours, we have beds made, dishes into the cupboard, and food in the pantry. Rita gets her table linens out so we will feel like we're home when we eat our lunch.

Dr. and Mrs. Brooks come by to see how we are and talk about when our baby might be coming. He asks questions to discern Rita's condition. He says, finally, "I think you are getting along okay. I see the baby is low, which means soon you will have it."

"I hope so, Doctor. It has seemed like a <u>very</u> long time."

This gives me a signal to buy some cigars to give out with the announcement.

In the afternoon I go to my hotel office to set things in order. I know word travels like wild fire that I'm back in town.

"Bing, I need you to buy me a couple boxes of cigars. I'll need them any day now." I hand him $10. I hope it's enough.

"Sure can do . . . but why do men give cigars when their wife has a baby?"

"Well, there are several traditions behind that. I'll tell you about a couple of them. Cigars used to be scarce and costly. The father of a son is saying, symbolically,

'I want to share my good fortune—my happiness—with you.' Sons-first has always been a man's choice."

"Won't you be happy if it's a little girl too?"

"Yes, I will be happy, but for a different reason, especially if my wife is all right afterward. And I really think daughters are nice, especially when I see how Rita loves her father. Another tradition comes from the American Indian, who thinks that tobacco smoke pleases the gods. When they burned tobacco and the smoke ascended to the heavens, the gods were pleased and would bless them with strong, healthy babies."

"Oh. So, there are lots of reasons and superstitions."

"Right, Bing. Just don't worry about it. It is just a pleasure man has after watching helplessly while his wife struggles. It's really his wife who can be proud."

"Huh! Sounds pretty funny to me. I'll buy the cigars right away."

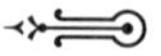

Several patients come in. Mrs. Shields says she's been waiting for me to come back. Then Mrs. Guthrie, who starts right in asking questions.

"Doctor Kenck, I've been thinking a lot about both you and Mrs. Kenck, for two reasons. Number one, I want to know how Rita is getting along. Number two, I have a molar that needs your help."

"Nice of you to be interested in Rita's health, Mrs. Guthrie. She is getting close to the time. Dr. Brooks says it will be very soon. Now just sit in the chair and we'll see about this molar that's bothering you."

"I certainly am glad you and Rita are back here. Her time is getting close. I plan to stop by your house every day to see her. Maybe I can help out some way."

"Thank you, Mrs. Guthrie. You have had children so you know what it's like before and after, I'm sure."

"Yes, I've had babies and lost babies. Life is not always what we'd like."

We get to work on that tooth. After I examine it, I let her know what I've found. "Mrs. Guthrie, that molar needs to be crowned."

"If you think so, Doctor, I agree. Can you start today?"

"Yes, today I'll get the tooth ready and take the impressions of it so I can make an exact copy at my work bench, to fit your bite. The gold I use is rolled from gold coins. That gold is harder than pure gold—it has a very small percentage of copper."

When the impressions are done, I say, "Don't chew hard on tough food on this side. The crown will be ready next Wednesday."

"Good. I'll come in then and, like I said, I'll stop at Mrs. Kenck's some time every day."

CHAPTER 30

BABY DICK'S ARRIVAL, JULY 27, 1906

"I'm pretty anxious," Rita says. And another busy week goes by. It's now Wednesday of the following week. Rita tells me this morning, "The ladies of our little circle are coming twice a day. I have no time to worry. One comes a while in the morning and another in the afternoon. Everyone says I'm so close. I can hardly wait for this to be over!"

"Mrs. Guthrie will be in to get her crown today. It's ready, so you can tell her when she stops by."

As I walk to my office, I meet Mrs. Guthrie. "Doctor, Mrs. Kenck is so very close. After I stay with her a while, I'll be in for my crown."

I'm at the office about an hour when Dr. Brooks comes in.

"I want you to know," he tells me, "I'm staying around town because I know something is about to happen with Rita. I want everything to go well."

"Thanks, Brooks. Sure is a different situation when the patient is my wife."

"Yeah, I remember when my boy was born. I thought I was having him myself."

As we were talking, hurried steps come up the hall. It's Mrs. Guthrie. "Doctor! Doctor! Rita's having labor pains!"

Brooks turns and dashes out the door, hurrying to his office to pick up his special birth bag.

"Thank you, Mrs. Guthrie. We'll do your crown to-morrow." I scramble out the door behind Mrs. Guthrie, dropping my keys while trying to lock the door. My hands are shaking! Oh, oh, I must hurry! I get home in a few minutes, calling for Rita.

"Rita? Rita? What's going on?" She is on the bed upstairs, looking uncomfortable.

"The pains—contractions—are coming every few minutes." Right then she has one. I know it hurts. "Remember, hold your mouth open and breathe as deep as you can. Doctor Brooks will be here very soon."

Now, the directions I had given to those at the births I'd been in charge of. Get a good amount of water warmed for washing the baby and mother. Strange how I must tell myself what needs to be done.

"Another one!" Rita calls. A quick look at my watch tells me it's been eight minutes since the last one. I go to the bedroom where we had laid out several layers of sheets for the delivery. Just then, Dr. Brooks arrives and takes charge.

"Have you got warm water ready, Kenck?"

"Yes. You'd never know I've done this several times before, now that it's happening to my own wife."

"Well, it's different when it's your own wife's labor and delivery. Stay calm. I'll tell you what to do if you get distracted. Basically, you are going to hold Rita's hand and coach her through it."

I hold her hands and wipe her face with a cool, damp cloth. I whisper close to her ear, "Oh, Rita, my darling, good lady. It will soon be over."

Dr. Brooks palpates her abdomen between contractions, keeping track of the baby's position. Then he checks the dilation. "It's five centimeters, so very soon now the head will show. You are doing fine. It will be over pretty quickly, I think."

He is right. The top of the head shows, and then the whole head is soon out. A small twist and the tiny shoulders are out. The rest is even faster. It's a boy! My own son!

Rita lies back with a great sigh. Brooks hands over to me this new little creature who is already protesting the cold new world. I wrap a soft blanket around him and carry him to the kitchen table where I have ready a pan of warm water to wash him. Here I am a grown man with great tears of relief, surprise, joy, and astonishment running down my face. I gently pour warm water over this little thing, washing off the birthing matter. He's yelling like this old world is a total shock. He has a strong voice and tight little fists. "Who are you going to fight, little man? I know it's a cold world, little guy." As soon as his bath is done and I've wrapped him in a new clean blanket, I carry him back to the bedroom.

Rita has revived considerably in just a few minutes. "Let me see him!" I take him to her. She looks at all his toes, fingers, tiny feet, and hands. I lay him beside her and she begins to talk to him, gently patting him. At this new attention, he stops yelling.

"Oh, Oscar, it's done!" Then she looks up at me. "How come you are sweating?"

"Oh, Rita, I don't know. I was trying to help. To be watching you in such pain is awful. Oh, my darling wife, you did so well!" Even though I haven't cried in years, the tears run down uncontrollably. Relief and joy all mixed in. "Going through this with you, I can't possibly brag."

"I don't know why not. You stayed right with me through it all. You must give your cigars away now. That's what you got them for."

After Dr. Brooks takes care of Rita and she's all cleaned up, he talks to her about nursing new babies. "Feed him when he's hungry—he will let you know. Feed him any time he wakes up and cries, but if he sleeps, let him sleep. At first, it will be irregular, but in time it will become regular."

Next, Brooks examines our little guy and puts a drop of silver nitrate in each eye. "This keeps eye infections away. All newborns should get a drop of this." Then he looks in his mouth, each ear, and tests reflexes. Finally, he says, "Kenck, looks like you got a healthy one. Also, he's got a strong voice. Good lung action."

"I need to find some lady to take care of things here during the day. Rita needs to take it easy for a while."

"Yeah, I think maybe you can get Mrs. Nadeau. She likes to help new mothers. She's even acted as a regular midwife."

"I'll send Bing to ask her. How much do I owe you, Brooks?" He looks at me with, for him, a rare broad smile and says, "I think we could do a trade deal."

"If that's what suits you, I agree. I'll take care of you and your missus. Your service has been invaluable to us today."

"It's a deal then, Kenck. Remember, I'm available whenever you need me. Don't hesitate to come right in. New mothers and fathers don't know everything." He smiles again, gets a basin of water and washes up to his elbows. He pulls down his shirtsleeves and says, "I think I'll go home now. It's past time to close the office. My nurse gal knows when to tell all those waiting to come back tomorrow if it's not an emergency."

Here we are, alone with this new wiggly creature. Wow! He's finally settled down to a feed job and seems to be catching on. Rita says after he eats we must burp him. I pick him up and gently lay him against my shoulder, and soon it's a "burp!" Then after I pat him gently a while, he seems sleepy, so I lay him carefully on his side in the basket that's been ready for a month. Rita drifts off to sleep. It's been a hard day. Labor *is* labor.

She sleeps in between baby crying and trying to nurse, but he falls asleep too soon. It's hard work being born.

"Oscar, what are your thoughts about a name for this little guy?"

"Nothing fancy, just a good American name. I've always thought my two middle names were too hard to explain. Oscar is all right, but 'Aliuvisus Maximillian' are too much. A bit European and grandiose. I think just name him after our fathers, Richard and Charles.

"That's good. I like both those and just like you said, 'Richard Charles.' He'll get nicknamed 'Dick' for short."

"To me he will always be 'Richard.' That way he'll always know who is calling him."

I stuck around home for three days. I figure Rita needs me in the house then. I get the lady Emma Nadeau to come help during the day. Then begins the cigar part. Even if it is an old custom, it gives me a certain pleasure.

Ed Corson, the man I rent the house from, comes in

often. Getting dental service for rent has spurred him to get his teeth taken care of.

"Hello, Ed. I'm not surprised to see you."

"Doc, I heard the news. You got a boy. Good for you!"

"Ed, I've got a little present for you, this cigar. I don't know the origin of this custom, but I know it's done."

"Oh, we all do a lot of things and we don't know why. Thanks. I haven't had this brand or any cigar for a long time. I got a cavity that's tellin' me things are too cold."

"Okay, Ed. Just sit up here in my chair. We'll take care of it." While doing this I'm actually surprised by another patient.

"Albright! I didn't expect to see you so soon, coming all the way from Augusta."

"This molar needs attention." He opens his mouth and points.

"Since a toothache brought you this far, I can give you the news. We got a boy last week."

"How are Rita and her baby doing?"

"It was an easy birth, if any birth is. Not till a wife goes through that does a person realize at the best it's a tough job. Oh yes, here's the cigar. Someone asked me why men give cigars at such a time, but I don't know where it comes from."

"Probably they are so glad a pregnancy is over. Beats me."

"I can take you as soon as I finish here. Dr. Albright, this is Ed Corson. He built the house we live in. By the way, have you heard from that Bateman fellow?"

"Yeah, he still wants to come but I doubt he'll get the money till next year. I'll hang in there another year. Then I might leave, regardless. I'm worn out."

As I look at Albright's tooth, I see it does need a crown. That calls for impressions and some time at my workbench. I go right to work, and by late afternoon I have it ready so he comes back about four o'clock.

"You are lucky. This day is not so busy so I was able to get it finished today. That usually doesn't happen."

"Kenck, I wouldn't have cared. I like to stay away. I get a little rest from my practice."

The days go by. It's a busy time and I'm really enjoying seeing our new baby grow. Rita says those smiles are not really such, but I see that he can smile in his sleep. October is here next week. The weather is sunny, cool nights and warm days. I need to catch up on work in Augusta, and Mama and Papa Auchard are anxious to see their latest grandchild.

"Rita, if you feel up to it, I think we should go to Augusta. Besides, your folks are longing to see you and baby Richard."

"Oscar, I'd love to see Mama and Papa, and I know they are anxious to see Richard too."

"Tomorrow I'll put a note on my door that we'll be back in December. It depends on the weather. We can't take chances on traveling in a winter storm with a baby."

"I'll be ready. I do so want to share our Richard with Mama and Papa. They will be so pleased."

"I need to go to Helena to get dental supplies and see how Mother is. I would like to take you, Rita, but I realize it's too difficult to take a baby. I'll be gone for a few days and then maybe I'll go hunting, if that's all right with my good wife."

"Of course you should go hunting, my dear husband. You've been working long hours every day, sometimes every evening at your work bench."

CHAPTER 31

WORRYING ABOUT ALBERT AT THE CABIN

In Augusta, before I go to Helena, Paul Bean comes to my office. "Dr. Kenck, us Beans are worried about Albert. We don't see him often and he didn't come along on the roundup last month. He looks like he's not taking very good care of himself. Ole told me when I said I had to get a tooth pulled and hoped you'd be here to tell you."

"Tell Ole and your brothers I'll come up to see Albert and find out his problem."

October 6, 7, 8 are full of people waiting a long time for dental work.

"Rita, I have to change my plan to go to Helena slightly. Paul Bean tells me the Bean brothers are worried about Albert, so I'll go up to see what's wrong.

Maybe I'll just take him to Helena with me."

On October 8, I go off to see Albert. I am shocked when he comes out of his cabin. "Albert, what's the matter?" His hair is extremely long, he's unshaven, and he just looks bad.

"Oakie, I don't really know what is wrong. I just keep draggin' myself around, don't have any will to do anything. I know I should be taking care of things."

"I'm going to Helena and I am taking you with me. We'll get a pan of hot water and get you cleaned up and shaved. Besides I'll cut off some of that hair. What have you been eating?"

"Not much, I guess."

"That is what's wrong. It takes food to keep up your

strength." I see a few empty whiskey bottles sitting around.

"Albert, this stuff does not give you strength. After cleaning you up, we'll start for Helena tomorrow early. I brought some bread and butter and eggs and an apple pie Rita baked for you."

Inside or outside the cabin, it doesn't look like he has done much of anything for a long time. I get the tub from where he hangs it on the backside of the cabin and bring it in filled with water from the river. While it's warming, I make us a lunch. He eats a little and seems to perk up. We do the bath job and I find no clean clothes, so I gather all I can find and give them a wash in the river, rinse and hang them on the bushes. It's warm enough that they'll dry before nightfall. Next is a haircut. I always have those barber type scissors in my pockets. Then a shave to get his face showing. He is exhausted by then and lies down on the cot and I see he drifts off to sleep. I can't decide what's wrong. No fever, just lethargy. When he washes up, I fry the fish I caught while he slept. He manages to eat some bread and fish and goes back to sleep.

I'm up at daybreak. Make coffee and toast what's left of the bread that Rita sent. I don't see much else, except we eat the rest of the pie. That will hold us until we get to Wolf Creek about noon.

I stuff the things I washed into a sack. Albert seems almost cheerful. I hitch up the horses and we're off. We pass Ole Bean's and then go to Clemons, the post office porch, and cross the Dearborn River. It's low this time of year. Albert is holding up better than I expected. Maybe his thinking of the pleasures of Helena has cheered him.

I have a good visit and tell Mama she is a grandmother. That does please her very much. I run into Mike Reinig in his store and bring him up to date on my life. I also look up my old hunting friend, Lou Woods, and tell him I'm not hunting this year because I'm too busy being a new papa. He is surprised I'm a family man now. As it turns out, Albert stays in Helena. I am thinking he needed to. Mama's cooking will strengthen him. The trip back to Augusta is uneventful.

I report to Rita about Albert and the visit in Helena. "Albert was in bad shape when I got there. Looked like he hadn't eaten, bathed, or shaved for weeks. I left him in Helena to be fed by Mama and get his strength back. I'm sure he had been sick and lost the strength to live. Of course, I can't rule out too much whiskey. There were some empty bottles around the cabin."

"Oh Oscar, we have to go out to see him more often. Living alone like that and no one to look in on him is not good. We could ask Ole to go to his cabin sometimes. I think he would if you asked him to."

"Yeah, I know you are right. Next time Ole comes in I'll ask him to check in on Albert if he doesn't see him every week, and I'll gladly give him his wife's dental service for no charge. Well, the thing is now he's in Helena that plan will have to wait until he comes back. Remember the Bible says we are our brother's keeper? I guess that applies here. Rita, I can hardly stay away from you and little Dick. I hurried to get all my business done so I could come home to you."

"Yes, my good husband and new daddy. A baby changes by the day in the first year."

CHAPTER 32

BACK & FORTH FROM CHOTEAU TO AUGUSTA, 1906-1907

Mid-December has especially mild weather, so it's back to Choteau for this dentist and his family. Little Dick is carefully snuggled in a basket, and we have blankets aplenty as we head out. After we cross the river, we come near a flat and a dry lakebed called Freeze-out Lake. Oh yes, I've been told a couple of homestead ladies lived out in this area one winter not long ago. They made a fatal mistake. They forgot to buy matches when they were getting winter supplies. They decided they must never let the fire go out. Well, it happened. They tried to keep warm but they were found weeks later huddled into all their blankets but frozen to death. I say always carry matches on your journeys in a little metal box.

After we get past the old abandoned shacks at Freeze-out, the west wind switches to the north. The temperature began to drop and the wind was cold on our faces. I gave a yell to my team and they really took off. We made it in time before the snowflakes, but that is too close to even be funny.

Our log home is very warm. We have two stoves besides a big fireplace. I have the Indians bring me several loads of wood every year. It's piled right near our door.

The rest of December 1906 it snows. Also, January, February, and March. Not until mid-April did the storms stop. This is killing thousands of cattle. They say Canadian cattle are drifting with the storms. The sheets of sharp ice on top of the snow cut their mouths and legs. If they get caught in a fence corner in the deep snow, they starve and freeze to death.

This bad winter is slowing business for everyone. Dr. Brooks sends the word around that if anyone expects a baby she must be brought to town two weeks before the due date because he can't get through to deliver out in the country.

We are not able to get back to Augusta till April 10, 1907. Little Dick will be a year old soon. He's wiggly and crawling around and pulling himself up on our couch. He's so happy and active most of the time. A real job for Rita to take care of him. Because of the long winter, we didn't take a chance of journeying to Augusta.

In Augusta, Mama Auchard is so happy to see Rita. She also tells us that Will has been having a toothache, that he can't eat hot or cold food. Rita gets right on him. "Mama says you've been having a toothache."

He responds bashfully, "Oh, it's not bad if I keep my mouth shut in the cold."

"Will, you get yourself down to Oscar's office tomorrow. What good is it having a dentist in the family if you suffer along with a toothache? Promise you will go to his office tomorrow."

"Well, if you say I gotta go, I guess I will."

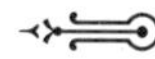

Rita's words have their effect, because the next day Will comes in as ordered.

"Hello, Will. I'm ever so glad to fix your toothache. You are always doing something for us. Sit down in the chair and I promise I'll be very gentle."

I get his mouth open and he begins to turn white as a sheet. "Will, put your head down between your knees." I give his head a push down and hold it there a while and then have a look at his face again. Yeah, the color is back. "Will, that happens every once in a while. Especially to strong men who do outdoor work. Somehow the idea of a drill on their teeth just makes the blood leave their heads. Don't let this make your blood drop to your toes because they want to run."

Will whispers, "I'll try not to. Kinda crazy to faint."

I keep up a running line of talk to keep his mind off

what's going on. He does seem to get over being afraid just as we are finished.

Ernest Bean, Ole's brother, shows up just then to pay for the dental work they had done last fall. He says, "Ole vants me to tell you vats going on. Albert, he come back to the Canyon. Vonce a veek he stops at Ole's on his vay to get a steady letter at Clemons Post Office and he sends vone in his vonderful handwriting. Every time Ole's vife, Ina, have ready vor him a loaf of bread and a dozen eggs, and she fill his lard pail vif fresh milk. Ole and Ina say they vill keep better track of him. They feel real bad he got so sick last fall. Albert tells he play violin in Helena at parties and he vill play for Bean parties."

"Thank you and tell Ole thanks too. I do appreciate you and Ole for caring about Albert. You folks are good neighbors."

When I got home tonight, I tell Rita the good news about Albert being back and what Ole and Ina are doing for him. Rita says, "Those Bean families are cer-tainly good neighbors. I guess they thought Albert wanted to be alone, and now they realize he needs to be included in the neighborhood activities."

Living in the Canyon wouldn't be half bad. Sometimes I think like Brooks: escape!

Grandma and Grandpa Auchard are delighted with our happy boy and are especially pleased he has been given Grandpa's name. When he carries Richard around, he tries to grab hold of his Grandpa's beard and has to be distracted. Rita tells me, "Papa brought a colt over from the barn. Will is gentle training that one for children who visit. Richard got so excited that his whole body wiggled. I had to hold tight. He reached out to touch the colt's nose."

1907: News that I'd be leaving Augusta May 15 gets around, and news like that brings in last-minute pa-tients who would otherwise put off coming. On May 2, five come in. Four on May 3 and eight on May 4. It's like this till the fifteenth, each patient catching up on the latest in the Kenck household.

"Hello, Clarence. Long time no see. How was the year at Gonzaga?"

"It was just like you said, a world apart. We boys were kept so busy that we didn't have time to get homesick. Schedule was everything. We sure had to do as we're told, too, and study. I used to think the Mission was too strict about conforming to routine, but Gonzaga has got them bested. Of course, we are practically adults, so they don't allow near as much time as at the Mission for just fun. The older students played instruments very well. I see where you learned about orchestra music. The parish ladies tried to teach us boys to dance."

"Sounds awfully familiar. Was the winter bad over there?"

"Snowstorms kept coming, and we boys shoveled snow from November till last month. But I don't think I'll go back. Dad's estate is almost gone. The rest of the kids—John, Matilda, Ursula, Rosetta and Helen—will have to go to the Mission for high school when the time for that comes, so it looks like I should go to work so there will be some money left for their high school."

"What do you plan to do if you don't go this fall?"

"I've a cousin whose husband has a big cattle ranch near the little town of Dupuyer. She says if I don't go to Gonzaga, they will hire me for as long as I want to work."

"What do you really want to do for your life work?"

"My ambition is to somehow get a store of my own."

"Just keep that in mind and you will get what you want. Now, let's have a look and see how your teeth are doing since you've followed my brushing program." Clarence slides into the chair and I have a look.

"I'm pleased with the look of your gums and how clean they are. I see two small cavities we can take care of right now." This I do in about an hour. After I'm finished we talk about another check-up when I'm working closer to Dupuyer. I tell him any time he's in Choteau to look me up at the Choteau Hotel. We shake hands and I wish him well. He's a natural for working with people.

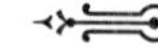

May 15, 1907. Back in Choteau

This changing from Augusta to Choteau is a bigger expedition with a baby in our family. He likes it and gets so excited to watch the horses. He falls asleep after a while though.

Brooks shows up at my office soon after I've opened up again to give me a report on some of the happenings while I've been away.

"Ed Dennis is an old-timer around here. About eight years ago he got married to a young woman about half his age. He's sixty something and—surprise—she had a baby last week, a girl. No one is more surprised than Ed himself. I told him, 'You thought you were too old to accomplish something like this.' He said, 'Doc, I'm a toothless old man and now I'm the father of a baby girl!' I told him, 'You can do something about that toothlessness. Get Doc Kenck to make you some dentures, and then you will look young enough to be Papa to a new baby.'"

Brooks was right. And sure enough, a man with no teeth comes in and introduces himself.

"I'm Ed Dennis. Doc Brooks told me you could make me a set of teeth. You see I've had a strange thing happen, not to me, but to my wife. I married Lucy about eight years ago and, lo and behold, last week she had a baby girl. I'm what you call 'dumbfounded.' I guess I'm a younger man than I thought. Doc Brooks said new teeth will make me look younger so when I carry our new baby around people will know I'm her papa and not her grandpapa."

"That is a good story, Ed. What did she name that baby?"

"*Alice*. After Teddy Roosevelt's first wife, I guess."

"Dr. Brooks tells me you've lived here a long time."

"Yeah, I was the second white man to file a homestead claim around here, north of town. I was here when Sam Burd and Dan Buck and a few others started the first irrigation project. Yeah, I've been around many a year. Where back East did you come from?"

"Ed, I'm not from back East. I was born right here in Helena."

"Well, I'll be darned. I don't meet many that are natives. I mean that are not Indian. I do meet a lot of mixed people called 'breeds,' but I don't like that name for them. I know a young one of those, and he don't know whether he's Indian or white. His dad was an agent on the Belknap Reservation, but he took that kid and raised him with his white family in Helena. His name is Ballie Buck. He says his name is Belknap, but he don't like it much. Helena folk got all huffy about an Indian kid going to their schools, so his dad, Dan Buck, brought him out to my neighbor, Sam Burd, who was married to a Piegan gal. Well, Ballie finished school right here at the Blackfoot Indian School. Not all Indians though. He got to be a darn good cowboy. Right now I hear he's runnin' the wagon for the Circle outfit out of Lethbridge, Canada."

"Ed, I think I knew that fellow when I was also a kid in Helena. He must have been that big boy, a little older than I, named Ballie, all right. He worked for X. Biedler at his horse barn. Just a big kid. He'd tell us younger kids to get out and stay out of the horse barn or we would get kicked. He sure knew horses. One day he wasn't there anymore."

"Ballie used to work for the S.T. That's 'Sands and Taylor.' He was the best young roper around these parts."

"Ed, let's get with the impression business for your new dentures. If I get that done, it will take just a couple of days to get them vulcanized and you will look a heap younger."

"Doc, I feel like I'm livin' life all over again!"

Dr. Brooks Leaves

A few days later, Brooks comes in to tell me about his too many night calls and other local news.

"How's that little one of yours?" he asks.

"He's growing well and is pulling himself up on chairs. Weigh him once a week. He blows bubbles and is happy when we put him in a swing made from a diaper and use the meat scales. Little Dick thinks this is real fun and makes all kinds of noises."

"Kenck, I've got something serious to tell you. We have decided to leave Choteau. I'm just killing myself with both day and night work. Margaret, my good wife, tells me that I must get out of Choteau soon before I keel over on the road somewhere. She likes Choteau but is willing, for my sake, to leave. Besides, I have more than one good reason to leave. I've never gotten to go fishing or hunting like you, and I'd like to do that a few times before I die."

"With you gone I can envision what MY life will be like."

"When we go, Kenck, I will bequeath my birth satchel to you, the instruments for a delivery, and medicines. I know since you've been with me several times the folks in need will insist on you before they will allow a strange doctor to touch them."

"Brooks, I wish the best for you. Just think of me when you go duck hunting and feel a twinge of guilt. If this life of service to my fellow man, and women too, gets too much for me, I'll do the same as you."

A Picture for Both Grandmas

"Mrs. Haugen is my name, if you don't know it already. I'm the one who owns the photo studio. It's right next to the Woodman's Hall. I bought it from Mr. Klingkenbeard. I told him at the time I don't know nothing about the photo business. He told me, 'You look like a smart lady. I'll teach you everything you need to know.' Well, I agreed to try to learn it. His teaching surely didn't amount to much, but I have learned from mistakes and success."

"Mrs. Haugen, what brings you here?"

"Dr. Kenck, I'd be real pleased to take your baby's picture. Maybe it could be a trade?"

"What would my part of the trade be?"

"Doctor, I have these two big teeth in the back that are giving me fits. I don't know if they can be fixed or if they need to come out."

"Get up in my chair here, Mrs. Haugen, I will take a look-see. But is that to be my part of this picture deal?"

"Exactly, Doctor. Real often I have to do what you call 'barter,' like what we kids called 'dis for dat.'"

"Mrs. Haugen, it's a deal. I've seen some of the pictures you have done and know your good work. Rita will be happy to get some photos. So, let's start on your teeth."

An exam shows the two molars that bother are badly

decayed, so I get to work right away and clean all decay out and then put medicated floors in them. I tell her we'll leave these with temporary fillings for a few days while I make the crowns. That way we'll know if they are going to behave with crowns on them.

"Thank you, Doctor. I've had several folks tell me you do good work. And I'll be expecting your missus with baby to come to my photo shop any day she can."

Rita gets little Richard dressed in the little garments she knit for him and puts him in the pram we got to wheel him around town. He is so happy. He loves to promenade. He behaved very well with Mrs. Haugen making a fuss over him to get a good exposure. Rita says she played peek-a-boo and made wonderful clucking sounds. The photograph sitting goes well and the pictures are fine. Little Dick is smiling wide and clapping his hands. Now we have just the thing for Grandma and Grandpa Auchard to show everyone.

Little Dick, approx. 9 months old

October 10, 1907

The hunting urge has come over me, mostly because Lou Woods writes to stir me up. But, I'm too busy most of the time. It will be hard to get away. Is it the hunting or is it escape? Probably both. I leave a note on the office door: Dr. K will be back after the first of the year.

Lou and I get an outfit together and take off for Charlie Dorrance's. He's expecting us. We should be able to get a handsome big bull. It's a little late and the bulls might be bunching up and catching the sun on early mornings. Dorrance tells us the bulls are beginning to head up, like it's getting close to the end of the rut. We think it's a shame to get the big one on the first day.

By waiting and watching, we can see where they go and the best place to put one down, besides making hunting simple. We will wait for fresh snow.

Up a different draw every day spreads out our time. On our third night, exactly as we had hoped, about three inches of snow puts a sound-suppressing blanket on the whole basin. Nothing equals the silent splendor of the first snowfall in mountains like these, and the tracking is easy.

Lou and I decide to go up the draw that has a substantial creek and also a cleared trail. We walk a ways and then stop to listen and watch. After the second mile, another stop. The only sound was our own breathing, which, in that silence, seemed terribly loud. Suddenly the shrill, piercing, bugle call of a bull split the air. It was so close it gave us goose bumps. We look at each other with a knowing eye signal. We took a few steps, and there was the big track where he had crossed this trail and plunged down the creek bank. We stood scanning the area. There he is! Standing in the creek now with his head stretched to start another bugle call. We both raise our rifles and shoot. We caught him as he had suddenly realized his danger. Both shots hit him as he whirled to take flight. He kept whirling and crashed on the same motion. What a giant. What a crash! Lou was speechless as he looked at the giant rack of horns. The bullets hit his lungs and I think his lights went out before he knew what happened. Lou and I were satisfied because this huge creature will be big enough to share. It is such a magnificent head and antler structure that Lou wanted to take it to a taxidermist, and of course I was willing he should have it. I am so busy that I don't have time. Besides, as yet, I have no place to display it.

That is it. The rest of our ten-day trip in the mountains is without further excitement. I'm happy to have a few quiet days, for some reason I can't explain, except a few days without being called away at night or even during the day to do the things a medical doctor should be doing.

CHAPTER 33

CHRISTMAS IN AUGUSTA, 1907, AT THE AUCHARDS

When I get back, we pack all the baby paraphernalia up, and it's Christmas at the Auchards this year. My Augusta Hotel office is in fine shape. We plan to stay here until the first of the year. Papa and Mama Auchard will have it no other way but we will stay with them. Little Dick has totally captivated them. Since it is the holiday season, we would like him to get in on the goodies as well as the downright joyfulness to have family and friends around. Brother Will had brought a good-sized fir tree from the mountains last week. Rita and Mama Auchard get the decorations from the attic and trim the tree when Dick is asleep. The decorations had to be out of his eager finger's reach. Rita tells me he is clasping his hands and letting out streams of excited sounds.

December 21, Saturday

Band concert day. No snow yet. Rita and I put our instruments in the surrey when Will brings it up to the house. Papa Auchard puts on his horsehide coat. Mama has her long wool coat and bonnet. Rita has her heavy, black, fur-collared coat and fur-trimmed hat with a wool scarf to drape over the top. I put on a wool vest under my suit coat and put on my Russian beaver cap. Baby Dick gets to wear his sleeper, because no doubt he will sleep on the way home as usual, and is wrapped in a soft wool blanket and thick wool cap his Grandma Auchard knit for him.

We park the surrey downtown. Papa takes his team

over to Nett's stable. He's put two foot warmers in the surrey with blankets to keep them warm as they listen to the band. For the concert, twenty or more dedicated players gain no more reward except applause and satisfaction that we can make music together. If someone doesn't show to hear the concert, he has a good reason. Christmas brings special effort. It's pure joy to make music then.

The concert being over, Papa Auchard gets his team from Nett's. He and Mama take little Richard home. All of us who played in the concert are rewarded with a big feed at Tomlinson's house. It turns out to be roast pork sandwiches made with fresh baked bread Matilda had made. For dessert we gobbled up pumpkin pie and coffee with big dollops of whipped cream.

Along with the players were all the people who helped out with the concert. Lots of talk goes on catching up on what had happened during the fall and winter months, and what was about to happen, like weddings and certain events you might guess usually followed.

Bud says, "Doc and Rita, I expect to see you at the Christmas Dance."

Quickly I accept. "Bud, it's been so long since we danced, I'll have to be extra agile not to step on the lady's toes."

"Ah, Kenck, I've seen you dance and know that's not possible for you to forget." He grins at Rita and she nods her head affirmatively. Bud is certainly right. Rita can dance all the steps and she teaches me all over again.

Dick and Victoria Adams, the newlyweds, are here. Vic is the pie maker for these good pumpkin pies. Dick says, "Oscar, we want you and Rita to come over to our place. I have my two-seater buggy already hitched in my barn. Then we want to take you out to the Auchard Ranch."

"Do you mean to tell me, Dick, that you don't get enough driving with your steady mail stage runs?"

"Oscar, I don't get you folks in my rig often these days, so it's a privilege."

"Well, we would be pleased to go along. We are happy to see you two married."

"Kenck, I'm like you were with Rita. All of us

wondered why you didn't marry her. I finally realized if I didn't ask Victoria someone might come along and snatch her away." He put his arm around Vic and gave her a squeeze. We agree to meet at the dance.

In the house we find Papa and Mama Auchard sitting near the cozy stove with its fire showing through the isinglass windows.

"When did Richard go to sleep?" Rita asks.

"As soon as he drank most of that warm bottle we had with us. It was still warm, wrapped up near the foot warmer. By the time he was off to a sleep so sound that when his grandpa lifted him off my lap he didn't wake up then nor when he laid him in his crib."

Next on our agenda is the Sunday School program on Wednesday, December 24. Families will come if the weather holds. Santa will surely make a stop.

Joe Bush is missing at the program, someone whispers. Joe has to make sure Santa lands near here.

Everything is going well. There is a scene of the stable as Mary and Joseph stand and look down at something that's supposed to represent a manger. Then three youngish looking wise men come slowly in from the side of the stage. A song they sing is very faint. The last is some children reciting short poems they've composed, "What I Want for Christmas." Three little stair-step Bucholtz boys come out together. They recited as one voice, "What We Want for Christmas Is a Baby Sister!" A snicker goes through the audience. Mrs. Bucholtz, everyone seems to think, is almost certainly expecting very soon.

One little guy follows the Bucholtz trio. He doesn't say a word but begins to jump around and skip and flap his arms about. The teacher loudly whispers for him to say his piece. He pays no attention, just keeps on jumping and whirling about. Suddenly he stops and steps down off the platform and runs to Mr. Carmachael and loudly asks, "Can I have my dollar now?" The audience breaks into laughs. Carmachael digs down and hands him a silver dollar. "Thank you, sir," the little guy squeaks and scurries back to the line of children who now must finish their recitations.

The teacher then brings all the children to the front

of the platform and has them sit down to the tune of *Silent Night* from the organ. As soon as this is done, strangely the sound of sleigh bells can be heard coming from outside the church. Suddenly, in the doorway a huge figure with a red stocking cap and a long flowing white beard appears chortling, "Ho, ho, ho! I want to see all you good boys and girls. I'm on my way to your houses, but I want to see which ones have been good. I've brought a bag of goodies for each of you and then I'll spend the night going to your homes while you sleep."

With that he brings his big sack to the front and the teacher lines the children up to receive the little sack of candy and an orange from Santa. It's a little odd that Santa's voice sounds so much like Joe Bush, but the kids don't seem to notice.

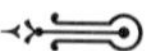

This day and evening are a taste of the good life. So good, I wonder if I'm dreaming.

In the morning we give Richard his new toys, but not all at once. Also, we give each other a surprise (sup-posedly). Rita has been knitting lately, not discussing what or who was to benefit. Nor had I asked her about her project. Ladies knit caps, socks, sweaters, etc., most of the time, but this time it is a sweater for me. The warmth of it feels good these chilly days. For Rita I had carefully hidden two pretty, jeweled, hair combs I'd picked up in Helena.

This evening we are in our dancing duds. The little one is fast asleep in his crib. Rita comes out of the bedroom and shows Papa and Mama how she looks in her purple velvet dancing dress, also how the jeweled combs hold her long brown hair in a pretty knot atop her head. Papa's eyes twinkle when he sees his beautiful daughter.

Brother Will brings the buggy from the barn. Solemn Will even smiles when he sees his kid sister looking so beautiful. I feel especially important to be escorting such a beauty.

Along with several couples we climb the stairs to the big Woodman Hall above Mrs. McKendrick's store. Tonight it is a ballroom. A familiar aroma, my favorite, tickles my olfactory senses. It says "mountains." As we enter, I can see why: evergreen boughs everywhere, plus two fir trees, set off the orchestra platform. Soft Christmas and dance medleys tickle my ears. A canopy of red, white, and green crepe-paper ribbons create a Christmas sky to dance under.

Mrs. Tomlinson, an elegant lady, is the hostess, selling the tickets and giving out the dance programs. Indeed, this is a Christmas Ball. The program indicates the first thing is a grand march. We realize that the Tomlinsons are bringing formal New England to the West.

Bud leaves his saxophone to be the marshall of the Grand March. I think there are forty couples to participate. Bud walks to the far center. "Ladies and gentlemen. Please line up here with your partners for the Grand March." So it goes. Beautiful ladies and nicely dressed gentlemen. The music sounds like *Under the Double Eagle*. Bud beckons to the lead couple and then stands at the bar to separate the couples to the right and to the left. We seldom get to do this so enjoy it immensely.

After all are abreast, he signals the orchestra to begin the dancing music, a waltz. Our programs were filled with the names of other couples, except every fourth one is for us. We can dance it or go to the punch bowl or do what we choose.

A lovely evening of dancing. We could tell we'd not danced lately but the joy of the occasion prevailed. Now we look forward to the usual local dancing on New Year's Eve.

'Tis a season to be joyous. Rita and I hadn't partied and danced for a long time, and with Mama Auchard to take care of the baby, we can take part in all the festivities. I did not get called out on any emergencies. Young Doctor Bateman is here and is available for any medical occasion that comes up. His office is at the same place as Dr. Albright's. I'm right glad about that since somehow those emergency calls in Choteau since Brooks left town were getting too regular, with very little remuneration because I cannot accept pay when I'm not a medical doctor. It was affecting my dentistry work. Too tired, never enough sleep. I'd begun to think something was wrong with me with all that getting tired out so easily.

Bud and Lizzie Tomlinson are happy and Bud tells me, "Oakie, it's really great to have you folks home again."Christmas this year is most memorable because it's little Dick's second and the celebrating community is busier than I've ever seen it. The weather is much milder than in previous years. Joe Bush is also in town and comes over mostly to talk.

"Kenck, we sure miss you when you stay in Choteau. Mighty glad to see you folks around. Since Dr. Albright's gone, we miss him too, but the new young Dr. Bateman that got here in July is fitting right in. He seems to know what he's doing and delivers babies about as well as you do."

"Yeah, Joe, I heard you have a new doctor. He's sorta fresh out of college but has all the latest knowledge of what to do for diseases. We'll have to get acquainted. How is your family and that lively little girl?"

"We named her Orpha, but we call her 'Billie.' I guess we did want another boy to take the place of the one we lost. She's four now and is the busiest little crea-ture. She bumped her mouth last July when she fell from her perch in the window of my shop. The tooth turned black and she is wiggling it. Could you take a look at it?"

"Tell her to come see me. I'll fix it or remove it. If it bothers her, she'll get a new one maybe next year."

"I'll bring her in to see you."

After Christmas, I make a special effort to find Dr. Bateman. At last I see him as he goes to the post office.

"Howdy, I'm Kenck, the dentist here."

He really perked up and said, "I've been wanting to catch up with you. People have been telling me stuff about you."

"Yeah? Sometimes they weren't able to find Albright so would beg me to do something. When I knew for sure that Albright was out of town, I'd go do what I could."

"You must have done pretty well. They tell me about some cases you've taken care of. I hope I can get to be as well thought of as you are. Are you going to stick around here now?"

"No, as a matter of fact, I'm leaving for Choteau tomorrow. The weather this time of year is 'iffy' so my wife and baby are staying with her folks about a mile up the road. The Auchards."

"So, I know you'll be back."

"Right. I'll practice in Choteau and then come back to my office in the hotel here. Choteau is a busy place. There's enough work for two medical doctors, although there's just one doctor there now that Brooks left. Also, there is another dentist besides myself. Since Choteau is the county seat, it has plenty going on at times."

"Kenck, it's good to talk with you. I've got some people waiting. Maybe we can get away sometime when you are back over here. What's the weather like here in January and February?"

"Last winter was fierce. It didn't warm up until the end of March. Lots of ranchers lost heavily. Dead cattle everywhere. I'm hoping this one will be better."

Bateman sticks out his hand to shake mine. "Kenck, it's good to know you are in this territory."

"I'm Oscar. We'll meet again."

When I get back to Rita later, I tell her about Bateman. He's young but sure seems serious about being a doctor. If anyone needs one, they should not hesitate to go to him.

Next morning I take off early. I just hate to say goodbye. I'm thinking that I should not have to leave my family. I'll figure out how to quit spreading myself so thin that I have to spend so much time away from them. Leaving them to go hunting is different. I'm always back in just a few days.

Before I go on to Choteau, I need to know Albert's situation. I ask at Beach and Wellman's store. Albert's neighbors, the Beans, come there regularly to trade butchered critters for supplies. I find Alva Beach. "Have any Beans been in lately?"

He says, "Not for a couple of weeks. I hope Ole or one of the brothers comes in today. I need a butchered beef and a hog."

"If one of them shows, please tell him I'd like to talk with him. I'm in my office trying to finish up the folk who've gotten started on their teeth lately. I've got to get back to Choteau too. Lots of people in that town for the Court session and they're expecting me."

"Kenck, you are a busy man. Taking care of the toothaches of the two biggest counties in the state, and not only that, I hear you are out on regular doctor calls when people can't find a regular doctor."

"I can't say no if there's no other doctor to help them. Maybe I'll have to do like Dr. Brooks did: just leave the country."

"Kenck, I'd hate to see that. We really need both a dentist and a doctor. We are pleased about this young Bateman deciding to come here." Beach goes right along cutting veal. "Yep, I'll tell a Bean you want to talk to him."

I'm not back in my office half an hour finishing up when Mrs. Brusgard comes in. "Doctor, vee be so very happy you be here ven us folks need you. Very bad toothaches very misable!" Then in comes Ole Bean!

"Howdy, Doc. Beach told me you are in and wanted to see me."

"That's right, Ole. Thanks for coming. Albert—have you heard anything about him lately?"

"Yes, just before Christmas he took off for Helena. He said he'd be back in a month or when the weather warmed up."

"I'm glad to hear that. Being alone and way out like that at Christmas is not good for him. I'm planning to get up to see him when he gets back. You tell him for me that I'll be coming and to write me a letter in Choteau when he gets there."

"I'll do that, Doc. We see him every time he goes by, kinda keep track of him since we know he's alone and needs milk and eggs. We've got plenty to share with him."

"Thank you. You folks are certainly appreciated. How is your wife, Ina?"

"She's pretty good. She had a baby boy in the middle of October."

"That's great. You folks got married a few years before Rita and me. What did you name him?"

"I let Ina name him. He's Wallace. A strong little guy. Just eats and sleeps so far."

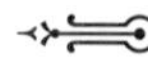

Not long after the New Year, here comes Joe with his bouncing sprite. She looks up at me with impish eyes. "No doctor!" she shouts. "I just have to wiggle it with my tongue for it to get mad. But I won't wiggle it anymore."

"Billie, get up in my chair so I can see why it hurts to wiggle it." Billie obediently climbs up but closes her mouth tight and refuses to open, so I must distract her.

"What do you think of my chair? It goes up and it goes down." I show her how the chair moves with the foot and hand levers, and then I hand her one of my examining mirrors.

"See this little mirror? Can you see yourself in it?" She doesn't answer but looks into the mirror and without thinking, opens her mouth to look at her teeth. I get out my large mirror and then she opens her mouth and reaches her loose tooth to wiggle it for me. Finally, I get her to let me feel this tooth. Actually all that's holding it in is a little bit of gum tissue.

"Joe, this tooth should come out. She might choke on it in her sleep. You'll have to talk her out of it. Tell her to put it under her pillow at night and see what happens to it." That got her all curious, and I quickly put a bit of oil of clove on the gum and had the loose tooth out before she could even think about it hurting. I put the tiny tooth in a little paper clasp envelope in her hand and she is down out of the chair and already out the office door.

"Billie, put that little tooth under your pillow tonight and be certain to check it in the morning to see if it has changed color," I tell her before she's gone.

CHAPTER 34

SPRING & SUMMER, 1908, TIME OFF, DOCTOR'S ORDERS

January 9, 1908—Back to Choteau, but I'm having more of the same trouble. Don't know what is the matter. I am tired, exhausted all the time. Can't seem to get enough rest to get my strength back. Doctor Brooks has left Choteau and people beg me to go out at all hours. The cases are mostly births. They tell me there's no one else to call.

This winter brings many cases of pneumonia. The medicine most effective is quinine, and I must take steps to get the patients to sweat, but not let them get chilled. Then the patients get up and out of the house too soon. Also, they don't drink enough water and there's been some kidney failure.

I decide to make the trip back to Augusta to see Dr. Bateman about my unexplained lethargy and exhaustion. I sleep in the stage during the thirty-mile journey but don't feel rested. I can hardly keep my eyes open or sit up straight for the exam. He takes a few standard tests, asks the regular questions, listens with the stethoscope, and then sits down with a somber look on his face.

"Kenck, this is serious." He's got my full attention now.

"You've got trouble. It's your heart. You've been working too hard without regular sleep for too long, and it's taken a toll."

I'm speechless. My heart? It's pumping awfully loud in my ears right now. Can't hear myself think.

"You must take time off immediately. If you don't, your legacy will be a widow and fatherless son. Will you do as I say?"

"To save my family, I will do whatever I must, Bateman. What do you prescribe?"

"Complete rest. That means no doctoring, no dentistry, no patients or work of any kind. I want to see you sitting back in your easy chair every day without a care for at least the next six months. With complete rest and proper nutrition, you may recover, but it depends on you."

The full weight of Bateman's prognosis starts to hit me sometime after leaving his office. Time off from helping people? What about my practice? Who will cover the emergency calls? Rita already has her hands full with Baby Richard. How could I ask her to care for a sick husband too? My head aches from the swirl of thoughts. I don't remember the rest of that day, except making the decision to go right home, without returning the thirty miles to my Choteau office.

Rita, my sweet wife, listens pensively to the information from Bateman's examination. But, when I start discussing a plan for temporarily closing the Choteau office and finding a replacement doctor, she smiles and gently places her fingers over my lips. "Dear husband, I will arrange it. Let me care for you now." I think to myself, how can I be so fortunate to have found an angel such as this? I rest, knowing our future is secure in her hands.

CHAPTER 35

THE CABIN AND FISHPOND

This spring is altogether different. We set up a temporary camp in the Canyon. Many things get done and I cannot tell you the details. The logs are brought to the spot I'd picked. I look again and they are all peeled. Notching and laying is done, but I don't remember when. Tony's partner comes up with a load of lumber and does the roof, even the tarred paper.

"Rita," I ask, "were you here when they did this?"

"Yes, dear. And so were you, but you were often asleep, and that is what Dr. Bateman wants you to do. Seems like you are making up for all the hours you were out on emergency calls the past few years."

"Is that what happens, Rita, my good lady? You are wise."

Building our cabin

"Oscar, it's a good thing I've come up here to camp with you while our cabin is being built. I can see what's going on and answer the questions of the men. Albert knows the plans too, but he's busy and tells them to 'Ask Mrs. Rita.'"

'Tis the middle of summer and the river is low. We decide then where the fishpond should be. We borrow a scoop from Dick Bean. It's his road-building equipment. Using the two horses we just got, Tommy and Gyp, Albert takes on the job of scooping out the pond and building the banks. Water from the spring will fill the pond, and then we'll place a fine screen on the outlet to the river.

Next we need fish eggs to start our fish-raising project. Ole Bean has heard we are making a fishpond and will need fish eggs. It isn't long before he and wife Ina, and also their little guy Wallace, come to see us.

"Vee hear you fellows gonna raise fish."

"That's right, Ole. We now need to get the eggs."

"Von place vee get dem is Ovanda, over across divide."

"Did you go all the way around by Helena?"

"Oh no. Der is a trail across the mountain dey call 'Lewis and Clark Pass.' It is okay to go. Vee go in cool vetter. Dey no sell egg in hot vetter. Ven you get pond, fill mit vater. You bring tubs und barrel and get grass from my lake. The eggs und little fish, dey need some places to hide."

I tell Ole about how I got fingerlings shipped by train from Bozeman to Craig and took them by wagon and then by packhorse to Benchmark six years ago in 1902. He is impressed. I also tell him I appreciate him teaching the local Indian boys how to make hay and ask when he'll be putting up the next crop.

"Vee hay mebbe July. Mebbe one month or so."

"Someday I expect to have them help with my own crop of hay. I'm buying the meadow above and below our homesteads."

"Kenck, vee know you vill haf cows and vill need hay."

When the Beans' haying time comes around, our cabin is ready. It is two rooms, one for kitchen and eating, and one for sleeping. We are happy to have a place of our own and in the mountains. If anything can make me get strong again, it's these mountains. What is that Bible saying? 'My help cometh from the hills.' Somewhere in the Old Testament, I remember.

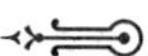

During the early spring, before the cabin is finished, Albert and I talk about bringing in the fish eggs. Albert suggests we get the younger Indian boys to help transplant lake plants for our pond. We ask Garvais about Indian help on this, and he is willing and collects a few of them to earn a little money through this project. We gather washtubs from the families and they make an expedition. Before long they had brought a load of lake moss and other plants and spread them in the shallow waters of the pond.

Now to add the eggs! The hatchery at Ovanda has answered my letter and told us when our egg order would be ready.

"Albert, I'm feeling pretty good. I think we ought to do a trip. Ole tells me we can go across on the Lewis and Clark Pass. It's just a single trail so we might have trouble. It's still early enough in the season for some deep snow, but it might be our last chance until next spring. Next spring means waiting another year to get our fish started."

Albert isn't sure. "Oakie, you sure you can do this?"

"I've been feeling so much better lately. I don't even feel sleepy like I did all winter."

"I sure hope so. I don't want you to overdo it, by no means."

"Well, if I get tired, I'll just rest awhile."

"Oakie, let's give it a try right after the last spring moon. We know that often brings a short snow or frost and then the weather is usually good after that."

Albert has good ideas, so that's our plan. We get some horses from the Beans' herd that are broke and gentle because hauling a load of fish eggs has to be on the gentle side.

For the trip, bedrolls are packed, a grub box, a tarp, barrels, and an air pump. It's the first week in June and we have directions from Ole and the Indians and take off to get our fish eggs.

It's only a trail, not a real road, so we look at every hill and gully wondering how it will be as we are coming back with our delicate load? At last we arrive at Ovanda. Their boarding house looks mighty good to us—especially a meal from the cook as we were plenty weary of our fry-pan cooking. We needed baths too. What a luxury! A nice big tin tub and buckets of hot water. I feel so much better afterwards that I ask the lady for a sheet of paper and envelope. A letter to Rita from me in Ovanda will surprise her. Hope she gets it before I get home.

In Ovanda we mostly rest the first couple of days, talking with the fish hatchery guys because what we want to do with these babies is let them hatch and grow and hatch some more ourselves.

The departure day soon arrives, and we get our barrels all soaked and ready in the bed of the wagon. Then the hatchery men fill them with fertilized eggs. Four barrels is all we can handle and keep running air through them. Reminds me of when I picked up those fingerlings so many years ago and went through the hassle of getting them back to Wood Lake and the headwaters of the Sun River.

Weather is favoring us. Cool nights and days of late spring, not too warm, but not completely freezing at night either. Across these prairies, this side of the Continental Divide was fairly easy until we started climbing up to the summit. It's a hard pull, a week's worth of work, especially considering the many stops to pump air into the barrels to keep the water oxygenated that floated our precious fish eggs. We don't begin to really worry until we go over the top and start down the other side. I worried so coming up the mountains that I didn't give the descent as much thought, but woe is me, here's a downhill place and the brakes won't hold all the way. What shall we do? I went ahead a couple of hundred yards and this looks like trouble. I know we can't do it the way we have the wagon.

"Albert, the only way we can do this one is absolutely backwards, so we must turn the wagon around and both of us winch the wagon to a tree and keep the horses from being dragged backwards too fast by the weight of the wagon." By then I was wishing we'd bought only one barrel of fish eggs.

We gathered big rocks to block the wheels at each interval, allowing the wagon to back down the slope just a few feet at a time. The downhill progress was much more difficult than the climb.

At last we reach lower elevations and make much better time, arriving home after four weeks away. Rita is overcome with relief that I'm back, and I'm feeling better too after a good rest from our fish-egg trek. Come to think of it, I am feeling much better. I never even thought of napping all the way home.

"Rita," I say as we are feasting on roast, potatoes, and gravy, "I just happened to realize I'm feeling much better."

"That trip must have been good medicine. I worried all the while thinking it was too hard for you."

"My good lady, I never gave it much thought, but now I see it was the right treatment for what ailed me. Next time I see Bateman, he'll probably agree that's what it takes sometimes—a task that gives a person great joy. I've a question though. Did you get that letter I sent you from Ovanda?"

"Really? Did you write and send a letter?"

"Yes, I did. Albert, you verify that's a fact."

"Rita, Oscar did certainly write a letter soon after we got there. He got some paper and an envelope from the lady who runs the boarding house and she said the stage picks up all the mail every day."

The days are getting longer now and the nights warmer. The eggs are hatching at a regular rate, and the tiny fry are too quick to get a good count. The water from the river runs through a mesh screen, but we have to devise a good way to feed these baby fish some baby fish food.

Ole had explained he used a fish-feeding platform when he first started growing his fry. Even now his fish get extra feed. He rigged a wire box nailed to boards that are strung out to the middle of the pond. In this wire box he threw some rodent carcasses, fish guts, and meat trimmings, and the blowflies lay their eggs on the stuff. The resulting maggots that hatch from the flies drop down and make delicious bites for the young fish.

Albert gets busy right away constructing a wire box like Ole's. His supper-table contraption is sturdy and will provide years of use.

Before we know it, summer has come and gone and the days are shorter. Winter is upon us. Not so cold yet but snow a few inches deep. The pond gets some ice around the edges but stays clear where the pipe from the spring bubbles up near the center.

About November, Albert says, "Oakie, I'm itching to go into Helena like I've been doing the last few winters. Will you be all right here, you and Rita and little Dick?"

I had been thinking he might be lonesome for Mama's cooking and the Kenck uncles' Christmas celebration, so I say, "Albert, of course we'll be all right. I'm getting better every week, I can tell, and you should go back to your home and have a good Christmas with the family."

Albert checks that there is plenty of wood and that Ole and Ina know he'll be gone so they will come up to check on us every few days. Often they bring our mail, but the letter that I had written and sent in Ovanda has still not arrived.

CHAPTER 36

CHRISTMAS WITH GRANDPA & GRANDMA AUCHARD

Our log cabin is plenty cozy. The wood logs hold the fire all night. Snow holds off but when December comes, we begin to think of Mama and Papa Auchard. That does it. It makes us think of where we should be this time of year. My little hatchlings needed to be fed, so the Garvaises were happy to do that. It was easy for them to put some rabbit or muskrat carcasses in the wire boxes.

Yes, we decide that's where we should be at such a time as Christmas, Grandma and Grandpa's. Winter clothes and blankets are piled into the buggy. Our faithful team, Tommy and Gyp, lead off through the thin layer of snow. Right soon we stop at Ole and Ina's to tell them we'll be at the Auchards until after the New

Year. They'll keep the mail for us while we're away. So, off we go snugly wrapped in coats and blankets. Richard is so wrapped up that he can't bounce around like he usually does so is off to sleep in a mile or so.

At last, just as the winter sun is starting to drop towards old Sawtooth, we turn in at the pole gate. Grandma and Grandpa are all smiles and so happy to see Richard. He starts strutting around just like he hadn't forgotten a thing about their house. Brother Will is happy too. He can't take his eyes off "The Kid," as he calls him.

Grandma says, "Oscar, you do seem better. You don't look so tired now." Turning to Rita, she says, "What did you do or feed him? He looks so good!"

"Mama, as you might guess, I fed him all the good stuff you helped me put up and taught me to cook too. But most of all, I think his being in the mountains and thinking about his pond made him quit worrying and gave him something to do without hurrying and going out on urgent calls late at night."

"Well, we'll feed him plenty all the time you are here."

"Mama, you always get us to eat more good food!"

"Well, daughter, a person never knows when he or she will get sick, and then more body is needed to get well. Oscar does need more strength now."

"Mama, I've worried enough for both of us and he is so much better. He isn't near so tired all the time. I now have to tell him to come and rest for a while." I hear this conversation as I'm bringing in our bags.

At supper, Grandpa Richard says, "What about Albert? Is he still at the ranch?"

"No, Papa," explains Rita. "Albert is in Helena, like the last several years. We think there is a special attraction there. We don't know just who though, someone he writes to regularly. He does have beautiful handwriting."

"I'm wanting to see Dr. Bateman," I pipe up. "Is he back yet from Iowa? He told me he was going there for a very special reason this fall."

"Oscar, I think I saw his buggy when I went for mail the other day. He did have Dr. Albright's old office there by the post office."

"Rita," I say, "let's go into town tomorrow. I need to have a talk with him. I hope he did what he planned."

Papa asks, "What do you mean? What did he plan?"

"He told me he was going to ask this girl, or lady rather, to marry him, because, number one, he needed a wife, and also he needs a business helper—basically, a slave."

"Yes," Papa nods his head, "a professional man needs to have a wife. I mean a good wife." Rita gives one of her little giggles and says, "Papa, you are so right!"

Papa and I retire to the sitting room and discuss the

national and state politics. His Republican philosophy appeals very much to me. Roosevelt, although fond of free enterprise, is disturbed at how the railroad and steel industry is really monopolizing interstate trade. He proposes antitrust legislation on many occasions. He also announces that the meat packers are not keeping the slaughter process clean, and there is a lot of protest over how little they are paying immigrants from Southern Europe. "Teddy" also wants to show the world the U.S. has a big Navy. He is sending several of our new battleships on a world tour to remind other countries that we have the might to enforce the Monroe Doctrine.

The next morning, Rita and I drive in to town. We take Mama's list of needs. She says, "Getting low on yeast and cranberries. Should be in now. Also, we need some jars of oysters."

Papa is carrying bundled-up Richard up to the barn to see his Uncle Will work with the horses. He says Will can't help but smile when he sees how excited Richard gets when the horses are running around in the corral. He catches a colt and brings him close so Richard can touch his nose and soft muzzle. All this Papa relates when we return from town. He asks if we found Bateman. "No, but we saw his new wife," explains Rita. "She is his new office lady. A very friendly person too. We asked her if they would come out and visit us on Sunday. Mama, do you mind?" Mrs. Auchard is always happy for more visitors. And that's what happens the following Sunday.

Bateman says, "Oscar, I brought my stethoscope. I want to listen to your heartbeat." So, we go into the front bedroom, and after he listens, "I'm amazed at the strength of it. You must have done exactly as I prescribed."

"Yes, Howard, I did that for several months. Lots of stuff happened those months and I must have slept through most of it, but now I'm awake a lot more."

"Rita must know what to feed you and made things happen that caused you not to worry."

"Yes, I've got a good one and I think you have too. Effie seems to be totally committed to you. Speaking of improvement, I think soon I'll start my practice here in Augusta during the week and go back to the cabin on weekends."

"Well, Oscar, I'd say let the ones who really want to get work done come to you on the weekends awhile out there on the Dearborn."

"Well, that's an idea. I'll try that for a few months and see. I know I'd be saved from that long drive on weekends and could see how the boys, the neighbor boys, are cutting my hay and taking care of the stock I've put together."

CHAPTER 37

A LITTLE BIG SURPRISE, OSCAR JR., OCTOBER 3, 1909

So it is in the spring of 1909 that some of my patients will drive so far for my dental care. When these folks arrive, Rita is burdened with extra mouths to feed, but the ladies jump right in and help with the work, and besides, they usually bring all kinds of food—butter, cheese, and bread, as well as meat, like chicken and ham.

By the beginning of summer, I decide the dental work must go back to town. The interesting fact that we are expecting another person in our family made me think that Rita should not have all that work and hubbub. She's the one who needs the rest now.

By September I'm having office hours at the Augusta Hotel on weekdays and come home to the Can-yon on Friday nights. Rita has one of the neighbor girls to help her and take care of our three-year-old. He's a busy little guy.

Bateman stops by my office about once a week now. He is so very concerned about Rita.

"For such a little lady, she is certainly gaining weight. I worry about her. Have her come to Auchards soon and stay. She should be closer to town."

Friday when I get home to the ranch, I see that Rita is getting pretty weary. "My dear good lady. What I really want is to take you back to town. The time is getting close, and I want you near me and also near Dr. Bateman."

"Oscar, I agree. I'm the one now who's getting worn

out. This time is so different than the last. I know Mama and Papa are worried, so if I'm close, they will be eased a bit."

"All right, honey. Let's get everything and little Dick packed and move you back to Mama and Papa's for the rest of your term before this little one comes." I hold her close and smooth her beautiful hair. Such a wonderful wife and what trials a woman has to go through in this life.

The rest of September she looks like it might be twins, but Bateman listens to the baby's heartbeat, explaining, "No, it will be just one."

"Oscar," he tells me when we are alone, "Rita is going to have a large baby. It won't be easy but I certainly want you to be there and, of course, I will be there. Her pelvis is narrow so it may be a difficult birth."

"Howard, what in the world can I do? This scares me. I love her so much. I swear this will be the last pregnancy for us."

"There are ways, Oscar, to keep from this hazard and I can tell you how. For now we'll hope and pray for the best."

"Howard, I didn't worry so much about not living through this past year, but now I worry about Rita making it through this."

"When she starts labor, I'll stay right with her and do the very best I know."

All of Bateman's counseling helps some, but I'm still very worried. Mama is worried, Papa too. Little Richard is our main distraction from this worry. It's good someone is not worrying. He's the happiest little three-year-old.

October is the month that the baby will enter the outside world. I can hardly leave Rita to go to the office, but Will has promised he will come get me and Dr. Bateman if anything happens. He explains, "I keep one horse speed-saddled and ready, and when I let him out to pasture, I keep Pete saddled and ready, day and night."

October 1 starts with a bang.

"Oh, Oscar! The pains are starting!"

"Rita, my darling, it will be over soon. How often are the contractions?"

"You time them by your pocket watch, dearest."

"Let's see. That's been a few minutes ago at three a.m. Do we have everything ready?"

"Yes, we have all things in readiness, except getting Bateman here when the pains are ten minutes apart." The present contractions are about twenty-five minutes apart for some time, and we doze off to sleep again.

Morning comes and the contractions continue at the same frequency. I'm worried, but I don't voice my concern.

When I hear Mama in the kitchen and Papa stoking the fires, I get dressed and tell them it's going to happen. I must go tell Dr. Bateman, but I must keep track of the time between contractions too. It is very early in the morning on a Saturday.

Papa says, "I can go fetch Bateman. I'd like you to stay by her."

"Okay, I'll get Will to bring the buggy.

In about an hour, the MD is there and examining Rita.

"The opening is not nearly large enough yet. It will be several more hours at the earliest. Could even be another twenty-four hours. She has a huge baby, no doubt a boy. I'll be at home. I will not leave town until it's over. Have her walk around here. It will help relax the muscles as much as possible to let the opening dilate."

He is right. Sunday morning early, no real change but the contractions are now reduced to fifteen-minute intervals. Bateman comes to visit again and gives Rita a muscle relaxant. The poor lady is getting weary. She drifts off to sleep between each spasm, only to be awakened with sharp pains in a short fifteen minutes, exhausted.

Early Monday morning, the contractions speed up again. The pelvis opening widens and Dr. Bateman arrives before breakfast. "Oscar, it's really close now. I'm going to have to do a surgery so she won't tear, and we'll give her some anesthesia when we stitch it back. She has suffered too much.

The water breaks and the head appears. After much pushing on Rita's part, out it pops. Shoulders follow, first one and then the other. The rest is easy, but Rita is so exhausted she passes out. Bateman explains we must keep her awake at all costs. I talk to her constantly so that he can gauge the amount of anesthesia needed. We give her several breaths of ether while Bateman does his sewing. He explains she may feel it a wee bit, but she won't remember it. I hope he's right. This is too much. It's a lively, hefty, fair-haired boy. Probably will be nine pounds when we weigh him. I wipe him off and get the meat scales to find out. Sure enough, nine pounds and four ounces. His head is a little pushed, but that will straighten.

Rita is so tired she drifts off even while she tries to talk. Not until the next day, October 4, do we finalize his name.

"*Oscar*," she insists, "after you and *Auchard* after Papa. That will be almost a junior, so he can use 'Junior' when he needs to show he's your son." Rita sleeps soundly after her huge effort.

I certainly was grateful to have Howard there when we needed him.

"Howard, I owe you."

"Oscar, never mind about that. You'll pay me back dozens of ways over the years. Another thing I want to discuss with you. Dr. Long, the MD in Choteau, stopped by a while back and he's urging me to move there. Says he has much more than he can do."

"But what about this town?"

"Yes, this town does need a doctor, but I'm thinking that a doctor will come here anyway, especially after it grows, because of the Great Northern putting a line in through here. In the meantime, between Dr. Long and myself, we can take care of a large territory. In Choteau we can get a hospital going if we work together. Anyway, Kenck, don't you worry. I'll be around a while longer yet."

We stay at the Auchards the rest of the winter. By spring 1910 I'm really feeling better and start more practice in my wagon office that I've had moved to the ranch. We decide to go it this way for the summer so I can be closer to Rita and the boys.

People are coming with their tents and camp gear to stay by our house to get their dental work done. Rita gets one of the Pocha girls to come help with the babies. As usual, all ladies who come pitch right in and help with cooking and housework. I'm sometimes working with the Garvais and Swan boys with the hay crop out in our meadows.

Besides dental work, other things are taken care of here at the ranch. A fellow came during haying time in extreme pain. It appeared to be gallstones. I tell him as soon as the stone passes out the bile duct the pain will stop. I give him a hypodermic shot of morphine. Soon he goes limp with the pain gone, and he lies on a cot for a few hours on the porch. I take off to work with my haymakers and leave him there asleep.

Later, Rita tells me what happens after I've gone. The man sleeps for another hour and then suddenly rises up yelling and grabbing his side again. "Oh, Missy Kenck, where is the doctor? He needs to give me another shot!" She tells him the doctor has gone way down in the fields. "Oh, oh, oh," he howls. "Another shot. Please, Missy Kenck. You can do it, you can." She explained to him she didn't know how to handle the needle. "Oh, oh, oh," he kept howling. Rita thought of my sack of poultice bran and put some water on to heat. She dumped a couple of quarts of bran into it, and then when it thickened, she put it into a cloth bag and told him to lie down again so she could lay the hot poultice around his middle.

The man did as he was told. Rita arranged the wet sack around his middle, and he did keep moaning for a bit after that but soon drifted off to sleep. He just woke up before I returned and thanked Rita for saving his life, calling her "Miss Doctor." She told him it was only bran, and he promised to get some before he got that pain again.

By the fall of 1910, I'm feeling my old self again. My strength is back and I'm working full capacity every day either doing ranch work or dental work on patients who are still coming and camping near the house.

These patients bring me messages from others who are asking me to come back to my office in the hotel. Rita and I talk it over.

"I'm puzzled, Rita. What to do. No way do we want to give up this ranch. Our boys need this kind of life and I do too, when I can take the time off from dental work."

"Oscar, maybe we can do both. For example, you open your office weekdays and come back up here on weekends. Just limit the dental work to weekdays. Saturday and Sunday just be at home with no dental work. I'm sure I'll be all right with the Pocha and the Garvais boys to do the chores and help with the children, and Richard will start school this fall."

"I'll think about it, my good wife. Oh, how I do appreciate your good-natured willingness to do so much. One thing though, there must be a telephone line to the house, regardless of what we decide."

Albert tells me he will not be back here next summer. He says, "Oakie, you got your ranch and fish-ponds. You really don't need me here."

"Albert, I never thought of our deal including whether I needed you or not. I thought you'd get to like this life almost as much as I do."

"Oakie, no, I needed to get out of town when we started this, but now I'm thinking of staying in town. Been writing to a lady named Esther and visiting her during my winters there. We have decided we want to be together and she's right. So, we'll get married before long."

"Albert, life is lonely. You do need somebody. Also, I can see you do enjoy being in town. You work at times when official documents need beautiful and precise writing like yours and also like playing your violin at parties. I'm sure you'll find plenty to do. When you decide for certain and get married, we can settle up what I owe you for your land and work here. Let me know when you want to settle it."

Fall 1910. Albert gathers his things and I drive him to the stage route as it comes by the Half Way House.

Dick Adams is still driving the stage. "Kenck, I'm glad to see you better. When do you plan to be back to your old office in the hotel? Lots of people are hoping it will be soon. Just when you educated all of Augusta on how to take care of their choppers, you had to lie low for a year." I tell Adams that maybe I'll visit the Augusta office soon. I turn to Albert. "So long, kid. Good luck and we'll keep in touch, aye what?"

"Yeah, Oakie, big brother."

CHAPTER 38

HOME AT THE RANCH ON WEEKENDS

Dick starts school along with the Garvais kids. A lunch bucket was a lard pail but now packs a delicious lunch. While Dick starts his first year, I start my practice in town again. Rita and Oscar, who is now two years old, are home alone, yet not alone. Mr. Pocha comes every morning to check on Rita. "Mizzy Kenck, you need me do something?" he always says when he brings the milk from the cow shed.

If the wood is low in the wood box, she says, "Yes, Mr. Pocha, some wood please."

Always he asks, "Doctor, he telephone?"

"Yes," Rita tells him. Every day I call once, sometimes twice, to see how things are.

When Friday afternoon comes, I'm glad to get Tommy and Gyp from the stable and head out for my mountain. I take only an hour and forty-five minutes in good weather. Also, everyone in town has learned I disappear on Friday afternoon.

Joe Bush comes into my office on a Monday morning. "Kenck, I tried to find you on Friday, but I missed you by a few minutes. I had this Indian kid who run away from the Fort Shaw Indian school. He was in agony with a swollen jaw. It was a bad tooth, I think. I finally got him to open his mouth so we could pull the tooth with the pliers. He did yell something awful, but my wife put a warm wet towel on his face and he finally went to sleep."

"What did you do with the kid then."

"Next day I took him back to Fort Shaw. I sure do feel for those lonesome Indian kids."

"One thing about it, Joe. They go right back being an Indian and forget all the English they've been taught when they get out."

"Kenck, we sure missed you when you were staying out of your office last year."

"Well, I'm much better now but I still have to get rested up on weekends. For a while I'll be at the ranch. Going to get a few head of cattle and make like the life of a rancher. It's work but not the same as going out nights on baby runs."

Most days I go down to Barnard's telephone right in their store and call Rita. She is sure to be near the phone to get three longs and three shorts that Mrs. Barnard can surely crank out on her office phone. Dick is sometimes standing on a chair so he can tell me what he's been doing. "Dad," he says, the first time we talked, "someone brought a skunk to school and put it under the school house."

I said, "Dick, who did that, do you know?"

"Yeah, but I can't tell on him."

"When I get home Friday we will talk about that."

I tell Rita when I get home, "We better not say much about trouble at school over the phone. We'll settle it when I get home at the end of the week." Rita says, "That's a good idea. Let's not give out secrets on the phone, because many up this way on that line are listening. If something is critical, I will tell you in code."

Every Thursday or Friday morning early I call home to find out what the good lady needs from the store. Even though we stock up on staples like flour, sugar, coffee, tea, and bacon, there's usually something that runs out. This time it's yeast cakes. Every so often the yeast needs a boost of some new critters. New things come into the stores, and I'll surprise her with something from far away. Today I'll bring oranges.

Dick's first year of school is full of stories of what goes on and who is there. "Dad," he says, "I'm pretty sure I know who brought the skunk."

"Try not to know things like that because if some-one asks, you don't have to tell."

"Okay, Dad, I'll just plug my ears when someone starts talking about stuff. But tell me, Dad, what kinds of trouble you and Uncle Albert got into when you went to school?"

"First I want to tell you about the school. It was a boys' school completely. No girls, and no lady teach-ers either. A boys' day-school. We all had the same kinds of clothes and we had to behave very politely. We said prayers every day because the priests of the Catholic church were our teachers. Good manners like saying 'please,' 'thank you,' and 'excuse me' were so very important."

"Oh Dad, they were really strict, weren't they?"

"Yes, Dick, strict and they had to be. Especially be-cause Albert and I didn't have a Dad around to keep us behaving right."

"Where was your dad?"

"I've been waiting for you to ask that question. After supper I'll tell the story of your Grandpa Kenck and what happened long ago. Mother has supper ready now."

The news of the week gets told at the table, about Joe Bush and the runaway Indian boy, and that J.C. Manix decided to buy out Mrs. McKendrick's store. He had told me a while back when he came into town after working for his uncle in Depuyer that ranch life was not for him. He came into my office and told me. "That's not all, either," I explained to Rita over supper. "He and Helen Nilon are going to 'get hitched,' he told me. She's a good one for him too. He didn't need to have a matchmaker either. J.C. is a good judge of people. The marriage will be sometime next year."

I bring Rita the local newspaper so she can read news about the people she has known all her life. Some of them she has taught in the log school near her home just out of town on Elk Creek. The road has a "Y" near the old log school. To the left is the stage route to Craig and to the right is the way I take with Tommy and Gyp on a fast trot to get home, and the horses know it well.

CHAPTER 39

THE STORY OF GRANDPA CHARLES KENCK

Now is story time. Little Oscar still has an early bedtime, but Dick is waiting impatiently for the promised story, so we settle by the warm fire.

"Dad, you promised a story all about my grandpa that I never saw."

"Yes, Charles was his name and we gave it to you for a middle name, so you have that especially from him. I'm not sure where to start, but since you are curious about the Indians and him, I'll start there. Other parts can come later.

"He and Leah Kenck, your other grandmother, lived in Helena. He was a businessman there like his two brothers. It was the year 1877 which was just two years after Yellowstone Park was set aside by the government in Washington, D.C., to be a national park for all people to come and see the geysers and wonderful scenery.

"Many people in Montana heard that a large area of Wyoming where it borders Montana was lately set aside for a national park. The year was 1875. A national park was a new idea. The President has the power to do it—not Congress. That area has many strange things—'wonders' some call them. They are geysers, spouts that shoot high in the air. One is called 'Old Faithful' and shoots high every hour. Also, there is a very high falls that roars down a rocky canyon, and there are pools of hot water of many colors."

"Dad, can we go there someday?"

"Of course, we will go someday, for several reasons. Now back to the Grandpa Charles' story. Ten young men in Helena got camping gear together, like tents, pack and riding horses, and grub packs, but they were very sure to put in fishing gear because they planned to feed themselves on fish that they would catch in several streams, like the rivers that join at the Three Forks: the Madison, the Jefferson, and the Galliton.

"It took several days to make the trip, and they finally got to Mammoth Hot Springs. From there, they go to the Yellowstone Falls, which are so very high. Near the falls a campsite by a creek appeals to them. If they set up camp some place, some of them can stay by the stuff while others can go out on horseback to see the sights.

"One man, a black fellow, was along to cook. The next morning after they set up camp, all but three men went out to do just that. The cook, Grandpa Charles Kenck and his friend, a violin teacher, stayed at camp. While they were cooking breakfast, gun shots began to fly near them. The three men ran towards the creek. Two of them made it, but Grandpa Charles was hit in the head by a bullet and died right there.

"The music teacher and the black man stayed hidden in the creek underwater, except for their noses, till the Indians finished stealing their food and their horses. There were only a few of the Indian warriors, but they took guns, ammunition, and the big ham."

Dick continued to ask questions, but I told him I'd resume the story the next night. So, he scrambles up the ladder to his bunk, and I carry Oscar. He's already in his sleeper.

The next night I resume the story.

"At this same time, an Indian tribe called the Nez Percé were made to leave their homeland in eastern Oregon, an area called the Wallowa Hills. General Howard told Chief Joseph he had to get all his people across the big Snake River in one month or his soldiers would come and drive them to the Lapwai Reservation forcibly.

"Joseph asked General Howard, 'What's the big hurry? Why can't we make this move in the moon of falling leaves when rivers are low?' General Howard said, 'No, you and your people must go right now.'"

"Dad, why was General Howard so mean to Chief Joseph and his people?"

"That is a puzzle. In earlier times, Howard had been more kind towards them, but my suspicion is that the General was reprimanded by the Department of War for being too lenient toward them and he was told if he didn't get tough then he'd get an early retirement from the Army."

"But Dad, why did they have to move anyway?"

"That's a big question. Some white people wanted that pretty valley because they thought there might be gold there. Gold was being discovered in many places in the West then. Also, Wallowa was a good place to raise cattle and horses. It has meadows of lush grass and good water."

"That wasn't fair, was it?"

"No, son. Fairness doesn't always happen. The thing that happened that started the big trouble after Chief Joseph started to obey the order to get all his people across the river in rafts was that some white men who were anxious for them to leave stole some of the Indians' horses."

"That was a dirty trick."

"Yes, it was. They had special horses called Appaloosas. Each horse born from their mares had a different design on its hide that looked like a blanket or a special patch. Kind of like that pinto pony the Beans have, only not so bright."

"So, what happened when those bad men stole the horses?"

"That's the thing. The young Indian men were really angry. Chief Joseph heard them say what they wanted to do. It was to get even, but he told them, 'No killing. It will only mean war. Our Nez Percé people have never killed a white man.'"

"Is that true, Dad? They never killed any white men?"

"Yes. When the first white men they ever saw came to Nez Percé country, they helped them with horses and boats to float down the Columbia River to the Pacific Ocean."

"Dad, who was the first man to come to their country?"

"The first white men that we know came to see them traveled through in 1805. Lewis and Clark were their names, and they had a crew of men with them. They were on their way to the Pacific Ocean. It was called an exploration trip. President Jefferson had persuaded Congress to buy a huge piece of land from France, which was called the Louisiana Purchase. He asked Captain Lewis to get a crew ready and take a trip through the area. Putting it all together took a while, but finally they headed out. It took two years to get from St. Louis to the Pacific and not quite two years to return. The Nez Percé Indians helped them both coming and going, but this story about them starts about 1870. Oh, 1877 was the exact year.

"Now, about the young Nez Percé warriors. They are very angry. I mean mad. They decided to revenge the horse stealing. After dark they slipped away to the settlement of white people nearest their camp and, of course, they have guns they had traded for from the whites for years.

"When they got to the white settlement, they kept real quiet until they saw a man walking by a cabin. An Indian took careful aim and killed him. The second warrior did the same when he saw another white man moving, and he shot too. Then they rode fast and hard back to their camp. The friends of those killed knew sure enough why they'd been shot.

"The report went fast to General Howard's camp a few miles away, and the next morning Howard sent troops to catch the Indians and find who killed the white men. The war was on. The Nez Percé warriors saw Howard's troops coming. When they got close, they started shooting at the Indians, and this act marks the beginning of the famous Nez Percé War.

"The Indians were clever. They let the troops chase them into a canyon, and then the warriors climbed quickly up the sides. It was then that the General's men realized it was a box canyon with no other way out except the way they came in. The warriors had congregated above the entrance and shot any soldiers they could see, resulting in many casualties for the troops.

"When night fell, the gunfire ceased and the troops waited, trying to figure out how to get the rest of the survivors out of the trap. By morning, however, no

Indians could be seen, and in fact, the soldiers determined they were long gone. Chief Joseph, with his band, stopped for a short while at the reservation of the Cayuse but soon went on up the Lo Lo Trail and over the Divide.

"When they got to the other side, Captain Reines, who had heard by telegraph that the Nez Percé were on the run, had orders to stop them. He tried but they outfoxed him too and soon were on their way down the Bitterroot Valley.

"Son, next story time you'll hear what happened next." Dick is not happy to have to wait yet another day to get this story, but he acquiesces.

The next night we resume our story.

"The Nez Percé in the Bitterroot Valley stop at the town of Sevensville. The store there sells them supplies and ammunition because they have money to buy what they want. Then the tribe quickly makes its way southeast in the valley until they come up and over the hills at the southern end. There they drop down into what is called The Big Hole.

"It was here they rested. Their old people and little ones need a break from the hard travel. That evening they put up their teepees and cooked a good meal. Chief Joseph is trying to decide where to take his people. General Howard is always slow to move his Army so they do not fear him. After much discussion, Joseph and the elders decide to go east and talk with the Crow Indian people, and if they will not help or let them stay nearby, the Nez Percé will go on to Canada.

"All seemed like this would work out. The Indian people of the West did not realize, as they later learned, the U.S. Army of the West had 'talking wire' [telegraph]. At that time, 1877, they had some telegraph lines for the Army communications in Montana, through General Miles, near Miles City, and General Gibbon at Fort Shaw. General Howard is able to get the message to one of the telegraph offices and tells these generals to catch the Nez Percé wherever they are."

"Did he really do that?"

"Yes. Not every western Army fort had telegraph,

but the messages were carried very fast on horseback to all the camps.

"The next story time will be about what your Grandpa Charles, whose picture you've seen, is doing during the time the Nez Percé are trying to get away. Will you be going to school tomorrow?"

"Yes, Dad. We have lots of Indian kids at school. Do they know about Chief Joseph?"

"Maybe some of their parents know some of the story, but not very many children know. Most of our Indian neighbors came from Canada and were not around when Chief Joseph was here. Just wait until you hear the whole story before you tell your Indian friends, okay?"

"Okay, Dad, I'll wait. Good night now."

Rita and I talk a while before we turn in. Baby Oscar has been sleeping soundly for several hours. "Rita, who is the teacher at the school now?"

"Richard tells me she is mean, but I believe she is only strict. Richard gives me the students' point of view. Ha! I know kids, especially boys. Miss Bady is her name. He says, 'Miss Bady has eyes in the back of her head, and besides, she's seven feet tall.'"

"Yeah, Rita, we know kids have strange notions about adults, especially teachers."

"Richard also tells me there are lots of kids who come to school only a few days. He can reel off some of the names: Garvais, Swan, Pocha, and one family named Chicken."

"Do the Garvais boys go regularly?"

"Yes, unless there's important work for their father, like ice cutting for the ranchers. Dick and Ole have ice-houses, and they get a crew in cold weather to saw and haul ice. The kids have to shovel sawdust from the mill to pack it. Anyway, Miss Bady tries to see they learn to read and write and do simple arithmetic."

"How about Dick? Is he learning?"

"Richard knows how to read. He's been through *McGuffey Readers* up to level three. Actually, he's been teaching Oscar his letters and numbers when he isn't teasing him."

"Rita, my good lady, I sure miss being here lots of

days and evenings when I should stay. You are a brave and competent wife."

"Have you had many emergency calls lately?"

"If at all possible, I just patch them up and send them as fast as they can go to Choteau to see Bateman. When he moved there he made his house into a hospital for those cases. Last week an old fellow in the foothills tried to fix a bullet that didn't fit into his rifle and it exploded. He was a mess. Jackie Shadler knows him. Says he's as crazy as a loon. His friend called me over to his cabin on the creek, and one eye was hanging down on his cheek. Part of his face is gone. I washed the wounds and put iodine and glycerin on and then bandaged his whole face, leaving a breathing hole for his nose. The blood kept bubbling at every breath he took. I said to his friend, Old Pete, 'Get some fast horses from Nett's stable and a buggy he can lie down in. Take him to Dr. Bateman's in Choteau as fast as you can.' He did that, but I saw Bateman a couple days later and was told it was too late. He had died on the way to the Choteau hospital."

"How terrible. I remember that old miner who lived in the cabin near the creek. He of all people should have known you can't hammer on a bullet."

"Joe Bush helped me. We both knew the case was pretty much hopeless because of so much blood loss. Rita, honey, let's go to bed. This weekend has been a real catch-up one. You catch me up on all that's going on here, and I've tried to catch you up on everything that's happening in town. Sometimes I forget the important stuff."

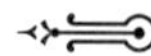

In the morning, Dick jumps out of bed.

"Dad, I gotta look at my traps. I got two traps. Garvais says I can catch mink by the river. He says he will show me how to skin them and get their fur on a stretcher frame."

"You are a trapper already, Dick. When you get some furs, you can sell them, yes?"

"You bet, Dad. I'm gonna be a trapper man. Garvais and Pocha said so too."

"Dick, one thing I want you to know. At school you must not cut up and tease the teacher. Miss Bady has enough with all those children to teach to read and write and do arithmetic without getting tricks played on her by the boys in the school."

"Tell ya what, Dad, I'll try real hard to stay out of trouble but I can't help but grin when I see the big kids do tricks on her. Then she thinks I am in on it and I ain't. Honest I ain't!"

"Okay, Dick, just make sure you aren't."

With that he's off to check his two traps.

CHAPTER 40

1912: RICHARD & HELEN AUCHARD MOVE TO HELENA

We of Augusta are all consumed with the fact that our banker whom we thought would help prosper the town has taken the bank to the new town of Gilman a mile away and at the terminus of the Great Northern Railroad. Other doings have gone pretty much unnoticed.

Will Auchard comes up to my office (it's unusual).

"Howdy, Will. What's going on with you these days? What's on your mind today? How are Papa and Mama?"

"That's why I stopped. Papa asked me to tell you he wants to see you."

"Something wrong?"

"I could say, but you best come out and talk with him."

"Is it urgent? Are they sick?"

"Not bad sick. But you better let him talk. Gotta get the mail."

"I'll come out this afternoon. I'll close a little early."

"I'll tell him you are coming."

Will's a man of few words, so this is probably more urgent than he says. I close up and get myself out to see what Richard Auchard needs or wants.

As I walk this way, I begin to think of the earliest times I have come along here. The mountain guardian of all this prairie and Elk Creek's tree line winds its way to join Sun River. I think of the times I walked expectantly to the Auchard pole gate. In my total thoughts those times, I didn't realize I was being drawn to bind myself to certain people and land and a mountain. Soon I'm over the bridge and then I'm at the gate. My thoughts leap back to when the precious little lady would just happen to be sitting in the swinging chair her father had made. I suddenly realized it was all meant to be—no mere happenstance. "What will be, will be"—*Que será, será*. I swing it open just enough to pass through. Soon at the door, Mama Helen greets me cheerfully. That eases my fears.

"Dr. Oscar," like she always says, "come in. I have a bit of tea and ginger cookies for you."

"Thank you, Mama Helen. You know exactly what kind of cookies I like."

Richard appears in the doorway of the kitchen. "Good afternoon, Oscar. I've been wanting to talk with you."

"Good afternoon to you. Will tells me you want to see me."

"Yes, I been thinking for some time now that I should turn the whole ranch over to Will. He's doing all the work anyway, and he's good at it. I'm thinking Mama and I should find a place to live in Helena and leave Will to run this like he's been doing for quite a while now."

"Mr. Auchard, I think you certainly well deserve to move to Helena if that's your wish. You have many friends there, especially in the lodge."

"The only thing is, I would appreciate a bit of help in finding the right house."

"Mr. Auchard, I will be glad to go to Helena for you. I've been thinking to go soon for several reasons. I'm sure Mike Reinig will be of great help. He delivers groceries from his store to almost every house in town. So he will know of houses for sale or rent."

Mama Helen is standing by to hear my answer. She smiles and says, "Oscar, you are staying for supper." It wasn't an order, but who can turn down a meal prepared by her? We talk further about living in Helena, over the supper of cold roast slices and fresh baked bread followed by rice pudding with thick cream.

"Richard," I explain, "I'll be going out to the ranch shortly after noon tomorrow. I will explain to Rita what you want to do. Rita will feel bad at first, but I'll explain and tell her we will go to Helena more often when you move."

I am right. Rita starts to cry when I tell her. "My dear lady, we will just go to Helena more often when the folks are there."

"But Oscar, I can't bear to see the home place without them," and she sobs.

"Yes, yes. I know a bit how you feel. I always think of the days I used to walk out there and see a pretty girl."

She manages to smile at that. "Rita, my brave lady, I'm with you and will try to help you through this."

"Yes, I guess Papa knows what he wants to do, and Mama always goes along with what he decides. I don't know what she thought when he decided to leave New York when I was just a little one. One thing, she was terribly afraid of Indians."

"Your Papa was always careful to please her and take care of her. He has probably prepared her about moving to Helena. Rita, let's look at it on the best side. Life in Helena will be pleasant for them. The lodge fold will take them right into their circle of friends."

"Yes, Dr. Husband, but I shall miss them. Going to town was mostly going to see them."

"Let's take time helping them find a place. Let's go next week—I'll have to take care of a few patients next week, like Monday and Tuesday, and then I'll let Wednesday and Thursday patients know I'll be gone the rest of the week. "I'll come home on Tuesday, and we can take the buggy down to Craig and catch the train."

"I think I'd like to go talk with Papa and Mama about what kind of a house to look for."

"Of course. Why didn't I think of you wanting to talk with them. Let's tell Dick and Oscar that we are going to talk with Grandpa and Grandma about them moving to Helena."

In the morning when we have breakfast, the boys are full of questions, mostly about why they want to leave the cows and horses. "How could anyone want to do that?"

"Well, Dick, when you talk to Grandpa, you can ask him the question." That seems to satisfy him for the time being. Oscar is too young to comprehend what it means to have them move into Helena.

Pretty much as we planned, we talk to Richard and Mama Auchard. They seem to be in agreement. Mama says, "I'm getting a bit weary of taking care of milk pans and churning butter. Yes, Rita dear, I'll miss the ranch, but I'm not as spry as I once was. What kind of house shall we look for? I know you won't remember our house in New York, but I want one nice like that. I hope you can find one. Although too many stairs will be hard for Papa, maybe me, too, to think of it. We have several preferences, if possible: two bedrooms, a dining room, a parlor, and a big kitchen."

"Mama, we will certainly look for such a house, and we also think you don't need lots of stairs to climb."

"Oh, Rita and Oscar, I needn't start telling you what I need or want—you two are wise about my needs. Always have been."

After talking with the folks, we tell our boys we are going to Helena to find a place for Grandpa and Grandma. Dick says right away, "Dad, can I stay home? I can take care of our animals and feed the fish."

"Dick, you are some kind of a boy—wanting to stay home and work. You are six, but I think you should not stay alone yet."

"Aw, Dad, I can do everything Mom showed me, how to cook mush even. And, 'course I can take care of all the animals. I can even milk the cow a part of a bucket. Please let me stay home!"

"Maybe you can if we can get one of Garvais' older kids to stay with you."

"You find out and I'll talk to him."

Come Wednesday, all things are arranged and I tell Dick and Clarence Garvais what I expect, and I say, "No experiments all the time we are gone. Do you understand?"

"Yes, Dad. We will not do anything that you will call an experiment."

Clarence says, "Mr. Doctor, we will not do anything—only chores."

"All right. You be real careful with the animals. Be real careful with the fire when you cook breakfast. We have some food cooked in the spring house and some bread."

"Yeah, I know, Dad. Mom has taught me how to fry taters and eggs."

"Rita, you have been really teaching him how to do this?"

"Yes, he wants to learn how to go camping, so I thought I'd teach him simple camp cooking."

So it is that we leave Dick at home while we go in the buggy with our fast team. We start off to catch the stage at Wolf Creek. First we stop at Ole Bean's place by the lake and tell them we left Dick and Clarence Garvais at the ranch, and to kinda check on them.

Ole says, "Vee sure vill sorta check up on them maybe vonce a day. Ina not feel too good. Maybe next week vee go to doctor in Falls."

"We will be back in three or four days. Let us keep Wallace at our house."

"Vee do dat. Wallace like Dick."

Off we go across the hills and then across the fields to the Half Way House and by the Barretts and Carmachael Ranch lands. At last we arrive at the Half Way House. We stop and water the horses and give them some oats and hay. We bring our lunch into the kitchen long table. Within an hour we are on the way again, aiming to catch the late afternoon train to Helena.

We made that train just in time. Oscar's eyes really got big when he saw the big black engine come rumbling to a stop. He wasn't sure he wanted to get near. After I got our bags onto the baggage cart, I gathered him up. In we stepped, up the foot stool and into the passenger car. Only after we sat down did he relax his grip on my shoulder.

In Helena, first the hotel and then we walked the few blocks to sister Mina and Carl Vandenburg's house.

"Surprise! We came to Helena on a special errand."

"What in the world is that?" Mina asked.

"Mama and Papa want to come to Helena and live. Dr. Husband and I are on an errand to find a place for them. Papa has made up his mind to turn the place over to Will. Papa is failing. I can tell. He just sits and dozes in his chair a lot."

"Well, that's too bad. How old is he anyway?"

"Well, he is getting up there—born in 1828."

"Oh my! That makes him 84 this year. How time does fly. It seems just a short time ago, Rita, that you were born. How we did rejoice for you—a baby sister!"

"Mina, how nice for you to say you were glad."

"Addy and I took turns holding you."

"Carl, do you know of any house for sale or rent fairly close to you folks?" I ask.

"We will just look around and see. I realize they need to be near us so we can help them anytime."

"Exactly our thinking on the matter also."

"Let's take a stroll around this neighborhood and see if there are any houses for rent. Mina would like it if her mother is close," says Carl.

As we walk around, I tell Carl about the days I lived in Helena.

"I'm surprised you lived here and went to school here too."

"Yep, I was one of those crazy Kenck kids. We were two of Charles Kenck's family, and we had cousins—other Kencks. My mother—we are going to visit her on Jackson St. We have never brought little Oscar to see her, or should I say for her to see him. She is still very German. Doesn't speak much English. Mr. Reinig who runs the main grocery store speaks German and interprets all the town news and events for her."

"I sure didn't know all that. Your brother, does he live here?"

"Yes, he does. Works for the government here and other agencies that want special printing, like certificates and diplomas. Also, he plays violin for many occasions."

"Look. Here's a house for rent. Looks somewhat livable. Let's knock and see if someone is available to tell us about the rent or sale of it."

"Okay, let's do that."

"We see your For Rent sign, Ma'am. Can you please tell us about that?" I ask.

"Yes, gentlemen. I'm renting, or should I say trying to rent it for my brother. You can examine the house and I'm here to answer questions."

"We want a house for my father-in-law and his wife. Not too big or too small. I'll bring my wife to look. It is her mother and father who want to live in Helena and not ranch anymore. Is the owner interested in selling the place? Or renting?"

"Sir, I don't know. That may be, so I can't say. He can be here to see your people tomorrow—he will be back on the early train."

Rita approves this house. "It's nice inside and close to Mina and Carl's place. Mina can check on Mother every day."

Where did summer 1912 go? When I ask, I'm amazed at what has been done with it. Moving the folks, especially Mama Auchard's lifetime collection of linens, dishes, and kitchen equipment. She has enough to leave some for Will and bedding too. The special dishes she and Rita pack with linens between the valuable dishes. Pans and kettles are packed with newspapers. Of course, milk pans and the butter churn she left for Will.

Will says, "I'm not cooking much. I'll be hiring a cook." Then with his deep chuckle, he laughs a rare time.

CHAPTER 41

THE HARRISON BASIN

Busy 1912 has rolled on. "The hurrier I go, the behinder I get."

As I'm driving Tommy and Gyp home towards my mountains, I begin to think about our plans to get more land. We do need it if we keep on with cattle.

There is another type of claim I can file: a desert claim non-irrigated. A 40-acre strip alongside our home place would just fit in.

At home I tell Rita, "We've been so busy we haven't had time to seriously consider that we need more pasture if we stay with cattle. Now that the folks are somewhat settled, on our next Helena trip I'd like to file on the 40 acres we've been wanting."

"Yes, we do need more land. The Harrison Basin you've talked about, let's find out who owns it and see if it can be bought. Ole Bean thinks so."

Oscar comes running in. "Dad, come to the barn! Come see!"

"What for?"

"Come see! Come see!" He tugs at my jacket.

He excitedly pulls me down the path to the barn. I hear what it is: lambs bleating.

"Three of them," Oscar starts saying. "Mine, mine. One, two, three. Mine, Dad."

"How are you going to feed them? They're just babies."

"Mama says 'milk'".

"Do they drink from a cup?" I ask.

"No, no, Dad. A bucket. Mr. Reeder says to put my hand in the bucket of milk and they will suck my fingers and milk too." He holds his fingers curled and demonstrates.

"Oscar, you got your work cut out for you. The lambs get very hungry before they learn how to suck up the milk.

Back to our getting land talk.

Rita asks, "If we can buy the Harrison Basin, how much land will we have?"

"Actually over 2000 acres."

Two weeks later, in Helena, I go to the land office in the courthouse. The owner is listed: son of the Harrisons who first filed and proved up on it—a desert claim. He is anxious to sell, so no problem.

On our way home I say, "Rita, we will take a pack trip this summer and see that basin and go on back to Donahur where the Bean family likes to go."

Back from Helena, I tell Dick, "The Basin is going to be ours." His eyes sparkle. "Can I go camping there all summer?"

"Sure, and you will have to take salt to the cattle and keep count of them."

Dick says, "I can't wait. Can I get kids to go with me?"

"Yes, if you will be responsible and do your job right."

Before long, the deal went through. Dick decided to get Jack Eberle. Jack had stayed with us from time to time.

"Dick and Jack get their outfit together to go up to the Basin to take salt to the cattle we had put up there. They wanted to stay several days—count the cattle and explore," I tell Rita.

She worries about them some. There isn't much they can get into because Dick says, "Dad, I'll behave 'cause I don't want to get into trouble."

The story about this expedition comes later. Dick had to tell. It is too serious to keep secret.

"When we got to the old bachelors' potato cellar, we decided to explore. We found dynamite caps in one of the potato cellars the old bachelors had made. We found the caps and dynamite and some old newspapers, so we made a long fuse out of the newspapers. Oh yes, we put a little kerosene on the string of papers and then we got everything ready. We knew the caps would blow up. We lit it way out at the end of the newspapers and then made our horses run as fast as they could. We were up the Canyon quite a ways and we heard an awful bang. We knew we better not come home for several days."

"Dick, you really pulled a most dangerous stunt. That blast broke windows as far as the Beans by the lake. Don't ever, ever mess with dynamite again. It's dangerous. What kind of punishment should I hand out to you two guys?"

"Dad, we didn't plan to do damage. We knew it would be a bang, but not like you say it was."

"Dick and Jack, I want you to promise me you will never mess with dynamite again."

"Okay, Dad, I promise I'll never mess with dynamite again."

"What about you, Jack?"

"Yes, Dr. Kenck. I promise I'll never mess with dynamite again, either."

"Now, I expect you fellows to keep your word. A real man keeps his word."

CHAPTER 42

THE CLEMONS SCHOOL

After the boys are in bed and asleep, I check to make sure Rita and I have a long talk. "What do you hear about Clemons School teachers, Rita?"

"I hear a lot from the parents and our kids about Miss Bady's practices."

"Is she strict? Does she give the kids a whipping?"

"Not exactly. She uses a stick flat like a ruler and raps them good and hard on the knuckles."

"If the kids misbehave, they deserve it."

"Yes, I agree, but there's other things. She makes them leave their lunches on the porch, and they freeze by noon. Also the dogs, Ole's and others, come and steal the lunches and then some kids don't have a lunch.

"That's not so good. Kids get so hungry, and if they have to go without lunch, they naturally think up things to get even."

"Yes, I've heard of some of the tricks they pull to get even."

"Like what?"

"Dick says some kid put a rubber comb on the stove and it stunk so bad she had to open the door. Finally, Miss Bady began to cough and choke on it and she told them to go home. But they do worse. They put gun shells in the stove. That's pretty scary, and the Mosher kids put a mouse in her desk one morning."

"Do you hear of the Indian kids doing stuff like that?"

"No, they must be afraid to try it. Besides, they are absent so much."

"How many kids are enrolled there?

"I don't really know. But, last week someone brought carbide to school and put it in an ink well. Then when Miss Bady wasn't looking, he spit in it. 'The rotten egg fumes were awful,' Dick says."

"It seems to me Miss Bady has the wrong approach if she does unfair things. Maybe she will quit in frustration.

"When I talk with the ranchers around, they are beginning to hope that will be the solution."

I decide to make it my business to find out what is really going on with this Miss Bady woman.

Not long after our talk, Dick and Carrie Bean are in my office.

"Mr. Bean, what is going on at the Clemons School?"

"Dr. Kenck, it's not good. Whether the teacher is good or not, I really don't know. We aren't going to send ours there when they get the right age. We will teach by the new correspondence method. The older boys are so rambunctious and so busy causing trouble that I don't want my kids going there. Besides, I need them to work. Leta is getting better and better with the cattle and with our farm machinery."

Along towards spring, Rita tells me Miss Bady left. She just got tired of the tricks the boys pulled on her.

There is a new teacher: Miss Myrtle Sorshalal.

"How's the new teacher doing? Do you hear?"

"Oh, yes, I hear Dick says the kids all like her. She plays ball with them at recess, and when it's cold has them come in and sit on a blanket by the stove to eat. She has made cocoa for them. When it gets really cold, she tells them that they can skate at recess. She'll show them how to play skinny. Dick is happy to go to school and is learning more and faster."

"At last a teacher who knows how to teach kids."

Dick and neighbor kids riding to Clemons School

CHAPTER 43

SECRET PLANS BEGUN FOR RITA'S CHRISTMAS SURPRISE

"Rita, I've got a good idea. Soon it will be Thanksgiving. Let's all go to your folks' new home in Helena for that whole week. I'm sure they'd be delighted, and we need to do this while Dick and Oscar are little so they can get to know their grandparents better."

"Oscar, you are full of good ideas. I'll have everything ready and also I'll see that Dick gets used to the idea. Already I can see he'll always be tied to his own world of trapping and outdoor chores around here and we'll have a hard time pulling him away."

"Right you are, wise woman."

Monday always starts with a bang or a thud or even a gunshot wound like last week on the way to town. I met Mrs. McGraw driving home and we stop. "Mrs. McGraw, pray tell why are you out so early?"

"Doctor, I just delivered a baby boy to Mrs. Chisholm. A good-sized one too. *Fred*, he's named."

"Did it go all right?"

"An easy birth compared to some. It is her second boy. She'll be fine. Now I can go home and get breakfast for James. Then maybe take an easy day. I'll not wash today!"

"You better not. Just get a few hours of rest, 'Doctor Lady.'"

"How are you, Doctor?"

"The truth is, Mrs. McGraw, I'm feeling terrific, but

the weekend here in the mountains at home with my family makes me even stronger for going back to work."

"Good day, Doctor."

"Same to you, Midwife Lady."

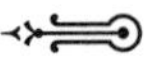

I open my office and then go to Barnard's. J.C. Manix steps out of Mrs. McKendrick's store. "Howdy, Doctor. I've got to tell you the news. Mrs. McKendrick is finally selling me the store."

"That's splendid," I say. "You will really make good in that store. We need a good mercantile here so far from a big city. When do you take over?"

"We'll sign a contract next Monday. Oh yes, and by the way, Helen Nilan and I are getting married.'

"Whoeee, all this excitement at once. Be careful, J.C." I say to tease him. "Congratulations anyway. You're on your way to the good life." On that note we shake hands.

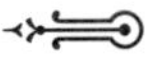

Today I have an idea about what to do for Rita for our Christmas this year. Between patients I'm turning it over in my mind. My main thought is I've got to get plans for a real house on the Dearborn. Later, Tony Pings comes to my office to get started on a couple of fillings he says are aching.

"Kenck, I'm sure glad to see you back in your office. Both Mabel and I need you."

"Let's look and see what needs to be done here."

"Okay, I'll take time if you've got it," he says.

I take a look inside Tony's mouth after he gets settled in my chair.

"You are right. I'm finding several cavities and even on these front incisors I'd like to put gold inlays. They will last longer than porcelain and are okay if you don't mind a little gold showing."

"Heck, Doc. I don't mind gold showing. It's better than toothaches!"

"What's going on with you these days, Tony? Are you right in the middle of someone's house?"

"I'm always in the middle of someone's house! Also, I'm getting plans ready for a decent, two-story, stone school for this town."

"Right you are on that one. I see the schoolhouse and can't imagine being the teachers of so many kids in just two rooms. I hear also that one class is held in the coat closet."

"Yes, true. But the problem is money. It's taxes that pay for schools, and we at this end of the county are not so many, nor is our property as valuable as around our county seat in Helena."

"That is a problem, Tony. So many, like our Indian neighbors, don't own property at all, and yet they have children and they want them to learn to read and write. There are sixty children in the Dearborn country that would like to go to the one-room school there by Bean Lake. The Indian children sort of take turns going. I think they have just a few pairs of shoes and have to take their turn at wearing them to school."

"The Indian children can go to the Mission school, well a few can, and they can go to Fort Shaw's government Indian school, but no way do they want to leave home. If I can get a bigger school built, that will help."

"Tony, I've a special request. Have you a few minutes to hear it?"

"Sure, Doc, I'll take time. I'm mighty glad you are back and working again. I can show you a bit of appreciation. You've done a lot for me even though you teased me a bit at my wedding."

"Tony, some of that was purely unintentional. But you notice Rita and I got married far away in Butte? We didn't want any tricks played on us here nor in Helena."

"Yeah, okay, spit it out. What's on your mind?"

"I want some help making house plans and I'd like to reveal them to Rita at Christmas."

"You come over tonight and I'll show you the plan I used for Bud's home or we'll draw one up for any way you want. I got a pretty good work light. Say about seven?"

"I'll be there, Tony, unless some lady decides to have a baby. I still sub for Bateman sometimes."

"Doc, put me down for some time next week, like Wednesday, and I'll shift work around and get here."

"How about nine a.m.?"

"Okay, see you tonight."

Next at my door is Mrs. Wellman. "Doctor Kenck, I'm so very glad you are better. This town needs you badly. How is Rita? I do miss her around town. She is such a lively, friendly person. Your children, how are they?"

"Mrs. Wellman, I'll answer your first question. Rita is doing very well. She is living in our two-room cabin, but I hope to get a decent house built next year. I plan to surprise her with the plans this Christmas. Tony and I are going to work on them right away. Maybe he'll show me the plans for your place and the Beachs' house. Oh yes, my boys are growing into fine youngsters. My first, Dick, is already going to Bean Lake School. He's learning how to trap. Our second son, Oscar, is anxious to go to school, but Rita spends lots of time teaching at home. He's really too young."

"Mr. Pings does a nice job on homes. You'll like the plan he does for you. I like the job he did on Bud Tomlinson's house."

"Let's see what we need to do for your teeth today."

After I finish with Etta's fillings and plan what else she needs, I ask about her son. Etta, what is Bing up to?"

"He's working steady. He's helping wire the country for telephones. Sometimes they even use barbed wire fences, but he's going to high school. A bit late, but he wants to do it."

"Tell him I remember about his milking so many cows when he was just nine years old."

CHAPTER 44

MONTANA SNOWSTORMS

When Mrs. Wellman leaves, I go right off to the post office. By this time the mail has been sorted. Mr. Barnard has been the postmaster way back almost to the first of the century. He's getting a little tired, as well as the mail is getting a little heavy.

"Kenck," he says, "I'm getting old enough to quit this job one of these years. I think I'll take to my chair and sit out the rest of life."

"Mr. Barnard, maybe it's time. You've been working steady ever since I've been around this country. I remember our very first conversation, up at the hotel. You've put in a lot of horse and wagon miles since then."

"Right, Kenck. Glad to see you are recovered from that bad spell. How's Rita? We miss her daily visit here. She and Lottie always had some funny-bone things to talk and laugh about. Here's your mail. It piles up sometimes. Packages too."

"Thanks, Barnard. I know my mail is taken good care of. Once when I went to Ovanda to get fish eggs, I wrote to Rita at the Clemons Post Office. She didn't get that letter for six months. It went to California before it finally arrived back home."

"Yeah, I know of some strange journeys the mail has taken. I've been at this post office since 1903 and some letters have traveled a heck of a ways."

"You just got so you are mighty good at shuffling the mail. But when the train does come into this area, there will be mail from two directions."

"Kenck, that's the trouble. Mail is enough as it is. I'd probably have to work all night when that happens. I'm getting too old for that."

"What about Floyd? He could do that for you."

"Oh no, Kenck. He didn't like school so he needs more book learning to do that. Besides, he won't do anything unless it's on a horse and is outdoors."

"To each his own, I guess."

"You bet, Doctor. An only son and an only child at that."

"Do you think this snow that's coming down will be the big one?"

"Could be. These early winter storms that start easy sometimes give us the deepest snow."

Very early the next morning I put on my snowboots to make my way to Barnard's phone. Sure enough, it's piling up steadily. I didn't want too many connections. Lottie's strong arm cranks the telephone transmitter. Before long she gets Rita, who tells me the snow has fallen all night and now it's at least three feet deep.

Little Dick will not be going to school today.

"The Beans are back in the mountains hunting and Ole is getting Brother Phil to start up the trail of the Dearborn Canyon to go after them and help get them home. I'm okay. Got the fire going and I'm baking bread. Richard is playing with Oscar to keep him happy, and he is happy because his big brother is actually playing with him."

"Stay in the house, honey, and don't try to go anywhere. Dan Garvais will come to take care of the cow. Bye now. I'll call again tomorrow."

The snow is so deep and not much goes on except the stage with their four-horse team and sleigh runners. The tinkling of the sleigh bells sounds loud, even in the fresh snow. Rita's mother used to get very worried about the stage in snowy times like this. She put a lamp near the windows so the driver could see that light as he came through in the evenings. Even when the snow covers the road, the horses most always know the way home. Early each fall Adams has someone put down tall stakes to show the road edges. Easy enough to see in daylight, but difficult at night. I keep thinking of the times I've been in the mountains in deep snow. Also, I hear Mosher's band of 2,000 sheep are back of Dearborn country and supposed to be on the way out.

This slowdown of activity brought on by the heavy snow gives Tony extra time too. He stomps into the hotel and up to my office. "Since everything is at a standstill, I thought I'd bring several plans to show you."

"Great! Neither one of us can do our regular jobs, so house plans it is. Tony, have you kept track of how many houses you've built?"

"Nope, can't waste time on that. Mabel might be able to though. I don't ask her about that."

We have a profitable session. I tell Tony I want a dental office room in that house. For now, I've hauled my old wagon office up to the ranch and people are still coming and camping close by for dental work. Also, we talk about how the kitchen needs to also be the dining room, so it must be large. We often have people, friends, or patients. Rita is a wonder to manage meals for lots of people. We get one of the Pocha girls to help with the little ones and the housework. I hope this snow will thaw by Thanksgiving week. The folks will be disappointed if we can't make it to Helena.

Several days pass. I call Rita every day. She brings me up to date on all the events out there. The Bean families did make it out. They had to follow the Dearborn River after they reached it because the snow was still three to four feet deep and drifted. Mrs. Mosher's sheep herder was going to quit and walk out without the sheep, but the sheep camp tender got out his rifle and said, "If you start down that trail without the sheep you ain't goin' far," so he changed his mind. They lost some, about two hundred.

The snow finally melts down into a wet mess before the Thanksgiving holiday. Dick Bean had to come to town. He comes into my office with an achy tooth.

"Dick, Rita tells me you had a bad time getting home from your hunting trip to Donahur country."

"Yeah, vee vas lucky. Vee got elk und vee had trouble

getting home. Carrie's little horse, Blackie, led us down the steep trail, even though covered mit snow. He vasn't the lead horse but pushed right up and took lead ven vee vas just tinking about what to do. Good, good horse."

"Well, it's good to see you and hear you got out all right. Now, let's see that tooth." I take a look after he's settled in the chair. It's obvious which tooth is angry with red gums around it.

"That tooth is about to abscess, and it's got to come out, Dick."

"Okay, go ahead, Doc. I don't need it if it's going to be more troubles."

I deaden the area. While we wait for that to take effect, we keep talking. "Your wife is a Barrett, isn't she?"

"Yeah, a Barrett. Very good vife too. I make sure I treat her right. Good vife very valuable. When I go to Falls, I always bring her stuff she ask for. Von time she say, 'Dick, sometime I need hat, this one too old and vorn out.' I go to Falls vif load of oats. Ven I come home and get to Adams' big barn, oh, oh! I tink, 'No hat!' so I turn 'round, leave wagon, ride back to Falls on Blackie und get hat. Takes extra day, but much happy vife!

"Also, I learn something dis year. Vee is so lucky to have a goot vife. I must show her I luf her. I tink of Ole how he lose Ina ven she die at Rochester ven Armond just a baby. Now Ole have two little ones. I be so sad for him. I vill try to make my voman happy every day."

"Dick, you are a wise man." We have a good laugh about the hat.

"I'm getting house plans from Tony Pings since he's built so many here. I figured he'd have several good plans, like Tomlinson's house up the street."

"Ya, dat look like a goot house. You put house on the Dearborn?"

"Yes, on the Dearborn. A cabin is too small for raising a family."

"You right. Vee had cabin. Then vee build on and on, just the vay Carrie vants it."

"I'm going to show Rita a few plans to see what she likes."

"Dat goot idea. Please da voman most important like you say. Vell, I be going home now. Vill see you sometime, Doctor. How much I pay?"

"Two dollars. Thanks." And he is gone.

CHAPTER 45

MORE ABOUT GRANDPA KENCK

The weather clears. The wind blows several days—a Chinook. The ground begins to show in spots, so we are able after all to go to Helena for Thanksgiving week.

Dick and Oscar are really pampered at Grandpa and Grandma Auchard's. Oscar is learning their names. He tries to imitate Dick but gets a different slant sometimes.

Dick says, "Dad, I want to hear the rest of that story about the Indians and my other grandpa." He crawls up beside me in the big chair and I ask, "Where did we leave off?" He gives me a rundown on that story that surprises me.

Dick pats me on the chest and says, "So, what did General Gibbons and his colored soldiers do when they found the Indian camp?"

"They hid in the trees just uphill from them. In the morning, the Indian horse tenders came out when it was barely getting light. The soldiers opened fire on them and the killing started. Now, General Howard still hadn't caught up to the Nez Percé. The Indians quickly ran to the bushes and began firing back at Gibbons' men. Quite a few Indians were killed, even some of Joseph's own family.

"By the end of the day the Indian warriors had trapped Gibbons' forces, so when night came, the Nez Percé buried their dead and slipped away toward the east. Joseph still wanted to see the Crow Indians living east of Yellowstone Park, and the decimated band continued that direction.

"At the same time, the Helena hunting group was coming to the Park and, of course, your grandpa, Charles Kenck, was with them. These men were camped by a creek and were making breakfast when some of the young warriors scouting ahead for food and horses came upon them.

"By this time, no one would blame them because Gibbons' army had really massacred many women and children. They were fighting a real war. In a real war, people on both sides do everything to win. Charles Kenck was cooking when the Indians attacked, shooting. He ran toward the bushes by the creek, but a bullet hit him in the back of the head. His friend Dietrich escaped the first attack but was killed later near the Mammoth Hot Springs. The cook, however, lived through it."

"Dad, what about Chief Joseph and his Indians? Did they catch them and kill them all? And what happened to Grandpa Kenck's body?"

"It's a long story and happened a long time ago, Dick. I was just two years old and Albert was a tiny baby. But I do remember later my mutter talking about the casket Grandpa was buried in."

CHAPTER 46

RITA LEARNS ABOUT HOUSE PLANS

We go to a party at the Masonic Lodge. It's really an extra Thanksgiving party. After the feast we dance. Whooo, it's been a while. The music gets down to my toes.

Dick tells me about his grandpa building boats for the Erie Canal. He says, "Grandpa told me someday when I grow up to go see the Erie Canal and the thing called 'The Locks' where they raise the great big boats by filling a deep empty bowl with water and then the boats just float out to a higher land."

"Yes, Dick. Someday you can go to where he used to build boats. Big ones."

"Dad, how old do I have to be to do that?"

"I saw them when I graduated from college, Gonzaga, and went on to the dental school in Chicago."

With wide eyes Dick says, "Golly, Dad, you've been everywhere. I'm going to see them too. You bet I will!"

"Dick, someday you will come with me to my office. I will show you what it's like and what you can do to help me when you get just a bit older."

"When will that be? Dad, you know I want to be a trapper."

"Sure, you will do that, but once in a while you can help your dad."

I'm having trouble keeping quiet about the house plans. I take them out and look at them when I can.

Dr. and Mrs. Kenck dressed up to go to the Masonic Lodge (circa 1920, see page 332)

One day Rita comes in unexpectedly and actually catches me looking at the plans. Whoops!

"Oscar, what in the world is that?"

"Rita, honey, guess I'll have to tell you now."

"Tell me what? Have you started to keep secrets from me?"

"I wanted to surprise you at Christmas, but now is okay too."

"I'm listening. I thought I knew everything you were up to."

"I just got these house plans from Tony, so here they are." We spread them out on the workbench. Rita is excited. "Oscar, you couldn't keep this secret very long!"

"No, I realized that as soon as Tony gave them to me. We are supposed to make any changes we want. See, this one is just like Tomlinson's."

We hug each other, so excited and happy to think we will have a real home where we have our fishpond and mountains so close.

"Tony says after we make the changes we want, he can order the lumber."

"You know I want a big kitchen to hold a big table. We have so much company and I want everyone talking."

"Rita, I can see that you won't want to miss a thing."

Tony stops by the office to ask how Rita and I are doing on the plans. Tony says to me, "Doc, get an idea of when you want the house built, and I'll make time some way to do it."

"I'll bring our plans to you and then you'll know the amount of lumber needed. I've got a two-room cabin we live in. Can the house be added to that?"

"Sure. I don't see why not."

"That's great, Tony. The fresh-water spring is really close to it and can be piped into the house."

Winter storms seem to settle down. Several short ones with Chinooks taking the snow off each time. When the March winds blow, the country gets dry. Tony looks at our list of changes and additions and puts in the order for all the lumber to be hauled in with several helpers, wasting no time. With the help of the Garvais boys, the frame was up in a week. Then after another snow and another blow, great progress is made. The next load is finish lumber, windows, floors, and doors, inside and out.

It really seems short to me. Of course, I'm in town working but Rita is there. She feeds the men. Bless her heart, she is a helper par excellence.

CHAPTER 47

THE HOUSEWARMING AT DEARBORN RANCH

The spring is a busy one, with the Bean family roundup and branding coming up. Also, the newspapers are full of news on the terrible earthquake in San Francisco. The poor people lost everything in falling buildings and fires. The town has mourned the loss of lives and loss of business. A few of my relatives are still in that city.

We decide to have our housewarming party on a Saturday. It looks like everyone has been collecting, making, and baking for weeks. Nice, soft, hand-braided rugs for each side of our bed so our toes won't ever feel the cold floor. Patchwork quilts for both Dick and Oscar. Carrie and Dick Bean are first to arrive, right after breakfast. Dick Bean explains, "Vee don't vant to spoil your Saturday, but vee want to see your new house und give vat de say, 'warming.' Vee haf a few tings vat will make you know vee so happy you haf home and vill stay here." Carrie explains when she brings in all the goodies they brought, "Here are dish towels for your kitchen and a bit of sweet for your biscuits. Strawberry preserves I made last year." We are stunned by this outpouring of welcome, but shortly others arrive bearing more gifts made lovingly by hand.

The McGraws arrive next with their gift of a setting hen on a clutch of eggs in a box. Mrs. McGraw says, "These are automatic deliverers, Doctor. These babies break out all by themselves," she explains, giving a knowing laugh.

The next week I find the brick layer, Henry. *Whispering Henry* he's called—a name he can't pronounce so people can understand it. The story about him is strange, but his voice comes out in a horrible rushing of air from the lungs. He explained to me once, "I gotta have special medicine to keep my throat oiled. Actually, whiskey or such." Even so, he can lay bricks, and we want the chimney built before snow flies so we can keep warm in the whole house.

Joe Bush is at the post office when I go there. "Joe, I need to find Whispering Henry. Gotta get our chimney built before fall."

"He hangs out in Gilman near the hotel and school. Ya gotta keep him oiled or he disappears from the job you've put him to do."

"Joe, when you see him, tell him I now have a job for him."

"Okay, Doc, that I will do."

Sure enough, long about five o'clock, this bushy-faced character comes stumbling up to my office. With a voice that would scare you if it was a dark night, he pushes air from a throat that vibrates like the foghorns I used to hear from off the lake in Chicago.

"Doc Kenck, Joe Bush says you want to see me?"

"Yes, sir, Mr. Henry, I need you to do a chimney job on my house up on the Dearborn about seventeen miles. I can take you and your tools and you can stay in my cabin until the work is finished."

Henry looks at me and then finally explains, "I busy for two weeks. Then I come."

"Mr. Henry, I will have the brick and mortar there for you." He tells me how much is needed for a chimney, so I get Clemons to haul this so it will be ready for action by Henry.

As per our agreement, in two weeks he is waiting with his work tools and an old valise that he carries like it is heavy. Well it is! He keeps it close by and I soon see why. Every few miles he fumbles it open and takes out a bottle and downs several gulps. "My medicine," he whispers, and not because he's being secretive but because he can't speak any other way. Evidently he's got an alcohol-blistered throat. He plans to stay until he gets the job done, and he will if his "medicine drops" hold out.

The next day Henry is up at breakfast. Who knows how many eye openers he has downed? Things go as planned, but by afternoon and several stops at the medicine bottle, he seems kind of unsteady. Unsteady or no, he keeps going back up the ladder. I decide to become a brick layer's helper and keep him supplied with mortar and brick so he won't have to negotiate the ladder too many times, but it still becomes too much for him. "Doc, I gotta stop for a while." That's when I decide to put a fence around the roof. When he gets up there, it could mean a fall. I sure don't want that.

Dan Garvais comes up for his Saturday talk. I get him to help me put a rail around where the chimney is to be. When Whispering Henry runs out of medicine, he says he needs to go to town. "Sure," I say, "I got some medicine and I'll let you have some."

We stretch out our supply of medicine, so I decide I'll have to bring some home the first of the week.

At last, the chimney is finished. I take a good look at it from all sides. It is definitely somewhat swayed. I say to Mr. Henry, "It's got a wave in it." Henry, not wanting to face the fact, yet acknowledging it, said, "Oh, de smoke goes better when he's crooked." Crooked or no, with the chimney built I'm more satisfied we are ready for whatever the weather will bring.

Dearborn Canyon—home, ranch, and fishpond

CHAPTER 48

THE GREAT NORTHERN RAILROAD—GILMAN & AUGUSTA FIGHT IT OUT

The big news this year is that the Great Northern Railroad is being built east from Great Falls. The plan is to cross the Divide after building along Sun River and the Canyon. They expect to meet on the other side at Essex, another branch of the railroad coming along the border of Glacier Park.

Every week I bring home the local newspapers. These have articles and editorials that encourage the people of the new town site of Gilman but provoke the longtime residents of Augusta.

The railroad itself instigates this quarrel. The primary instigation results from the railroad's desire to name a town in honor of one of its executives, L.C. Gilman.

No matter what, the railroad figures to have its way, and aren't we the primary benefactors of the area? They refuse with the excuse that to change their plans is not feasibly cost efficient. The Augusta folk certainly are not satisfied with such a lame excuse. No matter where the rail was to terminate, for the present it was to be a new town and named after their important man.

Augusta happens to have a new and ambitious resident who comes from Minnesota to make his fortune by starting a bank. Abram Lincoln Bradley is his name. The strategy of the Great Northern is to induce an influential business in Augusta to move his business to the new town site. This happens to be the president of the new Augusta State Bank. Bradley is helped by the

GNRR to construct an impressive brick bank building on the new Gilman town plat in an effort to influence people to move there from Augusta.

I gather by the grapevine that some residents of Augusta are influenced. The highhanded movement of the bank, without consulting any account holders or stockholders about the move or the changing of the name to Gilman State Bank, infuriates some of the bank's own stockholders, namely Alva Beach and J.C. Furman, who are particularly incensed at Bradley's actions. Furious is the word. There are others who are just plain mad. The editors of *The Augusta Times* and the new *Gilman Optimist* are having a word battle.

Rita looks forward to each Friday as I bring home the newspapers. "Rita," I caution her, as if she needed it, "we can't get too public with our opinion. I have several Gilman people as patients, even though my desires are in favor of Augusta."

"Yes, dear Doctor Husband. I will be cautious because you are in business that reaches many in the whole area."

"Rita, we can sit on the sidelines and watch the battle of the two towns. We do have our desires, but we will watch only. *The Augusta* news editor puts a voice and information to its readers."

"When they build a depot and the bank actually puts up a building, Gilman will have a start and probably others will come."

"Yes, that's true."

Each week *The Gilman Optimist* reports all the new business being built and the town is growing by leaps and bounds. All this activity does make it look like Gilman is a booming town.

When the two-town tug-of-war spills over into the school situation, the big promoter, A.L. Bradley, solicits the help of *The Helena Independent* editor, William Campbell. Gilman parents decide they should have a school district separate from Augusta. In the Helena paper's following edition, Campbell throws his full support to Gilman. He publishes all he can scrape up for the new town to have its separate school district, not only with words but also he goes to Miss

Herrington, the county school superintendent, and tries to influence her. The result is she agrees to come to a meeting for the Gilman school, and she refuses to allow the creation of a new district.

C.C. Covington, a county commissioner and also an Augusta school board member, first is against the separate district, but because of his political ambitions, changes his mind. The county commission authorizes a new school district. So much for political influence.

There is still the matter of Augusta trying to get the Great Northern to build a spur line out its way, but only time will tell.

Our newspapers now can go to bigger issues, like Teddy Roosevelt switching from the Republican to Populist Party. Even though Augusta loses the school issue, there are those in town like J.C. Manix and Dick Vaughn who are determined to somehow force the GNRR to put a spur to Augusta.

The story of Gilman and Augusta goes on, but Rita and I still plan to stay out of it, and mighty handy of us to do since we live outside either town. Life on the Dearborn is busy.

Today, Caleb Clemons and his helpers take Rita's organ from the Auchard place and install it in our home. We need some music and Rita misses playing.

I told her Monday it would happen. She said, "I'll get all my Saturday cooking done on Friday so I can play the organ all day on Saturday and Sunday. I really miss playing it."

Also, another thing I buy is an ice cream freezer from Beach's store. Since we have ice cut from the pond this winter and stored in the icehouse, we will be all set to make ice cream during the summer. Dick is eager to turn the handle while I keep putting rock salt and chunks of ice around.

Rita has made a custard of milk, cream, eggs and sugar with a spoon of vanilla. "Dad, I can make ice cream," Dick says confidently. "I watched them make it at Dick Bean's party. Mrs. Bean put in some strawberry jam. It sure was good!" The cranking started getting harder and Dick was showing the strain. "Dick, let me take a turn and see how easy it is."

"Dad, I can turn it," he says, straining at every word. I take over and realize it is just about firm enough. Not long now. I clear off the salt from around the lid and remove it, pull out the dasher and scrape off some ice cream with a spoon, and then replace the lid. Dick and Oscar take turns licking the dasher and get ice cream all over their faces. I pack more salt around the can. "Dad, when can we have more?" Rita is standing by to take the dasher to be washed. "Boys, we will have ice cream for dessert after we eat the dinner I've fixed." No urging this time to clean up their plates. They are sitting exceptionally still for them, and not even asking to be excused either. "Yep, Rita, ice cream works wonders, every time." Rita gives me a knowing giggle.

It is a happy day in spring. We usually have company when the weather is this nice, but this is a bit early to expect anyone. Rita is happy with the organ and sits down to play right after she and I put the dishes through the hot suds and rinse. Being Sunday and Dan Garvais has the day off, Dick and I go milk our cow and then feed Tommy and Gyp, my speedy team that can make it to or from town in record time.

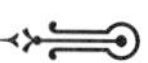

Following spring and summer and heading into winter, one morning Bing comes in to my office. "Looks like we are in for a bad winter. Hay is getting scarce."

"Take off your hat and coat and step up to my chair. Let's take a look-see."

My explorer catches in the decay.

"Yeah, that's the one. But be sure to look at all of them, Doc."

In between drillings we talk.

"Who else do you know would answer a draft?"

"At the LF Ranch, Tot Nett and Benny Jefferson. I don't know how Ballie Buck will get along without them. Guess he'll have to get back out of the house and ride and feed all day."

"All of us will have to if all of you working fellows are drafted."

"Others that might go are the Carmichael boys, Harold Brusgard, and Ben Arps."

After the first molar I say, "Bing, I think we'd better wait a day to do the other molar. Too much drilling might give you a headache. Come in tomorrow and we will do the other molar."

"Okay, sure, isn't much business at the store when the snow is this deep. How is your family doing on the ranch?"

"They are snug and warm. The Indian boys are good helpers. They keep the wood box full and take care of the chores. Rita keeps busy baking bread and other goodies because the oven is always hot these days. Dick goes out on his trap line every morning before he goes to school. Gervais taught him to trap and take care of his catch. He's got several pelts stretched already."

"See you tomorrow, Doc."

"Come in when you can, Bing."

CHAPTER 49

THE DEATH OF RITA'S FATHER, RICHARD AUCHARD, MAY 12, 1916

Tuesday afternoon, someone comes fast up my stairs and into my office. I'm working on a patient. "Dr. Kenck, excuse me for interrupting, but Mr. Dyer at the depot asked me to deliver this telegram: "Grandpa Richard died this morning. . . . Dr. says heart failure. . . . Masons taking care of funeral arrangements. . . . It will be Friday. . . . Please come as soon as possible. . . . Please answer. Anna Louise Vandenberg.

The boy who brought the telegram speaks. "Mr. Dyer said to tell you he will send answer."

"Of course." And I get a sheet of paper and write the answer: "Anna Louise Vandenberg: Rita and I will come tomorrow. . . Good you are with Grandma Helen . . . Thank you for the telegram.

I give the message to the boy. I give him a dollar. "Are you Mr. Nett's boy?"

"Yes, I'm Tot Nett. I work for Weston Howard. We met on the train. Mr. Dyer came out and asked Weston if I could deliver this."

Now thoughts start racing through my mind. I've been calm and collected for many deaths, but even so, when it happens to our own family, the thoughts start tumbling through the head.

First I put a note on my door. "Gone to Helena. Mrs. Kenck's father passed away. Will be back next week."

First to Nett's stable to pick up my team and buggy. I think then I'll stop at the ranch and tell Will (Auchard) about his father. Quickly, I go into the lane and by the house. I see his housekeeper lady, Miss Messenger, at the kitchen door.

"Miss Messenger, where is Will?"

"He's eating his lunch." Will comes out.

"Sorry to tell you, Will. Your father passed away early this morning."

Will said in his very low voice, "When is the funeral?"

"Anna Louise sent a telegram and the depot agent sent Tot Nett up to deliver it. I just got it half hour ago. I'm on my way to tell Rita, and we will go to Helena tomorrow. It will be a Masonic funeral."

"I can get the stage on Thursday to be at the funeral on Friday. I'll stay at The Harvey."

At that I said, "I've got to tell Rita, so we'll see you in Helena."

On the road next I must turn off at the Cottle ranch. Ida May Auchard Cottle, Richard's other daughter, besides Rita, must be told. John Cottle is at the corral, so I stop.

"John, I have sad news for your missus."

"How so?"

"Richard Auchard passed away early this morning."

"He was getting up in years. Ida is not too well either."

"Please tell her. I have to get home to tell Rita. We will go to Helena tomorrow. The funeral is Friday. Will said he would take the stage Thursday."

"Ida is not very well. She may not go. Thanks for stopping by."

Back on the road again, I begin to think of the life of Richard Auchard, especially how he has affected mine. Most of all by giving me Rita. He scared others away. I know why too. She was his pride and joy, and he wanted the very best for her, and he was going to make sure. The lecture he gave me rings in my ears when I seem to forget I have that precious gift. Not only that, his influence getting me to consider the Masonic Lodge.

Then again it overcomes me he is gone. As I drive past the lake and Ole Bean's, I prepare myself to tell Rita her Papa she loved so much is gone. She comes out the door—she looks surprised. I jump down to tell so she won't be wondering too long.

"Rita, Papa's gone. He died this morning." I reach

to take her into my arms and hold her. This is so hard for her, even though she knew he was failing.

"Oh, Papa. I'll miss you so. . ." Sobs and tears. I hold her for a long time. Finally between her sobs, "When did you hear—how?"

"I have Anna's telegram in my pocket."

"I answered. I said we will come tomorrow."

"This is hard to bear."

"The Masons will take care of the funeral."

Oscar comes running up. "Mama, what's the matter?"

Rita brushes her eyes with her apron. "Oscar, Grandpa Richard died this morning."

"Did he go to heaven?"

"Of course, he learned how from Brother Van. Just like I told you. His body got too worn out, so he left it here. And, his spirit that lived in the body went to be with God."

"Oh. Do we know anybody else there with God?"

"Yes, Oscar. I told you about Grandpa Charles who got killed by the Indians."

"That is good. He will see him there."

We got everything ready to take the buggy early next morn.

It is May. As we drive over to the road to Wolf Creek, we see the hills covered with spring flowers and grass. We catch the noon train at Wolf Creek. Richard and Oscar really like the rumble and swaying of the train and especially the whistle.

I have taken charge of several funerals around Augusta, but this one was being planned by the Helena Masonic Lodge. So I watched and listened to be able to use the ritual if needed.

Oscar and Richard were very quiet. I told them to act like grownups. They certainly did. We kept them apart. The folks in Helena associated with the Masons and Eastern Star, like the Auchards, gave a very special time to take care of all the needs of the Service. They plan to see that Rita's mother not be left alone or have any needs they can take care of. Anna Louise is with her evenings and all night.

Rita says, "I told Mama that soon we would come and move her to be with us."

After getting home we made the plans and fix the

little room off the kitchen to be Mama's bedroom. Dick comes in the kitchen the next day after we get home. Oscar is right behind him.

"Hey, Dad and Mom, can Grandma come to live with us?"

Oscar gives Dick a shove. "That's what I wanted to ask and you stole it." And he gives Dick a punch in the stomach. We have to separate them right away—a fight will go till Oscar is bawling. Fights start and unless they are separated, fists keep flying. Oscar never wins but he won't give up.

After the fight is settled and each one is sitting in a chair across the room from each other, Rita tells the boys our plans.

"Next week your dad and I will take the big buggy and go to Helena and bring Grandma home with us."

Grandma's friends she had made in Helena over the last four years were sad to see her move away. They stopped by the house the day before, and each lady gave her a handkerchief they had crocheted or tatted an edge around. They were a dear bunch of ladies, and Mama Auchard shed tears with each one as they left her to get finished with her packing.

All the while, Rita kept folding and packing the linens and clothes in their two trunks. We ship those to Gilman and will have them hauled out by the Clemons Freight Company.

After we got across the Valley, Mama began to cheer up and became interested in the mountains and trees of the Prickly Pear Canyon. With one stop overnight in Wolf Creek, the next day we made it to the ranch. Dick and Oscar are shyly happy to see her and soon warm up to begin telling her about everything they had been doing while they had made things all neat with the Pocha girl who stayed with them.

Every day I stop at Fishers' Drug Store. I want him to know how much benefit he is to this town.

"George, Rita and I are thinking we are going to be moving into town."

"How come? You have gotten quite a bit of land and cattle together. What will you do with all that?"

"That's our dilemma. True, we have worked hard

to get it, but we know that very soon we will be sending the boys to high school and we need to be with them. We've decided to not give the responsibility of watching them to someone else like so many who have boarded their kids with someone in town. Next year Dick will be ready for high school, so we will come to town for the school year. That year we will probably be part-time here in town and try to keep the ranch going weekends and summers."

"Yeah, I can see your problem. I think that I will just stick to one place to live. I can see it would be different if I had two boys instead of my two girls."

"George, let's make this winter go away so we can get together and give your house the proper treatment."

"It's okay, Doc. It doesn't know the difference."

The mail today brings a letter from the lawyer about the will of Richard Auchard. The Court date has been set for probate hearing of the will. I will be happy when it's settled. A few of the heirs are unhappy with the slow progress of probate. It takes a full year at least.

Will Auchard is buying out the other heirs and he is not in a hurry, of course, but some of the others are getting impatient with me even though I can't hurry it, no matter what.

I call Rita and tell her I'll go with Dick Adams on the mail sleigh to Craig and catch the train to Helena. Also, I'll stay with my German mutter. Then I trudge in the snow up to Dick Adams' house to tell him, "Day after tomorrow I will be on your stage to Craig—gotta get to Helena to get the Auchard estate finally settled."

"Okay, Doc. I'll be there at six with sleigh bells."

Now I get out my warmest clothes and the sweater and cap my German mutter made for me. I didn't realize that I have been lonesome to see my mutter. After my father's death she became a capable business woman—running the businesses he left. Of course, she had the advice of the Kenck brothers who were and are bankers and businessmen.

Even after I get back from Helena the winter storms keep rolling in from the north. Our plans for a housewarming for the Fishers have to be put on hold.

CHAPTER 50

SUMMER PACK TRIP

July 20 is Dick's tenth birthday in seven days. Rita and I discuss it. What can we do for a ten-year-old boy to celebrate? The answer is plain. Dick runs in the door, "Dad, you said we might take a pack trip sometime. Why not 'cause it's my birthday next week?"

That's it—our problem is solved. It doesn't take much at all to get me planning and getting a pack trip together.

I say, "Rita, how can we all take a pack trip? What about Grandma?"

"Well, we can ask her to see if she could ride that much."

Rita says, "Mother, we would like to take a pack trip back into the mountains to celebrate Richard's tenth birthday; do you think you could ride back in the mountains?

Mama says, "At one time I could, but I haven't ridden a horse that much, but I tell you what. I can take care of things here while you folks go."

I say, "Mother Auchard, I wouldn't think of you being here alone. We can get Alvina Pocha to stay with you and, of course, the Pocha boys to take care of the cows as they always do."

"Dr. Oscar, that's a real good idea. Alvina and I will have a happy time. I can teach her to sew herself a dress and maybe to knit."

Rita is hearing all our conversation and smiles with her usual chuckle. So we make plans. On purpose I get Dick involved so he will learn how to get everything ready for a pack trip.

I go over what horses we will take—three for packhorses. Of course, we will include Cerise.

Oscar jumps right into the planning: "I ride Cerise with no pack on her."

"Oscar, we need to pack her; she is the best for that. You can ride another horse that is easy to ride. Cerise will be along, and you can take care of her and make her happy with her oats."

"Oh, all right, Dad. I can take care of her and she will be a happy horse."

I have to take one more trip to town and put my vacation notice on my office door. I stop at the store for a few supplies and see J.C. Manix.

"J.C, I'm taking a pack trip back to Donahur country. Actually, we are celebrating Dick's tenth birthday. We will be gone a week."

"Kenck, what a splendid idea. That would make any age happy. I would like to do it someday myself. My boy is just three, but someday he'll be old enough for such a trip."

"What's his name?"

"Walter James."

"You will someday. It'll be good for you and the kid. I know because I really long to go back into the hills—exciting, exhilarating, relaxing. I'm in the office all day and tomorrow, but after that don't expect me near town. Here's my list. I'll come for it tomorrow about three o'clock."

"All right, Doc. It will be ready for you."

I'm working on a set of dentures that are due tomorrow when in walks Ballie Buck.

"Howdy, Doc. Here's Myrtle, my wife."

"I'm so very glad to meet you, Mrs. Buck. Ballie and I are ancient friends. Of course, he told you I was one of his favorite pests when I hung around the stables."

"Dr. Kenck, it is so nice to meet Ballie's friends. And I'm more than pleased you are a dentist. I do need such a doctor as you."

"Well, if that's the case, please put your hat on my little table and step right up and sit in my chair. We will take a look at the situation."

My mind tells me right away this is no ordinary lady. After an exam of her dental situation, I tell her she does have several teeth that need attention.

She tells me, "Doctor, I'll need to come in when Ballie comes to town for supplies and mail, but I'll need to be back in time to put supper on for the crew."

"Mrs. Buck, of course, that is the best anyway. It is too tiring to you to have more than one correction at a time. For one week I'll be gone; I'm taking my two little boys and wife back in the mountains on a pack trip."

Suddenly I see tears well up in her eyes, and she says, "We'll have to go now." And, I'm puzzled.

I say, "When would you like to start?"

Ballie answers for her. "We can start right after haying is done next month. I'll come by and let you know a few days ahead."

They leave then and I'm still puzzled—what did I say wrong? I have to put it out of my mind. These dentures have to be ready by five o'clock.

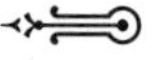

In comes Joe Bush. "It's close to five. Are they ready?"

"Yep. I'm just now running my foot machine to finish polishing the surfaces. Sit up and we'll put them in."

"Okay, Doc. I've been thinkin' you might not get them finished if too many came here and talked to you or you had to patch up someone who's been in an accident."

"No problem Joe. Only Ballie Buck, the new foreman at the J.B. Long Ranch, and his wife came in."

"Yeah, I met him too. He is one smart Indian."

"Let's try these. How does that feel? These will fit tight now and maybe there will be sore spots. I'm gone next week, so if they get too sore in spots take them out and rinse in warm water with salt in it and leave them out a while. I'll be back in ten days. We are taking the boys on a week's pack trip. "You wear them a while, and if they hurt too much, put your old ones in."

"Okay, Doc. I'll manage somehow till you get back. You have a good trip and be careful about bears."

"Thanks, Joe. I go prepared."

By noon next day, I pick up the supplies J.C. has all ready for me and my mail. Then I'm on my way. Guess I'd better stop and see Will. I need to tell him his stepmother will be at the ranch but will have a Pocha girl staying with her while we do the pack trip for Dick's birthday.

Will says when I tell him, "You need a packhorse or two? I've got several. I've got one that's special I'll give to Dick for his birthday. How old is he now?"

"He's ten."

"Soon be a man."

"First a baby and then soon a man."

Will, in his low, low voice says, "Then too soon old. I'm still haying." He motions for me to follow. I drive behind him to the corral, and he gets a halter and catches the horse he wants Dick to have.

"Name is Bill."

So, I tie Bill behind my buggy and away I go towards my butte and my mountains. My mind scans over my list: food and medicine kit—most important camping gear. It's been so long since I've gotten ready for a pack trip that my readiness smarts are rusty.

Driving in towards the barn, Dick comes running, "Dad, where did you get the horse?"

"Son, it's your horse."

"What? How come?"

"Uncle Will gave it to me to give to you. He says it's one good packhorse."

"Wow! What's his name?"

"It's Bill."

We get the pack boxes out and plan what goes where. By July 26, we are lined up: four horses to ride and four horses to pack. A week in the mountains is a big project.

Dick has gotten his new horse to realize he is his caretaker, and of course, Oscar long ago was Cerise's caretaker. We had to borrow a packsaddle from Ole Bean. I only had three.

At last we string out along the trail and wave goodbye to Grandma and Alvina. We travel up along the Dearborn River. We turn away from the river, or should say it turns away from the trail. Here we start up a slope. Soon it levels off into a meadow edged with forest.

Suddenly, the hornet residences come in full force towards us and pick out Cerise as their target. She breaks away and heads for the trees, jumping and bucking trying to escape them. She tries to get through a couple of trees too close together. She lets out some squeals. She is stuck. Her pack is holding her back, and she is frantic.

Finally, I get to her by cutting some brush away so I can back her out. We flag the hornets away from her. Only then can we handle her. I'm sure she has a few stings, so I rub spirits of turpentine all around her ears to ease the pain.

Everything then goes smoothly until we are close to the place we plan to make camp for the day and night. A long climb will get us up on the flat above. Cerise is tied to the horse's tail in front of her. She pulls back and breaks the rope this time and down she rolls. It looks like a disaster for sure. Little Oscar starts howling, "Dad! Dad! My horse! My horse!"

End over end she tumbles coming to a stop on her back. We get the pack off her back and then get a hold of her halter and pull her until she finally gets up.

Nothing broke in her pack except the lid of the Dutch oven. The jar of pickle relish in the oven didn't even break. Cerise was okay. She jumps up and we load her pack back on her.

Cerise's tumble reminds me of one of my hunting trips a few years back when I was coming down Scapegoat Mountain descending a series of switchbacks. Horses above would kick rocks on those below. Young Cerise saw one good size come tumbling and she jumped to let it go under her. She succeeded in doing that, but she landed wrong and went tumbling down herself and landed on her back in the creek below with all four feet in the air.

She is famous for these kinds of happenings so who can say nothing else will happen to Cerise this trip.

As I say this, Rita prophetically says, "This is two times already this trip."

"Rita, two times is a-plenty," Little Oscar says. "Nothing better happen to my Cerise."

We camp at the head of the Dearborn and get camp set up while Rita puts the food together. I cast a line in this small creek. Sure enough a hungry one grabs my bait. After putting our grub back in the grub box, we get the horses staked out. Not all, but Cerise and Billy for sure. The other horses will stay around because they know they will get another bite of oats.

"Dad, you said we are going back to some place that Dick Bean hunted elk one time."

"That's where we are headed. Tomorrow we will go on and get over that mountain." I point to the one. "Beyond that, it's called the Donahur country."

"Did Dick Bean tell you anything about that place?"

"Some, but he told me about the struggle they had getting home because of the snow storm that happened the last night. It was so deep their horse could only go by lunging into the snow, and the trail didn't show at all."

"Yeah, that would be awful and scary. I'm glad we are here in summer."

When we did get over to the Donahur, it was too beautiful (almost) to describe—meadows and groves of trees, streams and lakes."

"Dad, I heard something really loud and long. What was it do you s'pose?"

"It's a bit early, but I heard it this morning too. It's an elk bugle. In the fall bull elks call the cow elks, and also the bulls challenge each other. The sounds bounce off the high mountains around and echo back and forth."

We camp by a stream and fish right away. I get busy making a place for Rita to cook them for our supper.

Dick fishing

Dick and Oscar take the horses to the creek after we take off their saddles. Then Oscar gets a pan of oats for his Cerise and examines around her ears to see the welts the hornets made.

"Dad, let's put stuff on these bites. They are hot and need something."

After we eat our supper, we wash the dishes in the creek. When the sun goes down, we put our bed rolls on some pine bows. We bring our horses in closer to the camp and give them a pan of oats after a drink. We tie them to trees. Usually a pack string stays together. We hang our food sack in the trees—hoist them high out of reach of hungry bears. We take the saddle horses and take a big circle around the Donahur Valley. We surprise a cow elk and calf twice. No bulls. They must be higher up because the next day we hear them bugle a few times, but it is early for that.

By Thursday we are thinking of starting home. We have good appetites. The potatoes are almost gone and the beans too. We still have ham because mostly we cook the fish we catch.

We gather up and repack our packsaddles, and on Friday we start back the way we came. We've had no problems and are feeling very lucky. We get to the ridge that was difficult coming in and start carefully down. Suddenly, Oscar calls out, "Dad! Dad! Cerise is stuck! She can't move her foot!"

I look back and she is struggling for some reason. I slide down and run back. Her ankle is twisted and her foot is stuck tight in a rock crevice. She tries so hard that the first thing I see is she is down and her foot is twisting. It must be broken. I say nothing, but I'm thinking if her ankle is broken that I'll have to shoot her. Oh, what a disaster for us and especially for Oscar. He is crying—poor kid. "Dad! My horse! My horse!"

I say, "Oscar, I've got to get my hammer and rock breaker and break the rocks away from her foot."

I think, "Oh, how awful to have to kill that horse right here with Oscar seeing the whole thing. I hurry and get the hammer from my pack and another rock to slip in just ahead of her foot. By now she is sprawled out in an odd position and still struggling.

"Oscar, you get by her head and hold on to her halter. Keep her as still as you can."

Between Oscar's sobs and talking to Cerise, I get the rock into the crack ahead of her foot. What a strange position. Finally, I get the wedge-shaped rock into the bigger one, and I give it a real hard whack with my camping axe. Then another even harder, and "creak!" the rock breaks open and out pops her whole foot. It looks distorted. I think sure it's broken.

She steps down with it after she struggles up off her knees and gingerly puts it to the test. Wow! She walks slowly away. I am amazed. Oscar too.

"Dad, she's walkin' on it!" He was so happy that he grabs her around the leg and hugs it tight. "My horse, my horse!" Cerise is truly the star of our trip.

When we get to the trail by the Dearborn, we know we are close to home. What a trip with Cerise this time.

Grandma Auchard has expected us sometime this day and she has made a custard pie and a big kettle of stew with some meat and vegetables Ole Bean had brought over. Grandma tells us that Mr. Bean got worried about her and came over with food for her to make a stew. "Mr. Bean didn't know I had Alvina with me," Mrs. Auchard says. "Besides Ole, other folks came by.

I served tea and cookies three times at least."

We take the packsaddle off our horses and run them into their pasture near the barn and the river. Like horses often do, they roll in the dirt and give themselves a run around the pasture. Words don't say it any better—they are glad to get home.

The boys are running around checking all their play areas. Dick says, "It won't be long until I will be setting these traps, Dad." He checks them all as they hang on the corral fence.

We talk about the cow elks with their calves that we saw and the bull elk bugling.

Oscar treasures Cerise even more as he feeds her the oats ration. Of course, he puts a little extra in her feed pan.

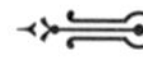

On Monday, August 8, I have to come off my mountain and down to earth. Back to the world of threats of war. Woodrow Wilson is nominated for a second term for the Democrats, and Charles Evan Hughes is nominated by the Republicans. When I'm back in the mountains, this seems of little importance, but man is a practical animal, they say. The saying of the Democrats is "He (Wilson) kept us out of the war." But with our ships being targets of the Germans, submarines make that saying very weak.

I'm back in my office in the hotel and expect those who missed me to be in. I hear footsteps.

"Mr. Buck, glad to see you."

"Doc, don't call me Mr.—I'm just Ballie to everyone."

"Ballie, when you folks were in, I was puzzled when I spoke with Mrs. Buck. Did I say something I should not have?"

"I came in a bit early while Myrtle goes to the post office. I want to tell you about Mrytle. You don't know about this and how could you? A few years ago, we had a baby boy and we lost him, and Myrtle has had a struggle to get over it. When she hears about someone's little boy, she breaks down in tears. It has been hard on her. That day, not knowing this, you spoke of your boys going on a pack trip with you. Her grief swept over her again."

"I am so very sorry. I would never have said anything like that if I had known."

"Doc, please don't feel bad. You couldn't have known. I hear her coming up the stairs now."

"How do you do, Mrs. Buck? We will take a look at your tooth problems. Put your hat right on my hat rack here and please sit in my chair."

As I examine with my explorer, I stop after each time and discover a cavity and explain what it is, and when I'm finished, I tell her what kinds of solutions are the best. It is probable that two teeth might not be saved but that a bridge is possible in both cases.

"Doctor, will you be able to start today?"

"We certainly can."

"I have no other plans and can be here until Ballie has to leave for the ranch."

So, I go to work on the ones that can be saved.

"Doc, I will come back in a bit to see how things are."

"I'm thinking two hours is about long enough for one time. I go slowly so as not to hurt too much."

Myrtle says, "Thank you for that, Doctor. I'm not so

delicate, but I appreciate your consideration. Now I will consider coming in with Ballie each week for as long as it takes. Whether that is a nice day away from cooking, I'm not sure."

"Sometime when you come, I hope my good lady will be in town to meet you."

"Doctor, I would be very pleased to meet her. Besides, several people have already told me how much they respect and like Rita Kenck."

"Perhaps we can arrange to be at one of the lodge doings soon."

September has been a busy time. We must, like other ranchers, get the cattle down from the mountains—fall roundup. Dick is anxious for snow and cold weather—two reasons, he says. "Snow means cold and the animals I trap get their winter fur coats, And, we can take the sleigh with Cerise to school and pick up the other kids who live our way. Our teacher this year is sure nice. We are a lucky bunch this time.

"For Oscar's birthday Mrs. Sorshalal brought a cake to school and we had a party at lunchtime. All the boys wanted to give him seven swats, but I wouldn't let them. We brothers sometimes fight, but I sure won't let someone else beat up on him. Mrs. Sorshalal played the piano, and we all sang the *Happy Birthday* song."

CHAPTER 51

OSCAR'S BIRTHDAY SURPRISE

Early in October it began to snow. Rita calls, "Boys, come look out the window." It must be something if Mother called like that.

Dick is excited, "Mother is Dad gone?"

"Yes, he went early to get down the road before the snow gets deep."

Dick says, "Now I can set my traps. Mr. Garvais says to wait till it snows and then the weasels turn white with a black tip on the end of their tails."

Later, Rita tells the boys that I called today while they were at school. "He said he is bringing a surprise for your birthday but not until Friday, Oscar."

Oscar says, "Did he tell you what it is?"

"No, because he didn't want to put me on the spot. He knew you would keep begging me till he gets home."

The weather stays cold, much to Dick's delight. He asks Grandma to call him at 5:00 the next morning. She responds with, "Yes, Richard, I will. When your grandpa was alive he always said I got up with the chickens." Richard says, about getting up at 5:00 a.m., that that is the way the rest of his life will be as a trapper man."

Oscar is getting impatient and keeps asking, "What day is it, Mom?" She tells him every day what day it is and what day it is not. But he keeps it up, "Do you s'pose Dad might come home today?" Rita tells him, "No, not before Thursday anyway because he has many patients with teeth that need to be fixed."

⊷⇒

Meanwhile at the office, I'm finishing up a bridge for Tony.

"Good morning, Tony. I'm glad you've come in early because I want to leave for the ranch as soon as I can because the weather might get tough traveling."

"That's just what I figured since I'm in between jobs, I'm not busy and thought you might be anxious to get out to your wife and kids. How are they doing?"

"They are doing well. They are going to Clemons School. Oscar is seven this week. This is his second year. Dick is all excited about his trap line. Dan Garvais has taught him a lot about trapping."

"Those Indian folk sure know their animals. They have made themselves a living with it and the firewood business. Good to hear about your kids. I thought we had enough, but along came another—a boy. We named him Phil after Grandfather Manix."

"Here's your bridge. Let's see how it fits in with the rest of your teeth. Bite down now. See if there are any high places."

I grind off a few high spots. "How's that?"

Tony bites a few tries. "That's better. No high spots now."

"I'm taking a birthday present home to Oscar today—a surprise."

"Yeah, what?"

"It's a dog—actually a pup."

"The kid will sure like that. This bridge makes me feel like I could eat a steak. I'll let you know."

Getting close to noon. I'll take off to get Rita's list and then get out to Will's place and pick up the puppy.

At the store, J.C. says, "Here are the supplies on your wife's list, even birthday candles."

"Very important. It's for Oscar."

"How old will he be?"

"He is seven next week."

"What do you get for a seven-year-old?"

"I'm going to pick up a shepherd pup that Will's collie female had two months ago. Oscar has gotten farm lambs from Mr. Recder, so he will teach the dog to help with them. Oscar is really good with animals.

Oscar, age 3, on Cerise

He sure knows how to handle his horse, Cerise—rides her all over the place—even when he was three."

At the Auchard ranch, Will's new cook lady meets me as I drive up to the house. She says, "I'm Miss Messenger, Mr. Auchard's cook."

"I'm glad to know you and to know Will has a cook.

That's really important to a hard-working man to have good food cooked for him. Where, may I ask, have you come from?

"I'm a friend of the lady who cooks at what they call the L.F. Ranch. Her name is Marie Bracket. She said in a letter that I certainly would be able to get a job in this country. Her boss is a man named Axel Swanson."

"Why yes, I know Axel. He brags about his cook. Where is Will?"

"I think he's at the horse barn. He said something about having to shoe a horse this afternoon."

Sure enough, he's at the blacksmith shop getting some shoes ready.

"Will, I come to get that pup you wanted to give Oscar."

Will lays down his shaping tools. "Good you come today—box is fixed. How 'bout two pups?"

We walk to the cabin where he keeps the pups.

"Okay, Will, I can take two—got two boys. That will please them both. I met your new cook. Glad to see you've got yourself a cook. That's one thing a working man sure needs."

"Right, Doc, since Mom left, I've got skinny. I got no time to cook and the stuff I cook tastes awful."

"Is she a good cook?"

"Ump, any cook is better'n me."

"If I take two pups, they will be company for each other and not miss the mother so much."

"Yep. That's what I figure."

As I leave with my pups in a box, they begin to whine, but before long they quiet down with each other so we make it home. I see why two pups are better than one. Besides, they keep each other warm. As we get close to home, the snow is surprisingly deep—one of the early winter storms.

I pull up to the barn. My good wife comes out. I know she is as curious as Oscar about what I bring.

"Rita, honey, I know you are anxious to see what kind of a present I'd bring for Oscar.

"You bet, my good husband. I do hope whatever…"

Just then the whining comes from the box.

"Just what I guessed, a pup! Is it from Will's collie dog?"

"Yep, a good wife is also a good guesser."

I open the box and the two little collies come piling out crying all the way with us to the house. Not long Cerise pulling the sleigh comes up to the house. Oscar runs to the house.

"Dad! Dad! You are home. What did . . .'"

Just then pups run towards him. "Two! Two!"

"Yes, one for you and one for Dick. One would be too lonesome at first and cry all night."

Oscar reaches down to pat the dogs.

"Oscar, because it's your birthday present, you can decide which one is yours."

"Oh, Dad, can I? Can I wait a few days?"

"Sure thing. Just decide by your birthday next Tuesday."

After supper the boys are comforting the pups in the cabin. Rita and I catch up on news.

"Has Mr. Fisher moved his family to Augusta yet?"

"Yes, Tony is building a house for them up the main street right next to Fred Walrath's house. The drugstore George has had Tony build is right by the Manix house. His wife is Laura Marsh, granddaughter of the Van Worfs in Helena. George came from Missouri to

Helena. He learned pharmacy in Helena working for two different drugstores on purpose to learn the business."

"Augusta is lucky to get a druggist and his store."

"Yeah, and so am I lucky to get help with all the illnesses that humans are prone to. He's having a good stock of basics like iodine, glycerine, epsom salts, castor oil, and alcohol. He also knows what doctors are ordering for pneumonia, typhoid, diphtheria, cholera, and tonics. He can order anything I might need and have it sent in one day on the stage."

"What about family?"

"Yes, he has two little girls about the ages of our two boys."

"Next time I go to town, I will call on her. We must make them feel very wanted in our town. I know. When Tony gets their house so they can move in, let's have a housewarming for them and invite all the town folks."

"I'll find out from Tony just about when he will get it done."

Dick and Oscar are totally absorbed with the new collie dogs. I hear their plans.

"Oscar, let's make them a warm bed out of a box to put on the back porch."

"Yeah, they will stay warm together and not be lonesome for their mother."

I hear them putting a cover on a big wooden box I'd brought freight in. They come in.

"Mom," Oscar says, "we need a blanket or something soft and warm. We already put some dry hay in their house."

Dick coaxes them to go in the door he made. Rita goes to her stack of old blankets and quilts and brings out one.

"How will this be, Oscar?"

He grabs the old blanket and hugs it to feel how it will be. "Yeah, Mom. Thanks. This will be just right."

The kids are worried.

"We'll stay awake awhile to see if they are happy." They try to, but when the pups quit making lonesome sounds, the eyelids got heavy. Sunday we will celebrate, because I will be back in town on Tuesday so will miss his actual birthday date.

Saturday, Oscar is watching Grandma in the kitchen stirring and stirring something in a bowl.

"What are you making, Grandma?"

"Oscar, I'll give you two guesses."

"A cake?" His eyes twinkle? "For me?"

"Right you are, and I'm going to put frosting and candles on it."

"Do we have candles?"

"Of course. Your father brought a box of birthday candles yesterday."

"How many candles should I put on your cake, Oscar?"

"Seven, but it would be okay if you put ten 'cause I'll be that old soon."

"Why do you say that?"

"'Cause that's how old I want to be."

"Tell me Oscar, why do you want to be ten?"

"Grandma, don't tell on me, but I'm going to buy a .22 because Dick got one this year and he's ten."

"Now the oven is right. I'll put a spoonful of dough in a pie pan and you open the oven door and I'll slide it in. This is a way to test the cake dough to see if I put everything in that I am supposed to. Now I'll grease the cake pans. When you taste the trial cookie and you say it's just right, we'll put the dough into the cake pans."

In a few minutes, the cookie is done. Oscar, you can be the cookie tester—I mean the cake tester."

Oscar says, "Now is it cool?"

Grandma takes the pancake turner and puts it onto a plate. "Blow on it to cool it. Count to thirty between blows. That is half a minute, Oscar. Maybe it's cool."

"Yes, Grandma, it's just right."

The birthday dough goes into the pans and Grandma looks at the clock to measure about thirty minutes.

Oscar waits patiently and soon the cake is done.

"Grandma, it's lots bigger!"

"Yes, that's because the soda makes it raise up."

Oscar decides right then that baking cakes is fun. Yes, I decide Grandma is a good addition to our family. Both the boys like the attention their Grandma gives them.

On Monday, we are all up early. Dick is back from his trapline. We all eat our nice warm oatmeal that Grandma put on the stove last night in the top of a double boiler. It cooked last night a while till the fire got low and cooked some more when I got up early and built a fire in the kitchen range. Warm oatmeal with cream will keep us going till lunchtime.

I tell the kids goodbye and warn them, "No tricks on the teacher today or this week."

Dick says, "It's not me, remember? It's the other kids who do that teasing, and I get the blame because I grin and can't look innocent."

Tommy and Gyp are harnessed in their stall, excited to be going. They snort and do horse talk. They like going to Nett's stable. It's like home to them.

"Goodbye, my good wife. I'll talk up having the housewarming for the Fishers. I will call you about anything special."

Oscar and Dick have the pups playing in the snow. "Bye, Dad," the boys yell from their snow play. Oscar will get Cerise harnessed right away. Oscar can get her to do just what she is supposed to. The sleigh is waiting for her to be backed into the shafts, the right position.

Just like he knew I needed to talk to him, Bud Tomlinson comes in my office door. "Dr. Kenck, good to see you this chilly, snowy morn. Reminds me of the place where we all came from in Connecticut. The winters were snowy and cold. What is going on with you and your family? We really would like to see you living in town again."

"Thanks, Bud. We do miss the goings on in town, but if I'm going to succeed in cattle ranching, I need to pay attention to it as much as I can."

"Yeah, and I miss you both in our music group. We plan to play for Christmas and would be pleased to have you and Rita playing with us again."

"That reminds me, Bud, Rita and I were thinking about stirring up some idea about a housewarming for the Fisher family. I think their house should be ready to move into."

"Great idea, Kenck. We are so pleased to have a druggist in town. And yes, I understand they are about to move into the house. Yeah, and they're really close neighbors to us—just one house between."

"Gotta be a Sunday so people can be free to come."

"Let's try for the third Sunday in October and hope no blizzard."

"Okay. That sounds like a good time. We can come

in and bring Grandma and the kids maybe. If we have to, we can stay all night at the Auchard place. Will doesn't mind having company. He's got a housekeeper now."

"When George first decided he'd like to start his own drugstore here, he had quite a time convincing his missus to even agree to come see Augusta and learn we had civilization here. A hotel, mail service daily, stores, a church, and telephone exchange. We had them come to dinner that day. My Matilda told her about the Eastern Star and Ladies Club and made her feel better about living here."

"Good for you folks. We need a druggist badly. Believe me, a happy wife is essential."

"Okay, Doc. I'll get out news about that—third Sunday in October. We will really warm up their new house. See you later."

Next day, I catch George Fisher unloading new stock in his store.

"George, we folks are so glad you and family decided to stay a while in our town. Several of us are going to give you a visit at your new house soon, weather permitting. Don't worry about anything. Our ladies are going to take care of refreshments."

"Doctor Kenck, you have already made us feel so welcome. I assure you, we don't plan to move away very soon. Thanks for warning me that people will come some day so I can make sure we have our furniture brought from Helena so there will be a chair or two for folks to sit in."

"Don't worry too much, George. All of us moved into Augusta at one time or another."

Tuesday night I call home, mostly to talk to Oscar.

"Hi, Dad. No, those kids didn't paddle me. Dick wouldn't let them, and the teacher kept them so busy they musta forgot." That was his explanation.

Dick said, "Dad, I warned them. I told them I can beat up on my brother, but don't you guys try it. I guess I scared them good."

I said, "That's what brothers are for. Good for you."

The weather is threatening about storms but still holds without a blizzard. It doesn't look good though—usually threats turn into blizzards—like the time the Beans went back to Donahur.

Sure enough, by October 10, the north wind quit

teasing and started to really be serious. Just one week after Oakie's birthday it started. I wasted no time—got the horses from Nett's and the box of my weekly order from J.C. and hit the road for home. Gyp and Tommy were excited too, snorting and doing horse talk.

Good thing I started quick 'cause by the time I passed Chisholms, no road could I see. But the horses were never confused. Of course, there are fences along the road. The snow wasn't coming down too thick until I got close to Bean Lake and then I had to just trust Tommy and Gyp. They were never confused. By the time I got by the schoolhouse, I could see no one was there. Wise teacher sent them home soon after it started.

Is this the beginning of a winter like 1886? I hope not. After the storm, I think maybe we'll have an open winter—the Chinook winds came and melted the snow down to a crust on the ground, but no that is just the slippery foundation of another dump of snow. Makes me think of the winter I took those fingerlings back to Benchmark—had to leave the harness—and then go back and get it—wasn't mine, had to get it back.

December 4—a brief spell of melting snow. I know I need to get to the office and also get supplies for the ranch. We have ordered skates for the boys so they can play skinny on the lake. We will make a run for the mail every few days. The sleigh is easy for Tommy and Gyp to pull.

I'm beginning to have thoughts of moving into town. This is just too much. Dick will be ready for high school. He'll balk at moving away from his trapline, but he could trap on Elk Creek on Will's ranch. There my mind goes—it's way ahead of me.

Finally one day I say to Rita, "Maybe we should consider moving into town for the whole winter. These snowy, stormy winters are difficult, to say the least."

Right away Rita breaks into a smile and even her old chuckle I hadn't heard in a long time."

"Oscar, how did you know what I have been thinking. I never said a word to anyone."

"Yes, my good wife, you have a gift of reading my mind even before I know it myself."

Strange, it seems now like my whole life opened up into a new chapter and I began to see a different future—what will it be?

CHAPTER 52

BATEMAN'S VISIT AND A POSTMORTEM

We can speculate, but what will be will be. *Que será, será.*

Mid-January, J.C. Manix comes in to see me.

"Howdy. Long time no see."

"Been real busy at the store. Walter Vaughn and I are trying to keep up and also to get ahead. He's talking about answering the draft call."

"I hope not, but it does look like it might happen."

"If the U.S. does get into this war, the government will take over the railroads, and we will have to wait with our Court action. Even so, I'm determined to follow through. That *Gilman Optimist* newspaper editor really fires my determination.

"How's that?"

"Last issue of his paper had a new map of all the area involving the Sun River Valley project. I looked for the town of Augusta. He left it out!"

The Gilman Optimist: Like their own prediction, they will make happen what they wish for. The town of Augusta has already faded out of existence."

"Really! What a slick way to get rid of a town!"

"I'll tell you one thing, Kenck, it does do it—fires my determination to carry through my Court plans even if this war lasts for years. The railroad will be extended to Augusta!"

With that exclamation, J.C. says, "Gotta get back to the store."

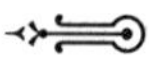

It's mid-March. Lately, the snow has melted and re-frozen several times by the Chinook winds. I'm working at my lab bench getting a set of dentures ready for the vulcanizing. The vulcanizer is at the ranch in my box-road dentist office, parked on the north side of the house. Dick is learning to watch over the burner to shift the vulcanizer and keep the heat gauge at the exact temperature reading. Sometimes when I'm ready for his assistance, he can't be found?!

It's still very early. I hear footsteps up the stairs.

"Howdy, Mr. Parsons. You are up very early."

"I'm up and have been all night. I brought Minnie in to Mrs. Riley Smith's last evening. This morning she had a baby girl."

"Is it good news?"

"Yes, Minnie's all right and now the baby seems all right."

"Two little girls is just fine. We thought it is fine to have two boys."

"This was an easy birth compared to the first one."

"Where did you leave little Ruthie?"

"Mrs. Moren wanted to keep her. The Morens are good neighbors. When their little girl was so sick and Mr. and Mrs. Moren were getting very tired, I went over and sat up with the girl who had diphtheria. I'd had it so I wouldn't get it."

"Minnie named Ruth after the name from the Bible and Amelia. This one will be Helena [Helen] and Elizabeth after my mother."

"Yeah, our two got named after their grandfathers. Do you plan to go into cattle on your homestead claims out by the Half Way House?"

"I would like to try dry farming awhile, but I'll work for the stage mail route till I get some machinery. This new idea of dry farming is really successful in some places in our state. But, a person needs to plow, disk, and harrow to keep the top soil loose to hold moisture under that top layer. To raise cattle, a person needs lots of pasture land."

"That's exactly what we are doing. We are getting what's called the Harrison Basin plus a 40-acre desert claim right close to the home place. The Basin will be summer pasture. It's a good day's drive to get our cattle up there every spring."

Hal turns to leave. "Hal, take care of Minnie and your girls. When we took care of little Ruth last year, Dick said, 'Can we keep her?'"

Sure looks like we will get dragged into this war. Our ships will be torpedoed and that will do it—no matter how much President Wilson tries to get the belligerents to negotiate a peace. We lucked out on that Mexican mess lately.

Nineteen sixteen, an election year, has a strange mix. The Progressive Party nominates Theodore Roosevelt, but he turns it down. Roosevelt then supports his old friend Hughes, but Wilson will likely get it. So far, he has avoided actual war. And he tries diligently to get Germany to accept a negotiated peace.

Spring is here, and the ranchers are getting ready to take care of their hay crops.

The last half of June can be an exciting time. The hay crew comes to our place. Able to do all kinds of work, the Indian boys and young men are eager to work with a hay crew. They try to outdo each other it

seems. There are a mowing machine, hay rakes, and a new kind of rig called a bull rake which picks up windrows of hay and drives up to the stack and shoves it onto the stacker rig and backs off. Then the stacker is raised by a pulley with a rope hitched to a horse which walks steadily pulling the stacker up over the stack and the hay slides off onto the stack.

In August after the hay is all stacked and the herd is up on the Harrison Basin. It is the time to have visitors this August. Our guests are Dr. Howard and Mrs. Effie Bateman. He says he has to get completely away every once in awhile to get a rest.

August is quiet time for me. I take most of the month off to pay attention to my ranch and family. Bateman brought a tent along.

"Kenck, I hear you have guests and patients coming up here to the ranch for your services. So, Effie and I thought we better come prepared."

"That's a fact. We've had tents pitched near our house."

"We brought some grub too, and Effie plans to help in the kitchen."

"We really appreciate your coming and your food and help. We have Mama Auchard with us all the time now. She and Rita are pretty busy in the kitchen."

"Yeah, I read in the paper when Richard Auchard died. I surmised, of course, you folks would make a home for his wife."

"If anything can help her over her grief, it will be living with Rita and the boys. She's happiest when they are around her.

The second day the Batemans are with us one of the Pocha boys came running in all out of breath.

"Mister Doctor! Old Indian John, he die! He die! On trail from the mountain. Dad not know what to do!"

I tell the boy, "I will come."

"Well, Howard Bateman, now you can see how my charity work is always lurking around. I'll tell the ladies we have to go to the Indian camp. Indian people are terribly superstitious, and especially about a dead body. They will probably be scared until we get the body all prepared for burial.

Bateman says, "Let's do a postmortem to see the cause of death."

"Well, if you want to, we sure can. When I embalm, they don't stick around so they won't know."

We get the body into an empty shed by the farm and take the time for this extra. Looking at the heart of this old man we couldn't understand why he lived. It was as hard as rock with calcification type material lining the chambers of the heart.

Bateman says, "Do you suppose we could replace the weight of it with something? I'd like to send this to my college path instructor. He would like to add such a thing to his human condition studies.

"I told him that we could replace it with something, I'm sure.

"Howard, I gotta tell about one situation with these folk who are hiding from authority. One time the Indian—dead and after I'd prepared him for the funeral and he is laying in the casket—the Indians keeping vigil like they usually do, all night—the body began to swell. It's hot weather. He's getting bigger and bigger, and the Indians are really beginning to become alarmed. One suggested that they call me back. They are really scared. They had put the lid on the casket, but it was rising up. They say 'He want out of there! Him come to life!'

"I tell them, 'No, no, hot, hot weather make him swell up. He's not alive.' Their eyes wide with fear, 'Mister Doctor, tell him no come back, too sick, too old.' I tell them, 'He got air in stomach. He still dead. I fix.' So, I make the air come out.

"However, if they find out that a part of this body is missing, they will shy away from asking me to help them bury their dead."

"Well, Kenck, we'll make a neat stitch and if they suspect something is missing, they will not know what."

So we go ahead and finish the postmortem. Bateman puts the heart into a big jar of formaldehyde. Next day the Batemans go home. He figures he has had a good break away from his practice.

CHAPTER 53

YOUNG MEN LEAVE FOR WAR

It's near the end of March, and finally I'm able to grab Tommy and Gyp and head for the ranch. They snort and jump around as though they know where we are headed, and of course they do. "Dad, Dad, at last!" both sons exclaim at once. Greetings like this tell me we had better make the move to town and live closer together. Pretty soon our sons will be grown and fly the coop.

"Rita," I say later after we are settled for the night, "I know what we shall do."

"I could guess, but tell me so I can see if I'm right."

"Rita, my good wife," and I hug her, "after all these years I know your thoughts are way ahead of mine."

"We will rent a house and move to town this fall. I know a house right near the hotel that will be empty that we can rent or buy."

"Oh, Oscar! Moving into town and being together. That's what I've been wanting lately. I miss you so, especially these long winter evenings.

"That settles it. I need you with me every day and every night. I think it's time we go to bed. Aye what?"

Actually I was going to suggest that we should go on a pack trip after the haying is done come summer, but this will do for now.

After this last storm and a Chinook wind helped clear the road, I get myself back to town to take care of all those who need a tooth pulled or filled. But somehow I have a peaceful feeling about the future, like it will be a bit closer to my good wife and I can see and be closer to my little guys. Life is too short and I don't want to miss any more than I have to.

⚬

I'm home again the next Friday and bring all the things that Rita said we are getting short of, like yeast. She and Mama Auchard bake twenty loaves of bread every week. Amazing how much bread a couple growing boys can eat.

"Rita, I never finished telling you last week my idea of what we should do next summer after the branding and haying is finished."

"Honest, Oscar, I have no idea this time."

"It will help us all about leaving this place we've worked so hard for."

"What kind of help do you have in mind?"

"I've been wanting to take a pack trip back to Wood Lake and Benchmark to check on the descendants of the fingerlings I planted in Ford Creek there in 1903."

Dick hears the words "pack trip."

"Hey, Dad, did I hear right? A pack trip?"

"Exactly, but not until we get the cattle up to the Basin and the haying done."

Dick runs upstairs to tell his little brother.

"Ya know what? We get to go on a pack trip again this next summer!"

"Honest? I'm gonna ask Dad. You try fooling me lots a times. Dad! Dad!" We hear Oscar all the way down the stairs.

"Are we really going on a pack trip again next summer?"

"That's correct as far as we know now."

"Where?

"We want to check on the fish in Wood Lake and I want to show you the Goat Rocks where I did my first hunting trip."

"Dad, will I be able to go if I get some bum lambs to raise too?"

"Oh sure, do like I do when I can't do the job myself. Hire one of the Pocha boys to feed them while we are gone."

"Okay, Dad. Do I have to use my own money?"

"Sure, that's your business, Oscar, so that's your

expense."

"I'll give him one of the lambs, not money."

"You are related to Uncle Will, I can tell."

"Yeah, he gives us animals, not money."

"That's a good idea. We have lots of time to plan. We can't go till the last of July."

It is now the end of March 1917 and we read in the newspapers that Germany's Kaiser Wilhelm has decided to take France, and his mighty army can capture that country. England is determined to keep him from doing that because she will be next.

We will be neutral, but we also see England will need our supplies. Can we do this and remain neutral?

Our rational thinking tells us "No." President Wilson assures he will try to stay neutral so our supply ships openly sail into English ports. Germany promises not to sink our ships if we paint them with red and white stripes and dock only on Sundays and depart by Wednesday.

Sounds utterly ridiculous, and of course it is. Before long our ships are being sunk by German U-boats. How naive we've become—absolute sitting ducks.

By April 1, we know we have become the fools for sure. Wilson realizes it's useless to deal with the Kaiser and asks Congress to declare a state of war with Germany. Russia has now surrendered to Germany, so we know the Kaiser will have all the more troops to capture France. We are forced to enter in order to end this war.

Even though our famous woman representative in Congress, Janet Rankin, dramatically opposes war and faints on the House floor, the vote is 373 yea to 50 nay following the Senate vote with only six negatives.

The young men around our county will know they are subject to the draft.

So, the day I finally get through the bad roads into town, Bing comes in and tells me, "This is it. We will have to go. I'm going to enlist so I can get the Branch I want."

"Good idea. I want you to tell the fellows you mentioned, who might be enlisting, that I will be glad to take care of their teeth before they go so they will not have the misery of a toothache while they are in the service. Will you do that?"

"Sure, Doc, that's real good of you. I'll send them in."

"How soon do you think you will be enlisting?"

"I'm not exactly sure yet, probably after the haying, toward the end of summer."

"I plan on being back in the mountains the last half of July so tell them to come as soon as they can."

"Okay, I will do that. Gotta get back to the store."

A few days hence Hal Parsons, Minnie Cottle's husband, stops in.

"Howdy, long time no see, Hal. How are you and your little family doing?"

"I can't say everything is fine. I've decided to reenlist in the Navy. I'll get in at officer level probably. Minnie is dead set against it, so she wrote her folks to come out to the place and get her so she is at her folks' place."

"That's strange, most wives are proud if their husbands become officers."

"She agreed to come with me to the Falls to have our family picture taken tomorrow. We will take the train. I'm going to try to persuade her that I should go back into the Navy."

"One thing we now know is that we are going to have to fight this war whether we want to or not. By the way, Hal, before you go, well, right now, let me have a look at your teeth. I want to take care of the teeth of all the local fellows who are going to enlist. I don't want any of the service men to be having a toothache while they are risking their lives for our country."

"Okay, let's take a look and see and if something needs to be done. I will come in when we come back from the Falls next week. I know they need cleaning and one tells me something when I take a cold drink."

"That settles it. Come in next week."

The month of April is half gone. Time to get the cattle together with the other ranchers around and brand the calves. They bawl around for a few days, but the comfort of their mothers' milk helps them get over the trauma. Then they are happy and frolicking around in the spring sun. Also, they are ready for their journey up to their summer pasture in the Basin. Dan Gervais will take Dick along and show him how to pack the salt up there and where to put the blocks like I did last year. Of course, the cattle will find it and so will the elk. Now we keep watching the weather, hoping for rain to get a good hay crop in the meadows.

Dan and the Pocha boys will get the mowing machines ready, and the hay rakes and the hay wagon need grease and repair. Warm weather brings Dick's trapping season to an end. His traps all hang in a row on the back side of the barn. Most of the help is now with the fishponds. He and Oscar help me build a fish-feeding bin out of chicken wire and make a rack to support it in the middle of the pond. Now we can feed the fish with rabbit carcasses and meat scrapings that produce maggots that will drop into the pond— yummy food for the fish.

"Rita, I think it's high time we stir up that party we promised to give the Fisher family."

"Definitely, Oscar. I've been thinking along those lines and knew you would be too."

"I'll try for next Sunday, because we cannot suggest such a thing and not go through with it."

Right away the next Monday I stop at George's drug store. "Howdy, George. I think and I hope the party we threatened to give you folks last fall will finally come to pass and we plan for it to be next Sunday. Will that be okay with you and, above all, your good wife?"

"As far as I know, Doc, I'll tell her about it, and if she has other important plans, I'll let you know right away."

Later in the afternoon I heard from George. All is "go ahead" so I call Rita and tell her. So, it shall be on the next Sunday of April. Reluctant, Dick and Oscar complain, so we compromise. "You kids can stay at Uncle Will's while we and Grandma can go to church and then the party at the Fishers."

They punch each other's arms in anticipation. "Don't get too happy yet; we have to ask Uncle Will first."

"Oh, Dad, you know he will let us stay there. He might be shoeing a horse and will let us help or something. Anyway, I like to watch the sparks fly all around."

"Yeah, Oscar, you know pretty much Uncle Will's doings."

The kids are right. Will is usually at the barn in the corral teaching a young colt to get used to a halter, and that's where he is when I stop by on my way home that afternoon. Having the boys stay over for the afternoon will be no trouble at all.

When we drop off the boys, we are welcomed into the house by Miss Messenger. Mother Auchard seems really pleased to see her old home so clean and tidy just like she herself used to make it. Then off we go to church where we see old friends and, of course, Rita is asked to play the organ as she always used to do.

Many folk are pleased to see us there together. Rita has been pretty much staying at home since she had the boys. People ask about them. We have to explain they like to visit with their Uncle Will so we let them stay there for the day. We all gather the food and gifts and walk up the street past the Tomlinsons' place, the Converse house, and arrive at the new house built near the Walrath place. Surprise! George has been busy. He built a footbridge across the ditch that runs in front of the house (actually Eberle's irrigation ditch that runs through several front yards in town) and look at that! He added a water wheel to the ditch. We get to the front porch and George comes out. I say, "George, you have been a busy man. What in the world are you doing with a water wheel?"

"Well, it's like this. I cannot do everything like you, a house in town and a ranch at the same time, but I can have a garden and that way it'll get watered. I talked to Mr. Eberle and he thought it was a splendid idea. Besides, my missus wanted one here since we had a little stream to show off." All the ladies with us ooo'd and aaah'd about the water wheel.

The ladies got busy after we were shown all around the house and got sandwiches and cookies they brought ready on little plates and passed the coffee and tea around. The talk was really buzzing, and the two little blonde Fisher girls, Virginia and Georgia, were pleased to pass the sandwiches again. After about an hour of catching up on all the news of the families and neighbors, we decided to make motions about going home. Actually, we didn't want to leave Oscar and Dick to bother Uncle Will too much.

When we get to the ranch, Miss Messenger invites us in for awhile. Inside she says, "I know you folks have had sandwiches and cookies so I have made for you a big kettle of soup, which should keep you going for your ride home."

The beef barley soup and the fresh bread were just the right thing before the journey home. The boys were bundled up in the back and drifted off to sleep by the time we passed the Chisholm place.

At home, I asked the boys, "What did you and Uncle Will do?"

Oscar immediately raised his fist and exclaimed as he pounded on Dick, "I'm going to tell about it this time, not you."

"Okay, okay, Oscar," I say. "Dick will let you tell it."

"It's a colt, I rode him around the corral. He's already broke, and I did it too. Uncle Will told me so. He's a bay. That means he's in between brown and red. He is so pretty. Uncle Will says we'll call him Babe, because he is a bay. Someday when I get big I'm going to raise horses. Right now all I can take care of is lambs."

"Oscar, I'm sure you will raise horses and cattle too. You have a special way with all animals."

"Yeah, Dad, Uncle Will told me that very same thing."

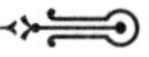

Just before spring roundup of the cattle on this end of Lewis and Clark, I begin to think ahead to the pack trip I promised the kids and decided I must see Ballie Buck and tell him we are likely to go by his outfit on our way to Benchmark. As I am thinking, this young Tot Nett (strange nickname for such a tough looking cowboy) comes in to my office.

"Howdy, Doc," he says. "Bing Wellman told me you wanted to see all us guys who are going to volunteer for the draft so we could get our teeth taken care of before we enlist."

"That's right. I did. So, I'm glad to see you for that and also I want you to tell Ballie that I'd like to talk to him the next time he comes to town."

"Sure, I'll tell him but he is in town today so you will see him today."

"Good. Now, Tot, let's look at your teeth and see what needs to be taken care of."

"One thing I do know is there're a couple that need attention. They told me so."

"You are right—two molars need fillings and then a cleaning. Also, I'm going to tell you how to brush your teeth. Most people don't really know. They think a person just needs to scrub the surface but that is only part of it."

"Okay, Doc. You are right. No one taught me anything. Just gave me a tooth brush."

"I'm going to take care of the worst decayed molar and then clean your teeth. The next time you come in I will do the other cavity and see how your gums are doing after your lesson."

"Okay, I'll see Ballie down at the pool hall and tell him you want to talk."

Before long it happens. The big man with the cowboy hat appears at my door.

"My man told me you wanted to talk."

"Yes, after we get done haying, Rita and the boys and I plan on taking a pack trip up Ford Creek, at least as far as Benchmark. We'll be passing by your place. Figure it will take us about one day to reach the LF. Would it be okay with you for us to make camp near the creek there?"

"Kenck, you know very well we would be so happy to have you come by, and by all means spend the night or more. Myrtle gets lonely to see a lady friend. Please do come and stay with us in the house and put your horses in our corral."

"There is a good reason to go up Ford Creek as far as Benchmark and maybe a day or so farther."

"A person shouldn't need a reason but what is it?"

"About sixteen years ago some other fellows and I, with the help of the forest ranger, got several barrels of fingerlings from the fish hatchery in Bozeman, and by a long tedious journey got them to Wood Lake and the

Benchmark area and planted them. I haven't been back for a long time to check on them to see how their descendants are doing."

"Well I'll be! It's high time you are checking on them. Besides stopping on the way in you must stop on the way out and tell us how the little fish are getting on. By the way, why did you plant all those baby fish?"

"I was in that country on my very first hunt and found no fish and learned from the old-time packer that the fish couldn't jump the falls of that branch of the Sun River. So, I talked it up with Judge Mayer, the forest ranger, and a couple others, and we soldered five-gallon cans together and packed them on horses with the fingerlings sloshing in the water in the cans. After we got them by wagon to Ford Creek, it was a job lashing those cans to packhorses for the final approach."

"Wow, that was a huge job. I hope the fish are still doing well and you have some fine eating up there. Very soon now the LF Ranch will be getting ready for the spring roundup. Nothing like the roundup in Alberta but a real job for a small outfit. A lot of getting ready. I always do this the last week of April so we can put the cows and calves on summer pasture after the calves have had a chance to recover from the branding and castration. Then haying begins. Good thing we found a good cook. A gal named Edith Fender and her husband will do the cooking and the chores. He's kinda sickly but able to do that. Main thing is she can really cook and Myrtle doesn't have to always be in the kitchen."

"I'll no doubt see you at a Masonic meeting one time before the last week in July."

"Sure thing, Kenck. See you then."

It's Friday and time to get out of here, but first the list for Rita and the mail. I see Bud Tomlinson in the post office. He agrees we had a nice party for the Fishers. He says he likes George for a neighbor and their ladies are getting to be good friends. Talking to Clarence (Manix), he says, "We can't do anything about getting the railroad extended to Augusta until the war is over, but my plan will work then either in the Legislature or the Supreme Court of Montana."

The rest of April we work with our cattle and get them headed to their summer pasture in the Harrison Basin and get set to cut and stack hay in the meadows. This year Dick will be big enough to handle a rake by himself and Oscar, on Cerise, the stacker horse. The Gervais boys and the Pochas do the mowing. It's a busy time. Rita and Grandma, with the Pocha girls, help with lots of cooking. When it is over we take a breather and make plans for our pack trip back to Benchmark and the South Fork of the North Fork of Sun River.

It's getting close to the end of July. We have a week to get our packs ready. I make a list of supplies to take. Several things I have to pick up in town. Also, need to put the note on my door that I'll be back in the office in mid-August.

As I collect all the stuff on my list, J.C. says, "Doc, too bad there isn't a cabin there at Benchmark. Then that could be a base for trips in lots of directions back in those rugged hills."

"J.C., you've got an idea there worth some serious thought. You'll hear from me about that later." Sometime I'll plant that idea in the kids' thinking. Now we can look at all our gear to see if we have everything to keep us going for a week in the mountains.

"Yeah, Dad, I remember last year we forgot pancake syrup. I'll make sure about that this time. Oh another thing so very important is matches. We had enough but barely."

"We have to see that all horses are shod too."

"This is how we will spread the jobs. Dick, you are the one to see to the packsaddles and pack boxes, Oscar, you will take care of the horse feed, saddle blankets, halters and hobbles. Rita, Mother, you will do what you do so very well, by seeing to our food boxes and cooking supplies. I will gather up all the loose ends like bedrolls and anything else that is missing.

"Oh, already I'm not getting the most important thing—fishing poles and tackle. I'm making a master list just in case something important is not left behind."

"Yeah, Dad, like the syrup."

"Dick, you make sure on that one so we don't have to sprinkle sugar on the hot cakes."

CHAPTER 54

THE FAMILY TAKES A TRIP TO BENCHMARK

On July 20 everything is "go." Grandma Auchard has her friend to stay with her and the boys to do any chores they need. We are strung out—four riders and four packhorses with Cerise in the lead. We follow the wagon trail along the skirt of Haystack Butte from the backside to the northwest side. At the rock quarry in Swallow Canyon we stop and eat our lunch Mother has packed in her saddlebag. A drink for us and the horses at the little creek and we are on the way again. A while longer we skirt the butte and come down toward the ranch buildings of the J.B. Long place. Their dogs spot us and two riders come towards us. Well I'll be! I soon see it is Mr. and Mrs. Buck. What a welcome we get!

"Well, well, at last you got here. Myrtle and I have been watching for you for several days. Every time the dogs barked we made a dash for our horses. We've kept them at the ready every afternoon."

"We didn't expect such a royal welcome."

"Come along. We will put your horses in the corral and relieve them of their packs and saddles."

We are expected to stay overnight. I am thinking that we might make it over the next hill to Ford Creek and camp there for the night. Bucks will not hear of it. I realize it is too late in the day anyway. Dick and Oscar get busy with the horses while we older folks watch. They are proud to show the Bucks that they know just how to unload and take care of the horses.

Ballie asks, "How in the world did you have time to teach them to do all that?"

"I have to admit they have had many teachers. Will Auchard, their uncle, is a horseman from way back, and Oscar is almost a carbon copy of him about horses. Of course, the Indian boys who help us all the time are excellent horsemen."

Myrtle and Rita walk towards the house while we talk by the corral. Ballie says, "Do you s'pose the boys would like to put up a tent down by the creek and sleep in their bedrolls there tonight? When Charlie Russell comes up from the Falls, he always sleeps by the creek. Says he likes the sound of the water all night long."

"Of course. They like to camp out any time. At home they often camp out a ways from the house. It's their very favorite pastime. That way they will be on their camping trip from the beginning.

"Hey, you kids, Mr. Buck wants to know if you want to camp down by the creek over there."

Both at once, "Yeah, Dad. We'll get our bedrolls and tent and make our camp ready. Can we cook too?"

Ballie speaks up, "Our good cook has a very special supper ready, and she can make the very best pancakes."

"Okay, Mr. Buck, pancakes are the favorite breakfast."

Supper is a real feast of fried chicken and lemon pie.

And yes, Mrs. Fender, the new cook, can really make some tasty supper!

Next morn early after breakfast with the Bucks and their crew—one I know well, Tot Nett, a patient of mine lately—we get our pack string and riding horses lined out and point ourselves over the hill to Ford Creek.

The Bucks are a true example of the code of the West. Need I say more? We won't forget they want us to stop on our way back out next week. Soon we go down the slope into the area called Ford Creek Forest Range pack station. Wagons are left here because the road goes no farther. Everything needed in the back country is loaded on packhorses here. The wagons just sit and wait for riders to come back out—like hunters with game and summer cattle herders to get salt and supplies.

We see a couple wagons by the supply shed, so we know there are others on the trail ahead of us.

The trail now runs alongside of Ford Creek. Soon we come to a place called "The Stairs." It is a rock hillside that has to be surmounted by our horses and us. I tell the kids how we had to use a special block and tackle to get our horses loaded with those fingerling fish cans up. It was November and kinda slippery from recent snow and freezing. It took the better part of a day to get those horses with their packs up so we made camp soon after the top. Today we have no trouble—thanks to our wonder horse, Cerise. She immediately moved to the side and started on the zigzag path that has been chiseled into that stone hill and, without hesitating, made her way to the top. Then she looked back and seemed to say, "That's the way; come on up." Then she turned to go on along the trail above.

Oscar says, "Dad, I knew she would know how. I've had her climb over rock places lots of times. She can climb places harder than that." We followed and rearranged the line-up.

At the place we had camped long ago, I explained how we had laid the cans of fingerlings in the creek above these falls to give them fresh water and air for the night.

After we eat our lunch Edith Fender had made for us, we decide that we will get to Wood Lake and throw in our fishing lines to check on the descendants of that long-ago planting of fish.

Dick and Oscar are in the lead now. Like kids they are curious about what's next. Dick calls back, "How far is that lake?"

"Not very far. We will be camping there."

At last the lake—a beautiful gem here in this valley between two mountains. I see fish jumping! We make no talk so they won't know we are here. We get poles out and in no time we have our lines in the water. Whoops! Every time, there's a fish, and a good-sized one too. In minutes we have eight and that's enough. The rest can live another day. These trout are feisty and plump. The planting remains a huge success!

We lead our horses a short way where we unload

and set up camp. I can see Dick and Oscar remember the process well. They know this is a pack trip for real and they perform. Rita is the one who rewards for good work. She is careful to stow away special goodies for all trips, whether just to town or a pack trip. This time it is little fold-over pies. My part is to make sure they thank her nicely for all she does for them.

The tents are up, the saddle bags of supplies are covered with the tarp, and the horses are hobbled so they won't decide to head for home during the night. We crawl into our bedrolls and drift off to sleep listening to the sounds of the mountains. Wood Creek that feeds the lake ripples a pleasant song.

Hot cakes with syrup and fish make a good breakfast. It doesn't take long to get our outfit all packed and on the trail again. After an hour on the trail we come to a another creek.

"This too is a place where some fingerlings got planted. It's called Benchmark."

"Why, Dad?" They both ask at once.

"Over there," and I point to a cleared spot, "is where the United States survey crew put a mark when they measured the area back when it was called the Montana Territory. It's still there if you know what to look for."

"Like what?" Dick asks.

"Long ago it was a charred post with a metal badge with U.S. and a number stamped in it."

"How long ago do you s'pose this post was put here?"

"If I researched or asked the ranger, he might be able to tell me. I do know that the survey was done after the Lewis and Clark expedition and probably after the treaty that established the Canadian boundary."

"Gee, Dad, guess I will have to study my history in school. Maybe I will find out some important facts about this place."

Oscar, who is interested in the future, speaks up. "Dad, I think there should be a cabin here so we could stay longer when we come up here during the summer and hunting season."

"Oscar, you are the guy that plans ahead. Next time we see the forest ranger we can ask about that."

"Okay, Dad, I'm not going to let you forget it. They

won't pay attention to me—not yet—but someday they will."

"Now we tell Mother we are going to fish a little to see how the trout I planted here in the South Fork of the Sun River are doing."

Dick chimes in, "Mom says she is going to see how the huckleberries are around here. She wants to put them in the pancakes if she finds some."

When we get together later for our fish dinner, I tell Rita about Oscar's idea of putting a cabin right here so people would have a place to camp summers and hunting season.

She says, "Oscar is a planner for the future."

"I agree, so let's plan for tomorrow. Let's take two trips farther into the mountains this time."

"Where, Dad?" Dick asks.

"First, the Goat Rocks area where I just about didn't make it out and then the Chinese Wall, which is awesome to look at." After this planning for the far future and the near future, we crawled into our bedrolls for the night.

Up at daylight we take off for the Goat Rocks. Dick

Pack trip to the Chinese Wall

takes a long look at this rocky mountain and says, "You must have been good at climbing those days. Could you climb that now?"

"Maybe, but it would take me too long. Also, there was snow on that mountain then."

"All right, I'll keep quiet so you can tell us the dangerous part where you almost didn't make it."

"See that ledge across that gully on the right side? There was a goat there. But snow was a big problem.

The wind had blown it into a big shelf on the west side above where the goats were so I crawled out on the edge of the snow—didn't realize it was just a snow shelf. I was lying on my stomach and was setting my sight to shoot a goat. I heard my friends shouting. 'Doc, Doc, don't shoot. Don't move either. You are in danger. Lie still.' Pretty soon I felt them get ahold of both my ankles, and they started to pull me backward on my stomach. Pretty soon they said, 'Now you can stand up. You were going to fall tumbling down this cliff. You would have been killed on the rocks.'"

Ballie and Myrtle Buck welcome us back with, "We expected you yesterday."

"Yes, we are a day late getting back. It was farther to the Chinese Wall than we thought. We might make it home tonight."

"Doc, you can do no such thing. We have planned that you will stay over with us. Myrtle has prepared special for you folks. So, now just let your poor horses get rid of their saddles and gear and have a good rest in our horse pasture."

We suddenly realize how tired we are. The supper is wonderful. Also, we are able to clean ourselves up and sleep in a bed. And the boys go for a splash in the creek and sleep again in their tent down on the creek bank.

Next day, the final leg home and find Grandma and a little Pocha girl having a good time with their sewing and knitting.

August, 1917

Back in town again to catch up on patients that have been waiting for dental work.

First thing, I go for the mail. I stop to talk to J.C. and tell him about being at Benchmark and how my Oscar said it would be a good place for a cabin for people to use in summer and hunting.

"Doc, you have a kid who really thinks about the future."

"Thanks, and it's a good idea. I'm going to give it serious thought. One reason is that Rita and I are seriously considering moving to town, and if that happens I will have to either get a manager for my ranch or get out of the business altogether. The price of cattle is so very low that to hire a manager it would probably cost more than I make so I will sell the place."

"After all the work and money you have put into the place, it's a shame to have to sell."

"Right now, I know, we've got to move in town by next year; Dick will be ready for high school. Besides, this past winter Rita and I spent most of the time apart. Snow and bad roads made it just plain lonely for both of us."

"What you gotta do, you gotta do."

"If you hear of a house, let me know. I'm beginning to look for one."

Bud says, when I appear before his post office window, "Doc you been playin' hooky and your mail has been piling up. Here, I put it all in this sack. Where have you been for the past ten days?"

"Rita, the boys, and I went on a pack trip back as far as the Chinese Wall. That is the thing to do in summer. Not in the winter."

"How was the fishing back there?"

"Absolutely great. With extreme satisfaction every time I threw my line in the South Fork of the Sun River, I would get a nice one. It was sweet pay-back for all my work of planting fish there fourteen years ago."

"This post office job is good and steady but not easy to take some time off. Someday I plan to retire, and then I want to move to the Bitterroot and have an apple orchard."

"I hope you get to do that. But right now I'm glad you are the Augusta postmaster. So long, Bud, I've got plenty of work waiting for me."

I set the mail aside right after I unlock my office door. Bing Wellman has followed me in. "Doc, I was hoping you would come in today. Tomorrow's the big day. Me and some other guys are leaving for Salt Lake City. The recruiting officer finally sent our train passes, but I need you to fix that cavity."

"Who else besides you is leaving tomorrow?"

"Tot and Benny. The three of us will go tomorrow. Harold Brusgard and Hal Parsons left last week. I can hardly wait."

"Well, Bing, the war will wait for you. Sit right there in the chair and let me finish the last of your fillings before you go." The filling goes fast. At least his teeth won't give him any trouble in combat. I'm glad to do anything I can to help out with our boys going overseas.

After Bing leaves, I then turn to my bundle of mail. The biggest part is the Helena newspaper. Each day's paper is a small roll.

Fall 1917

It's time to get the cattle down from the Harrison Basin to join the other ranchers of the Dearborn for the branding of any we missed last spring. Also, now we will sell some critters, especially the older cows.

One by one the young men of our area find their way in to tell me they are leaving. I read in the news the French people are excited to see them, but the French and English generals will not let our General Pershing have any say in strategy, even though they are in a stalemate with the enemy. The United States is able to get thousands of men to France in ships by using the convoy method to guard against German U-boats.

Before Christmas most of the boys who are willing to enlist are gone. This is a tough time for some families. Here in Augusta, to help ease the worry and loneliness, the ladies start knitting clubs—socks for soldiers and another club to roll bandages. I am asked to teach a first-aid course. Seems like the idea is to keep everyone busy, and that's not all. The government wants to borrow our money so the sale of Liberty War Bonds is added to my duties, which already include dentistry, sometimes obstetrics, emergency doctor, and funeral director. I might list a few more of my duties but shall not because it would look like I feel sorry for myself and I don't. I do all these things because I want to.

Rita and I now consider all these things and know that we will go ahead with the change we mentioned a while back. Next year, 1918, we will definitely move into Augusta.

We spend our last Christmas at the ranch. Dick doesn't want to talk about it. Neither does Oscar, who complains the loudest.

"Dad, I won't be able to raise my bum lambs if we move to town. Grandma and I can stay here. I can take care of the milk cow and my horses right here."

Rita steps in to reason with him. "No, my son, we would not think of leaving you here. We want both of you with us. We would miss you too much."

Oscar heaves a big sigh and puts his head into his hands. "Life is just plain tough."

Next week I stop at Ole Bean's. "Kenck," Ole says, "You have good trip last summer? How are the fish at Benchmark?"

"Yes, we had all the fish we could cook and eat. I saw that all my trouble in planting those fingerlings has really paid off. Soon as we got to Wood Lake we saw plenty of fish jumping, so every time we threw our lines in we got a nice one. We stopped at the LF Ranch both going in and coming out. Ballie Buck runs that ranch now. We knew each other in Helena when we both were kids. He told me that he helped Guy Weadick put on the first Calgary stampede. He's talking about helping put on a stampede here in Gilman or Augusta soon as some of the cowboys come home from the war."

"Vell, I got a few bucking ones he could use. I don't ride no more like I used to."

"Good. I'll tell Ballie the next time I see him. Ole, have you heard anything from your boy in Europe?"

"Oh, ya, one letter from France, but ve don't know vere dey are."

Ole is right. From our boys over there we hear very little. The newspapers are the only way. We know that route is not reality most of the time. Back to work at my office.

CHAPTER 55

THE INFLUENZA EPIDEMIC—1918

First month of the year I see J.C. Manix. "Kenck, I just heard of a house that will be empty soon. The folks that live in it plan to leave."

"Where is it?"

"Across the street from the young Barnards."

"The location is okay. I want to be close in. Who owns it?"

"I'm not sure. Ask Tony."

"That's too bad about Dick Adams. He's sure sick."

"No matter how he feels, he will drive the stage. I hope it's not pneumonia."

Later, George Fisher tells me there is a contagious and serious sickness going around. They say it was first in Spain. A killer type of influenza. Many in the cities are dying.

We are in the country; I hope it doesn't come here.

This very night I am with Dick. Vic and I take turns trying to get his fever down. Then his lungs fill up and he can't breathe and the fever will not go down. So very hard to see a good friend get worse and I can't stop it.

The next morning I talk with Fisher again. He says, "This killer flu has finally reached this town. I am going to get another supply of quinine and eucalyptus oils for rubs, vapors, and poultices. They help and sometimes work, I hear from the drug companies."

Early the next morning quick steps come up my office stairs. It's Floyd Barnard.

"Doc, it's my dad. He hurt his hand yesterday, but now he's got a red streak up his arm and he is hot and burning."

While I grab my bag, I tell him to get a fire going to get hot water, lots of it. I get right down there and I find an advanced case of blood poisoning. All day long I keep hot wet packs and carbolic drawing salve on Will Barnard's hand and also give him aspirin. By the end of the day, I haven't succeeded. He has become delirious and I can't get the fever down. I ask his wife, "Lottie, when did this happen?"

"I told him to get up to your office because his hand looked real bad. He just said, 'Stop worrying, it'll be all right.'"

"Lottie, I'm sure sorry, but he's not going to pull through. The poison has reached his heart."

She threw her arms around him and sobbed, "Will, don't leave me!"

By that time he could not hear nor respond.

Times like this I wished I would know more about the ills of man.

Will Barnard's funeral is on a cold and stormy day.

We bring the casket from church to the graveyard on the hill just north of town. We don't tarry long but gather with the family and friends. We mourn for each other the loss of such a good friend.

In the fall, the mortuary association has decided that I should have the instruments for embalming because in bad weather it would help them. Next time I'm in the Falls they want me to come in and they will give me the kit and the instructions I need.

The news is full of accounts of the many deaths in the towns and cities across America and of all the things people are doing to try to keep the disease at bay. All gatherings are stopped as much as possible. Only families are to go to funerals and only at the graveside. Schools and colleges all shut down; all places where people congregate together are closed. This makes me think of the stories of the plagues of Europe and in past history on the earth.

Today is the first Friday in March. By noon I finish my last patient of the week. Even my practice is suffering from the idea that people should not gather in groups. They stay out of town unless absolutely necessary. First the store and then the post office. Bud Tomlinson is not very busy either.

"Doc, these are terrible times. People don't hang around and talk to each other. It's a lonely time. I never saw anything like this or heard of such. I sure hope it lets up soon. I'm worried about my brother."

"I know you are thinking about him. I'm also thinking of my brother in Helena. He could be at risk also. He is not so very well either. This flu seems be getting the healthy faster than the sickly though."

While I'm at the store picking up Rita's order, J.C. says, "This flu is fierce. I hear three people on the Dearborn have been taken with it."

"Who?"

"Young Mrs. Frank Thompson and a couple named Reddic. They had three boys."

Back to my office and I pick up all the work I want to take home and then back to the Nett stable to pick up the buggy. Nett has my fast team harnessed, Tommy and Gyp, and they are making "going home" noises. Away we go! No need to crack the whip. In fact I have to slow them down as I turn at the corner by the Mayer house. Out across the valley and then up over the hill and I am by the Converse and Douglas places by the South Fork of the Sun River. Now I turn in the log gate of the Cottle place. Through the bull pasture and then I must get out and undo the wire gate that is the entry to the John Cottle Ranch.

I must stop there. Ida Cottle is the half-sister of Rita. She has been failing for a long time. Lately she has been worse, and John came to my office to ask me to stop by and see her. Maybe I can think of something to help her.

I drive around and down the lane up to their house and tie Tommy and Gyp to the front gate. They are anxious to get home because they know where they are going. I tie them well so they can't take off without me. Just then John Cottle comes out of the house.

"Kenck, I have sad news. Ida died this morning. I sent Henry to town to call the funeral director from the Falls. They will come tomorrow to take care of everything and arrange for the funeral. They say they are so busy that they won't be able to have the funeral until next week." As we talk, Minnie comes out to the porch.

"Hello, Doctor. I was hoping you would stop on your way home today. The girls and I are staying here with Mama and Dad. It is sad to see Mama go, but she was miserable for a such a long time."

"I'm sorry about your mother. Rita will be sad to hear her sister Ida is gone. Emma went a long time ago. But Rita still has brother Will and her other sisters, Mina and Addie, and her brother Jay. I guess Rita being the littlest and last she was loved by all of them, and she loved them. If Rita can do anything about the funeral be sure and tell her. She will be there." I turn to go but decide to tell them, "I will come by on Monday to see what we can do about the funeral and all. You are our family and we want to help with anything that needs to be done."

My team jumps to start on the road again. Back through two gates and we are at steady running pace again. As I get close to the ranch I see the smoke coming out of the chimney. It's good to get home again. I begin to think about living in town. The ranch horses see and hear us and they make welcome sounds. The kids come running out to take the horses and buggy down to the shed. Just then I realize that Oscar is getting taller, almost as tall as Dick.

In the house I tell Rita the sad news. "Your sister Ida passed away this morning."

"That makes me sad, but I have noticed that every time I've seen her these past two years that she has looked like she was failing. When will she be buried?"

"John told me it's not certain. The mortuary is very busy. There have been a record number of deaths around here and they are having several funerals a day, so probably next week. I will stop by there on Monday when I go in and I will call you. If it is next week, I will come home and get you and Grandma."

"If you see John, will you please tell him that I would like to play at the funeral some songs on the organ that Ida liked. Also, I would like to have the minister read the Bible verses that she loved best."

"I hear that in the big cities only the immediate family can attend."

"I'm sure glad we don't live in a big city. I'm a country woman."

"Rita, if you are a country woman, I am a country man."

"Dad, we are country kids too," Dick chimes in. Oscar has to add his twist on this family agreement. "Besides being a country kid, I'm going to be a rancher."

"Yeah, Oscar, we can tell without even asking. The animals we have all know who is the boss."

"One day next week you kids will be in charge here. Mother, Grandma, and I have to go to a funeral. Your Aunt Ida died and we have to go and help with the arrangements."

Dick speaks up. "Whose mother is she?"

Rita explains, "She is the mother of all those girl cousins and one boy that are the Cottle kids. But really, they are grownups now."

Oscar asks, "Do you mean all those cousins are relatives of ours?"

Rita explains, "Yes. All those cousins that are relatives to me are relatives of yours too."

Oscar scratches his head and says, "Gee whiz, I guess I'm stuck."

Rita says, "Don't feel so badly, Oscar. They are stuck with you too. The funeral for Ida will probably be Monday or Tuesday, and you kids will be in school."

On Tuesday next, the Cottles that live around Augusta gather at the church. The Methodist minister from Great Falls is there, but he must leave immediately for another Service in Ft. Shaw. Ida's daughters—May, Minnie, and Susie—and son Henry are here. Rita plays the songs her sister loved, and our families drive their buggies behind the hearse to the graveyard on the hill. The cold winter wind blows the words of the minister toward the snow-covered Sawtooth. We supply our own comforting words from the Spirit. Will Auchard, Ida's brother, asks us to stop at his ranch before our journey home. Miss Messenger has coffee and sandwiches waiting for us.

Will Auchard

At home that night the kids are interested about their cousins. We tell them the names of the cousins who were there and that Uncle Will was one of them who helped with the casket.

"What is the casket?" Dick wants to know. So, I tell him about the wooden box that we put people who die in to bury them.

"Where do people get a casket?" Oscar wants to know.

"Smokey Eberle has that log store in Augusta. He sells all kinds of things and caskets are some of them. He keeps them upstairs at his store."

Oscar pipes up, "Dad, while you were gone we got two new calves!"

"Were you there when they were born?"

"I sure was and one cow had a bad time."

"What did you do about it?"

"She was lying down and really groaning and struggling. I saw the hind legs coming out. I knew she needed help. So, I ran and got Dan and together we pulled and pulled and finally got the calf out."

"Oscar, I can see more and more you are the man

who will have a cattle ranch because you already know what to do when a critter is in trouble."

"Dad, I remember what you said you had to do when the baby wouldn't come out so I knew she needed help."

In the March days that follow, many more calves are born, and I quit worrying about the cows having attention when they are calving. Oscar is my watchdog.

These cold winds of March make calving very risky. Freezing wind can chill and kill a calf. Thanks to Oscar for losing nary a one. He had Grandma wake him early every morning so he could make the rounds of the calving corral to see how every cow is doing. One calf he saw was too cold. Dick was just back from his trap line. He and Oscar took their wagon to the corral and brought the calf to the kitchen where Grandma had a fire going in the range. She put down an old piece of rug for it and rubbed it dry with old towels till it got up on its wobbly legs and began to look for its first breakfast.

Now, in the warmer days of April all the newborn calves are frisking and playing in the meadow. Towards the end of April my main man, Dan Gervais, with his boys and my kids work with the Bean families to run the Dearborn roundup.

With all the calls from flu cases, I have trouble getting home even on weekends. How long will this plague last? Even though I'm not a medic, many sick ones insist I come because our resident doctor is too busy and exhausted.

I read in the papers that thousands are dying in the cities in our country and all over the world. Also, it's double jeopardy for our boys in France. Two of our boys have so far been killed in battle action—Harold Brusgard and Ben Arps.

At last warmer weather has brought grass on the hills and pastures. The kids and I took a ride up to our Harrison Basin. The snows are melting and the salt blocks we laid out for the critters are helping.

Dick has one more term at the Clemons School by the lake. He will have to take the state board test in order to go to high school. The county superintendent will come and administer these tests. He is getting sorta worried now for fear he can't remember what he is supposed to know. Rita was a teacher before our marriage and has decided to help him study the basics. It's a stressful time for them both. Sometimes I get called in to help out.

The last two days of May are the dreaded days. Dick's usually happy face has taken on a worried look, so I decide to tell him about the exam I had to take to graduate from Dental College. "Yeah, Dad, tell me about them again."

"The final test at the college would be the thing that would decide if we students were going to get our licenses to be dentists."

"You must have passed 'cause you have been doing it for—how many years?"

"About twenty years now, I think."

"So, why did you worry?"

"There was another fellow also taking the test, and he had a bad time with tests because he is always so worried that he won't pass that his mind will go blank. During the test I looked at him and his face was as white as a sheet, and I could see the sweat standing out on his forehead. The professor was dozing, so this student quickly held up four fingers. I knew what he meant. So, when the professor picked up his magazine and began to read again, I knew what his problem was—a formula. I scribbled it on one of my papers and held it sorta sideways so he could see it. I knew he got it because he calmed down and went on with the test with no more trouble. When the graduation notices were sent out to us seniors, the blow fell. I didn't get a notice that I was to get ready for graduation. At that time I just sadly concluded that the professor had seen me."

"Gee, Dad. What did you do?"

"At the time I was really disappointed. I said nothing to anyone and began to think—what in the world shall I do now. Then I remembered about another student who had gone to that school and he couldn't get a diploma for some reason so he went to Africa and had been a dentist for several years there. That is what I could do also."

"Something must have happened because I never

heard of you going to Africa."

"You are right about that. The week before graduation was to take place a few of the other graduates started sorta whispering to one another about my attitude. Finally one of them said to me, 'Kenck, why are you so quiet these days? Aren't you excited about graduating and going back to Montana to practice dentistry?'

"I finally said, 'I'm not graduating.' They asked why not. 'The main reason is I didn't get a notice like I heard you fellows did.' They all said, 'There is no reason why you didn't get a notice to get ready to graduate.' I didn't say anything because I didn't want to tell on my friend who I had helped in the test. They decided to go to the president's office. To their question, 'Why didn't Kenck get a graduation notice,' he replied, 'of course he did. I made it out myself.' They reported to me of their find that I had been sent a letter of graduation. Result was they began to look to see what happened to that letter. Sure enough, they found it had slipped down behind the officer's desk. So, after all that, I rushed around and got myself ready to graduate. The lesson is that it's too bad for the guy who panics when it comes to testing, but I had no excuse and had to accept the consequence. I couldn't tell or blame him."

"Dad, you sure got a scare. I can't panic myself nor help someone else."

"Your mother and I will work with you to help you learn the stuff to pass the test."

Dick grins and says, "If the test could be about trapping, I wouldn't be worrying one bit."

Summer is at hand and we concentrate on getting as much hay into stacks as we can. Last year's hay was not enough so we will work hard and cut, rake, and stack every blade of grass possible. Some of the cattlepeople had to have swamp grass hay shipped from Minnesota last January. We know that we will get a weed crop from that stuff.

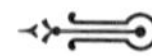

The war rages on in France, although the French and English generals have begun to respect our General Pershing's strategies. All the news of the war comes to us by the newspapers. Sometimes we hear the sayings of our boys, like: The first hundred years are the hardest. Also, the songs they are singing are like *Hinkey dinkey parlay voo, mademoiselle from Armatiers hasn't been kissed in forty years, you may forget the gas and shells, parlay voo, but you'll never forget mademoiselle.*

June 6, 1918: First participation of U.S. troops—27,500 infantry and marines attack German lines and recapture Vaux Bouresches and Belleau Wood by July 1. French name places don't tell us much but the word *recapture* certainly does. We know that when our boys enter the battles that words like that and *route* and *drive out* will appear more and more in the papers.

'Tis everyone's hope that the war will end soon and our boys can come home. However, the government keeps urging us to buy war bonds. As the one in charge locally, I'm amazed at the willingness of people to go without in order to help the war effort.

CHAPTER 56

MOVING TO AUGUSTA, THE WAR ENDS, INFLUENZA ABATES

The next time I am free enough to go to the ranch for the weekend I have good news to tell Rita. The Quinn house on Main will be available. At home after supper I say, "Rita, I have news about a house right in town. The Quinn house. What do you think of that?"

"I don't know what to say. I've not been in that house."

"My good wife, two things I assure you. One, it's only temporary. And, two, as soon as we can, we will build a house that suits you. I think for now I will keep my office in the hotel because in the back of my mind I want a building just for my office."

"I certainly agree and, of course, we will put that along with a decent house to live in also."

Oscar had been listening without a word until now.

"Every summer Dick and I will come out here and put up hay and keep this place going so we can come back here when we get out of high school."

"Oscar, you have good ideas, and we will decide about such things when we get to that place. You might have altogether different ideas when we get there."

"Dad, when Aukie (Dick's nickname for Oscar) makes up his mind, I almost have to beat him up to make him change it." For that, Oscar starts punching Dick, so Dick grabs both his hands and pins him to the floor."

Like usual, I have to stop the argument.

At the end of the summer I sell off most of the cows,

steers, and yearlings. Still kept our bulls—expect to sell to someone who needs new breeding stock. The hay we put up this summer will be stacked. If this next winter is like the last, we will get a good price for hay.

We get settled in the Quinn house. "Rita, my good wife, this is not the house I want for you, but for now I hope we can manage."

"Doctor, my dear husband, I can manage for now, but I know you have a better house in mind for us."

"I've got one in mind but not until I know for sure will I talk."

This year things are some better; we are encouraged about the war ending in Europe. Germany seems unable to stand against the Allies. Our troops, with the English, are holding the Germans from advancing to Paris. The influenza epidemic is not claiming as many lives, but even so, a valued local lady is taken, Mrs. Sam Larkin. We tried everything to no avail. She was such a fine lady. Poor Sam. We have learned ways to save people, and we must use all methods we know to save anyone who shows symptoms of the flu.

My mind runs ahead—across the street from this house is a piece of ground just right for a dental office. Next time I see Tony I'll tell him. In the meantime I'll think about the design. I know that the work window must face north—the best light for working in the mouth.

A few days later I see Clarence. He says, "Kenck, it begins to look like the war will soon be over. I'm going to see my lawyer to learn what kind of action I need to get the railroad to lay rails to Augusta."

"No doubt you already know just what that will be."

"Yeah, first see the State Railroad Commissioners and then I will know what else I can make happen. One thing is for sure: A.L. Bradley cannot and will not be able to bury Augusta."

It is fall, and Dick and Oscar spend time at Uncle Will's—Oscar helping with the horses and cattle. Yes, he has his Cerise, and Dick has his horse that Uncle Will gave him. Dick likes to work in the blacksmith shop getting shoes ready and his traps ready to use along the South Fork. They spend as much time as they can out there.

School for them is different and it shows. Oscar has very little to say, but Dick is complaining. He is really puzzled. From what he says, so am I. The teacher he has is really strange. She handed those few freshmen just one book; it's about slavery. He expected subjects like mathematics and science. If it doesn't change, I'm going to see what this is all about.

Ballie Buck comes in, mostly to tell me some of the details about the Gilman Stampede that he and the local cowboys put on.

According to him it was a real success—nothing like the Calgary Stampede that he helped with in 1912 but a good start for this part of the country.

"Ballie, is your missus in town with you today?"

"No, but she plans to come next time, probably Friday."

"Rita wants to see her. We are living in town now."

"Tell me where so I can tell her."

"Just up the street in the Quinn house."

"She will be glad to have someone to visit with when she comes in with me. The fact that you and your missus came by on your pack trip really made her happy. She needs other ladies to talk with. She wants to join the Eastern Star and I am for it."

"When she visits Rita, they can talk about it. That lodge will certainly appreciate a lady like your wife."

"Yes, I agree. Also, we men have to make a good woman happy."

One day soon Sam Larkin comes to my office. "Doctor, I want to tell you how much I appreciate all you have done through this sad time of losing my wife. If there's any way I can show you I mean it, let me know."

"Sam, I am so sorry I could not save her. When a man loses a good wife, it is terrible. I cannot imagine it nor even think about such—it's too much."

"I will gladly do anything I'm capable of. I've got good horses—especially one named Prince. He is the smartest of any horse I've ever had. Have you got time to hear of the time he proved it?"

"Sam, I always have time to hear about a good horse."

"It happened a few years ago when we had driven in to the Christmas program at the church. It was late when we started home. Prince was hitched to our good buggy—with our little Ethel between us, with her sack of Christmas stuff. It was about eleven o'clock—too late to be out on a dark winter night. Suddenly it started to snow from the north—actually, a blizzard. It got really bad. I couldn't see anything, but we kept on going. Pretty soon I decided we should turn towards the east even though I couldn't see a thing. Prince kept turning back to the direction we had been going. I tried three times and he still refused to go that way so I tied the reins around the buckboard and let him have his head. Not very long we were driving in our gate that I could barely see."

"That is my kind of horse. That's a good story. If I need an especially smart horse I know where to go."

"Sam, are you going hunting this year?"

"I don't think so. Most every fall I do that but this year I won't be going."

"I won't be going either—too much to do with working for the war bonds and flu patients. But if the war ends soon next year I will go. There is usually a party of ten or so. You could think about coming along. We generally make our headquarters at the Cow Camp near Wood Lake."

"I would like to do that, and I will furnish any horses you or others in the party will need. I will be in on it. Dr. Kenck, I will be looking forward to hunting with you. By fall the war should be over and so should the flu rampage."

October 1918

Oscar gets me cornered. "Dad, let's you and us kids take off this Friday with our bed rolls and camp gear and go up to the ranch and see how things are there. We'll take our saddle horses so we can roam around and check things out."

"That's a good idea. We can call that our birthday celebration." That's what we do too.

"I think we ought to see if we can get someone to come up here and live, take care of our place, and raise a few head of cattle and a few horses. I don't like to see it empty. It will go to pieces. The rats will take over the house."

Oscar says, "I wish I was old enough to come here, and I could live real easy all by myself." Dick chimes in with, "I'd like to come here and live all winter and run my trap line. Some day I'm gonna do that—live in the mountains all winter and trap for fur."

Sunday we pack up and go back to town. We tell Mother and Grandmother about our good time and talk about the things we'd like to do. "Rita, I do think I'll try to find somebody to live in our house up there. It should be used for humans to live, not just the mice and rats."

Rita asks, "Did you see any elk or deer?"

"Yes, we went up to the Basin and they were around there. We could tell they had been trying to get at the salt left over where it has been put so many times."

"We saw some of the Indian folk. Oscar and Clarence Paul had a good time riding around the country. It's hard to leave those people. The kids sure were glad to see each other. I realize we need to go back often. We talked to Ole. I told him when it's time for his Wallace and Armond to go to high school that we want them to come in and stay with us."

Rita says, "You are certainly right. We do want them to stay with us then."

November 1918

Will our boys have to spend another miserable winter in the trenches? If the bullets don't get them, sickness will.

Soon we read the news: GERMANY ASKS FOR ARMISTICE. I guess they don't want to fight in winter. The Armistice is signed in General Foch's rail-car headquarters.

Next we read the American troops begin to gather at the seaports. They sing *"Lafayette, we are still here."* Even so, they know they have beat the Germans to a stand-still. Yes, the war is over.

We in the United States are happy about the Armistice and begin to realize the war is over. But still we don't celebrate too much because our enemy, the terrible influenza, is still taking lives.

Living in town with my office in the Furman Hotel, Rita can get the news in a minute when I come home from work. "Rita," I say, "since the war is over, I think a bunch of us can finally get away to go hunting. I was talking to Sam Larkin this week, and he mentioned that if a group of us plans on going hunting that he will supply the horses.

"Also, Oscar, you missed out so many times on hunting because of the war and the influenza epidemic that it would be just wonderful if you could get away for a nice hunting trip.

"I will let the fellows know and see what kind of response I get." I send out notes this week and get quick responses. "Rita, it looks good. Everyone I contacted is excited about a hunting trip. I've also contacted Ed Druckmiller (hunters' guide) to see if he's open, and his answer is Yes."

As I was going out the door to see Druckmiller, Oscar grabs my pant leg. "Dad," he says, "I want to talk." This makes me stop. "Dad, I'm only ten, but there are things I want to do, like hunting, but now I want you to talk to the other guys about a headquarters cabin for hunters." I remembered that Oscar talked about a cabin at Benchmark during our family camping in that area two summers ago.

"Well, one thing that I will do is talk to the hunters about definite plans for building that cabin."

Oscar says seriously, "Promise?" I nod yes. "Then, shake on it, Dad." I shake hands solemnly with my youngest son, promising I will talk to the other hunters about getting the cabin ready.

The crew begins arriving in town. George Hildebrandt from Helena, Tom Baker from Lewistown, and the two Drs. Wright from Great Falls and Havre are here to team up with J.C. Manix, Sam Larkin, and myself.

Sam plans to come into town with his wagon and the extra horses he is bringing for packing and riding to take us all to Ford Creek Station at the end of the road. With the horses and the wagon loaded with all supplies, we head out for Ford Creek where we will meet our guide, Ed Druckmiller. He will bring some of his packhorses in case we need more.

We head out towards the mountains. We waste no

Dr. Kenck, leader, and hunters ready to start on a trip to find meat.

time and get to Ford Creek Station fairly early. But, like a bunch of anxious kids, we quickly pack and load horses and take off up the Ford Creek trail to camp headquarters at the old Cow Camp on Wood Creek.

Actually, the weather is too nice for good hunting. We get busy and set up a good camp and take stock of all that we brought. We put up two poles for tents and another taller one for hanging grub sacks.

We hunt the next day, but it's too warm for this time of year. We don't expect much. No snow, no elk, yet.

After three or four days of fishing and quietly looking for signs of elk, the weather begins to turn cooler, with a little dusting of snow—just enough to find and follow the tracks of the big elk. A few of us have luck over the next ten days. Bring in four, which we agree to share. Some even decide to stay on for another week into late November.

While everyone is here, one evening I bring up the idea of a hunting cabin being built around here, with enthusiastic response. But only Ed Druckmiller makes an offer to spearhead the project. He offers his experience on such structures. He will snake out the logs needed with his team in the spring when packer business is less.

The hunting camp is a success, possibly because I took over as the breakfast cook. Every morning I am up mixing up my big batch of hot cake dough while Ed rounds up the horses we had staked in the meadow by Wood Lake. I got a bit of razzing about my willingness to do breakfast. So, I told them about my personal commitment to my good wife to cook breakfast every Sunday morning. I assured them that was one good way to make a happy home.

With the cool weather comes the first flurries of winter, and a fine layer of snow makes tracking the wily elk a simple thing. We fill our packs and packhorses with a good supply and head for home. Back to town with winter meat and good stories.

"Catch me up with the news," I ask Rita. "What about Brother Van? Just before I left the news was he'd had a stroke."

"The news is bad because on the 19th he had another one. They brought him from Chinook to the Deaconess Hospital in Great Falls. He is so sad he cannot move except to talk some. Mama consoles herself. She says between her sobs, 'We shall see him in heaven.'

"They tell that he has his hundreds of Christmas cards all ready to send, and he told Mama that if he went before then that they should print on them 'First Christmas in Heaven.'"

Day by day, *The Tribune* reports his condition. He is failing fast.

On December 19, Brother Van woke from the coma he had been in for several days, and as he said he would do, he raised his right hand just a little and in a whisper said, "Home, home," and was gone. Now all of Montana is in mourning.

The funeral Service in the Great Falls Methodist Church is so large that many stand during the long Service. After the long lines of mourning people had passed by with one last look at the body that Brother Van needed no more, the casket was closed and taken to the train waiting to carry the often-time passenger for the last time to Helena to be buried in Forest Vale Cemetery. It is the day before Christmas.

The Helena Independent reports that the children of the Deaconess School who loved Brother Van, and of course, he dearly loved them, came with their teachers bringing a little decorated tree to put on the grave and they sang Christmas carols while standing in the snow.

CHAPTER 57

NEW HIGH SCHOOL, EASTERN STAR, & THE GREAT NORTHERN RAILROAD

Town life settles down this winter and spring. Everyone seems more relaxed since the end of the war and the Armistice. Talking with patients, I learn families who live in districts farther out are wondering how their children will be able to attend the new school. I tell them that several town families will make room for kids from out in the country. Also, we are considering using the Rock School as a supervised dormitory. We plan to have a couple of the school staff live in two rooms of the main floor. Several townspeople have volunteered to take in those students who live too far out instead of spending weeks at a time in Helena away from their families.

It's time to think about our own high school. The question is how to find the money needed to build and maintain it. The idea begins circulating to consolidate the five school districts of Augusta, Clemons, Mountain, Riebling, and Gilman. This would give the district a large enough tax base to get the school built and maintained.

After some discussion and negotiations, Consolidated School District No. 45 is born. Gilman is not the happiest participant over the union, because they had been verbally promised that the location of the new school would be between Augusta and Gilman. The actual placement of the high school turns out to be in Augusta, only one mile from Gilman, but a sore mile for the Gilman contingent.

The prime public-spirited men responsible for making the union possible are Mr. Brandt and Mr. Ogden. With the creation of the new and expanded district, a new school board is commissioned, and I am elected as a board member, as are G.H. Gonser, Fred Eder, Malcolm Chisholm, and C.C. Covington. The first superintendent elected is Charles Troyer. We hire the first principal, Miss Mary Stewart, and the first two teachers, Misses Esther Drenckhahn and Norinne Murphy.

The new high school is constructed this spring and summer. We incorporate a gymnasium and locker rooms, theater stage, indoor plumbing, science room, domestic science department, and a business department. The first floor's southwest corner is a large manual training-mechanical drawing room. Four other large rooms are double classrooms. A small future library, a general assembly, and English room is on the southwest second floor. Being on the school board makes me knowledgeable of our new school—one of the best and most modern schools in the state.

The new high school seems a success. By September we will have a new superintendent and no criticism from the Gilman folk.

J.C. Manix comes by my office today.

"Howdy, Doc."

"Doing just fine, J.C. What's the news?"

"Even though we have had to wait so long to finish our project of getting the rails to our town, it has paid off. That the State Railway Commission has been set up *for our benefit* is the thing."

"How so?"

"I figured I could get our legislature and governor to establish <u>that</u> to make the Great Northern comply with what the state wanted. So, now the state can overrule the G.N. That's exactly what will happen."

"You surely know the process of government, J.C."

"I've talked to our legislators and governor a good deal to learn the ways of getting what we need. It surely has paid off."

"Thanks for giving me the inside dope. Keep in touch. See you later."

Since we live in town, Rita is the one who goes to

the store and gets the mail. So, unless I have a specific need, I depend on the news she gathers. This evening I have special news when I get home. At supper I tell what Oscar has been anxious to hear.

"Ed Druckmiller was in today." I can see Oscar really jerks to attention. I continue.

"He had some good news. 'Doc, I gotta tell you what's been going on in the hills.'"

"'How so?' I say."

Oscar slumps down in his chair with a sigh.

"Oscar, cheer up, it's good news."

"But, Dad? You make me wait so long."

"Ed said, 'Will Stecker and I went over to the Cow Camp and we snaked in enough logs for a good-sized cabin and for boards to be reved out for the roof and floor.' He also said that Will came with him because Ed had helped him build a cabin a couple years ago. Besides, it's better that guys work together logging in the woods."

Oscar happily raises his right fist with a shake and a "yeah!"

Then I add, "Ed also promised that next spring about this same time he and Stecker will go back and peel the logs." Oscar is a happy boy indeed.

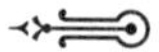

A few months later, just as J.C. said, it comes to pass that the Great Northern Railroad is forced to extend the rails to Augusta. The Montana Supreme Court refuses to consider their case. This calls for a great celebration. Naturally, it will be held in our new modern high school gym.

"Rita, have you any information about getting an Eastern Star going in town?"

"I surely have. Several of us ladies have made progress. The main ladies are Alice Cunniff and Mrs. Fisher, who is an Eastern Star in Helena, but she really wants us to have the lodge here."

"We Masons would like that very much so we could have some nice times with our wives in that lodge."

"We ladies want that also because we don't like staying at home any more than you like having just men's meetings."

We are in complete agreement, so soon things begin

to happen. It turns out that the chapter is instituted June 20, 1920. It is called Sun River Chapter 94.

Rita says, "We received our charter August 21. So, now we are ready to elect our officers. Our meetings are above J.C. Manix's store—same place as you Masons meet. We got nineteen members to start. First we have an election to fill all offices:

Worthy Matron: Ethel Wellman
Worthy Patron: Frank Mitchell
Associate Matron: Alice Mitchell
Secretary: O.A. Kenck
Treasurer: W.H. Warden
Conductress: Rita Kenck
Associate Conductress: Maude Fisher
Chaplain: W.D. Vaughn
Adah: Augusta Berube
Ruth: Sadie Clemons
Esther: Jessie Nett
Martha: Ruby Miller
Electa: Alice Cunniff
Sentinel: George Fisher."

"So, now Olive Chapter 10 of Great Falls assists us with installing all the officers. At this time we have twenty-four members. With this good foundation, the Eastern Star can look forward to many years of good meetings and good parties that will keep our Masonic wives happy. One thing though, we will some day change the name to Augusta Eastern Star Lodge.

Now that Rita has been successful in the Star project, she wants to take part in the Civic Club. The ladies of the town meet in a small house they bought from a lady who had used it for a hat store. This is the second time this building is moved. It will be the Civic Club's meeting place from now on.

Rita tells me the ladies want to buy a piece of land for a city park. After searching, they heard Mrs. Bushels would sell them a piece of land near town and also near the river if they promise not to commercialize it. They paid $250 for it. Got picnic tables and made a fire pit plus an outhouse. They fenced it and made a gate too. Our ladies cleaned it regularly. Rita tells me that each year the club organizes a clean-up for the town and hires Mr. Clemons to haul away trash to a gully

George Fisher and the fire-warning bell

on the hill sorta northwest of town.

One project we accomplish is a fire-alarm bell. Mr. Quinn agreed to make it, but the problem is where shall it be so it can be most quickly reached? Finally, Maude Fisher solved the problem. "Since my dear husband was so anxious to name our club "The Hen House," we elect his store roof-top to be the place of the fire bell—which also means he will be mostly responsible for the sounding of it."

The next time we talk, George says, "My smart mouth got me cornered." George will never call it "The Hen House" again.

"Rita, today your niece Minnie and her two little girls came in."

"How is she?"

"She seems to be fine. Ruthie was having trouble getting a tooth to come out to make way for a permanent incisor. That little Helen is a happy child. Minnie says, however, that Helen has too many earaches."

"What are the rest of the Cottles doing? I don't hear much since Ida passed away."

"You may be surprised, but maybe not. Minnie said

she and her girls went with Susie and Henry to Livingston last month and they were married at a double wedding at sister Etta's house. Henry married Helen Arps and Susie married Bill McManus."

"I'm not surprised except that they went so far to do it. It was May Key who told me that was going to happen sometime soon."

"Minnie said that Susie stayed at Jessie Cottle Bicket's because Jessie came down with a mastoid ear infection. But she has come back to Augusta by now."

"Now I can say all of my nieces are married, except one of course is getting a divorce."

"That's too bad."

"My dear husband, I have an idea. I wonder if Susie and her husband have any place to live."

"Are they staying with Minnie at the Cottle Ranch?"

"When Minnie talked to me she did not say where Susie and Bill are living."

"What I'm thinking about is our talk of having someone live on our ranch. Do you suppose they might be the ones who can take care of it and get a few head of stock started for a herd of their own?"

"I will give that some thought."

Next day early I drop in on J.C. as he is in his back storeroom opening crates.

"Good morning, Kenck," he says as he works on prying off boards. "What brings you out so early?"

"Do you know Bill McManus?"

"Not much. He's Walt's brother, but that's about all I do know. I guess he's been working around at different outfits. What is your reason for asking?"

"Last month he married Susie Cottle. Rita and I are thinking about getting some couple to live on our ranch. We hate to see it empty. So, we are considering asking them if they would be interested in living there. I can't pay them but maybe they can use the place to get a start in cattle."

"Well I think Susie is a nice lady so all a person can do is give them a chance."

"I'll find them and see what they say."

A couple weeks later I see Susie at the post office and I ask her if she and Bill would be interested.

I tell Rita, "Susie said, 'I will tell Bill. I would like to live in your house on the Dearborn. Right now we are staying with Minnie and Dad on the ranch while Bill looks for work.'"

Rita says, "I have always liked Susie. She is a nice girl and a hard worker. Maybe they can get started in some cows and even some bum lambs."

Couple days later Bill comes in and we talk over a deal for them to live there and see that people don't come in and strip the place. I tell him though that I probably will have to sell it but we aren't ready just yet. The Gervaises and the Pochas are watching it, but they are not always there and some stuff has come up missing.

I tell Bill, "The kids and I will take a drive up there this Sunday and see what is there and tell the Indian families that you and Susie will be moving in next week."

Bill says, "I'm helping Mr. Cottle with some fencing for a few more days now."

"By the way, Bill, I want to tell you the Bean families will be good neighbors to you folks when you live there."

"Thank you very much. Susie and I appreciate your kindness of providing us a place to live and get started."

I tell Rita that Bill was in and I talked to him about the place. I also told him that we might sell the place if we could find a buyer, but that might be a little while.

Dick has been quietly listening and suddenly blurts out. "Dad, did you tell them not to bother stuff like our things in the upstairs that are still there?"

"No, but you and Oscar go up there with me Sunday and we will write down all the stuff that we left there that we don't bring home with us."

"Okay, I'll write down all my stuff."

"It will be much better if you bring it all home. Maybe you can store it out at Uncle Will's."

"Ya, that's a better idea."

Later, when he and I are alone, Oscar says to me, "Dad, I don't like the idea of someone else getting to live in our place."

"I don't either, but it will help us to let it go when we build a cabin up at Benchmark."

"Yeah, Dad, but I'm sad. And maybe mad too."

"Life is hard, but we have to go on, son. You are a man."

Before we plan the work party, we take care of one of the reasons for our moving to town from our ranch in the Dearborn Canyon, the graduation of Dick from high school. Being chairman of the board it gives me great pleasure to give him his diploma, something not many dads get to do.

By 1924 at last we are able and ready to build the cabin since Ed Druckmiller and Will Stecker have gotten the logs and boards all ready. All the work crew, plus the tools we know we will need, have been collected and sent to the road-end place at the Ford Creek Forest Service packhorse corrals.

CHAPTER 58

THE CABIN, ELECTRICITY IN AUGUSTA, & OUR OWN HOME

Our superintendent, F.F. Sparks, is one busy man. Our consolidated district has thirteen rural schools to oversee. During some terms not all are in use: Reibling, Clemons, Ostrom, Willow Creek, Fairview, McKelvey, Half Way, Warden, Elk Creek, Thompson, and Gonser. To visit them regularly is a big order. He is furnished with a Ford. The country roads are either too rough or too muddy for a buggy.

At the September board meeting, Sparks gives a report of his visit to the Ostrom School. "Our board member, Ogden's daughter, is the teacher." He reads off the written report that she gave him. "You local people probably know the families. Her students' names are Betsy and Lanier Sallee, Bob and Laura Arps,

Elton Converse, Susie Reichart, Izzie and Eddie Goss. Miss Ogden seems to be a good teacher. The children behaved very well during my visit. I had not expected a written report of the education level of the students and am pleased that she prepared one for me. It will be a good service if all our rural schools will do the same." We board members realize Sparks understands our school system.

Now it is time to begin thinking about our cabin and what we need to take to get it ready for winter and hunting. I must write George Hildebrandt, Dr. Wright, and Red Mahood. They are also needed to

initiate our cabin. Answers come fast. Now I've got to work on my list of what we are going to bring.

About mid-October, Sam Larkin brings his wagon in and leaves it alongside of Fred's lumber store. We begin to put certain things in it for the cabin and put a tarp over. Finally, the time arrives and Sam brings the horses in. We put pack and riding saddles in a second wagon. The guys get all their hunting gear into that one wagon. I check out with most of the fellows to make

Front row—Guys at our cabin: Dulaney, Kenck, Wright, Mahood

sure they have the essentials. Early the next morning we wind up the road towards Ford Creek horse corrals where, like always, we load the packhorses and head up the trail.

As we ride along, I think about Oscar and Rita. Oscar just turned fifteen a couple of weeks ago and I hate to leave him, but school is his work for now. His time will come that he will hunt. Rita has got Mrs. Swanson eager to start the quilt that she and Mama Auchard planned to keep Mrs. Swanson from worrying about her husband Fred going hunting and leaving her alone. She is a real worrier, and Fred Swanson never gets to get away with the men hunters.

Besides the quilt project, Rita is busy with the town's Civic Club and the Eastern Star. Also, if anyone needs my dental services, she can tell them when I will be back in about two weeks from the time we left. For now I can breathe the smell of these mountains and relish the sights—the groves of golden aspen fluttering their leaves in the slightest fall breezes and hear the creek gurgle beside us as we wind up towards Benchmark and our cabin that we had dreamed of for so long.

Our cabin at Benchmark

In late afternoon we finally arrive. J.C. is just ahead of me. He is stunned. "Kenck, you didn't tell me what it's really like! You guys did this in ten days?"

Fred Swanson chimes in, "Yeah, they did it but I don't see how."

"Fact is we couldn't have done it but we had three ladies cooking, and they did more than cook too. They really helped with everything. So, we can't take all the credit."

After we unload, stake the horses, and sling some grub, we make a plan for the work projects in the warm days ahead.

Some of these are to chink the log walls, make an outhouse, cut some wood and stack it near the door, and design and make a porch. These are just a few. Each of us chooses what jobs we will do. I know I will cook some of the time. We get our bedrolls and turn in with no trouble getting to sleep. A pack rat rattling around in the night didn't alarm us too much. We hunkered down with more covers over our heads.

For about a week we keep at our self-appointed jobs. After several warm days, snow comes softly in the night—several inches. This changes our whole program. Hunting overtakes all. Okay, we have done more than we had planned. We now realize how a cabin will give us more time to hunt.

Time to leave comes too soon. These days apart give us a refresher from the job of earning a living and being the men we try to be. We share the meat and make sure that everyone signs the logbook. Then we lock the door with a nail and a hammer and give a shout, "WE SHALL RETURN!"

At home we find the town all excited. We will get electric wire service in the spring of 1925. This news causes me to think of building my office. However, the work will be in the spring. Now I draw up my plans.

In November, Dick comes home from his summer and fall work at Allen's Ranch. He tells us that many of the dudes are not only odd but also green about horses and pack trips. "We wranglers were warned we could not play tricks on them. It was really tempting sometimes."

"Dick," I ask, "what do you plan to do next?"

"I'm thinking about going to welding school—maybe next year. Right soon, like in February, I want to go back to Benchmark and set my traps there."

"Yeah, that would be okay, but Mother will worry if you will be alone. So, I insist you get someone to go along."

"Dad, you know that I can trap by myself. I'm eighteen."

"Yeah, I know, but I don't want to hear two women worry."

"I get you, Dad, so I will see if Ed Druckmiller is interested. Anyway, for now I got a job coming up. I'm pretty sure."

"What are you talking about?"

"I just saw Del Walrath at the store and he asked me if I am a good climber. I told him. 'Sure, I'm part monkey.' He's got a contract to wire the town for the power company, and he needs a helper who can climb and also learn how to do the job.'"

"Yes, I've heard that we will soon have power. So, good thing I'm going to build the office I've wanted."

"Let's start right away. Maybe we can get it done

before the main line gets here."

"Okay, I'll get out the plans and get Fred Swanson to order the lumber. Dick, you are going to be one busy man."

This evening I read in the paper that Congress has passed a law that makes all Indians citizens. "What do you think of that, Rita?"

"Probably most of the Indians around here will not know what it means nor will they care at first. Maybe someday they might realize what it means. They live in their own world and know little about federal laws except those Indians who are forced to stay on reservations."

"Well I'm wondering why the government has decided on this action. I think they should have been given this many years ago. Our Indian policy has been wrong a long time, but this act won't change things much. Our Indian folk around here have mostly escaped from Canada, and they try to stay out of the reach of any U.S. laws. By the way, I have a bit of news I think you will be excited about."

"Dear husband, don't keep me in suspense."

"The news is that Bud and his family are buying an apple orchard near Hamilton in the Bitterroot Valley. Sad to see them leave Augusta but the good part is that they will sell us their house here."

This is a strange one. A sadness that will bring joy. Doesn't often happen but it grants one of my secret wishes, a nice house in town. When Bud comes back from his trip he will arrange to have all his furniture shipped there.

"Rita, let's take a few days in Helena to get the finances arranged to buy the house and to build my office. I've been wanting to check on my German mutter."

We find that my mother is getting frail. She has a lady who takes care of her. Mother's helper says, "Mrs. Kenck is getting forgetful. She thinks that Albert is still alive and wonders why he doesn't come to see her."

I tell her, "When you feel that she needs more care than you can give her, let me know and I will find a nursing home for her." Mama calls me Albert so I see what she means.

Mother talks to me in German about her life-long puzzle. She has always been in doubt that the casket that was brought home after my dad was killed in the

Yellowstone Park area wasn't really her husband. She says, "He be tall—the casket so short—not fit him—maybe someone else in that casket."

I say, "Mama, sometime in better weather I will come to Helena and investigate your puzzle."

"Please do, son, I so long vant to know."

Rita says to me after we leave, "Oscar, what do you think about this worry of your mother?"

"It's not a new worry of hers. She has talked about this before and I have heard from my uncles the same story. Someday I will look into getting a Court order to look so I can keep my promise. I wonder about that myself." [I did handle this matter eventually and found Mutter was right to some degree. It was my father but the manner in which it was preserved did not necessitate a longer casket.]

Now Rita and I can look through the Tomlinson house. It has three bedrooms, a dining room, a study, living room, large kitchen, sun porches both front and back. Besides the two bedrooms upstairs, there is a big room the whole width of the house at the top of the stairs. All the room we will ever need.

In the partial basement there is a furnace and a canned-food storage room.

"My dear good lady, now you can begin to plan what furniture you will be needing to fill up so much more space than you have had."

"Yes, my dear doctor, my mind is really working. The first thing I plan to get is dining room furniture."

"Yes, and you shall have it. You have been so patient. It will please me to see that you get just what you want.

Augusta home bought from Tomlinsons

BIG CHANGES IN AUGUSTA—NEW OFFICE, NEW HOUSE, NEW SOURCE OF POWER, NEW PEOPLE, AND HOUSES AND BUILDINGS FROM GILMAN

January 1925 is a busy month as we gradually move into the Tomlinson house just up the street—the second house east of Fishers' house. The boys are happy to have their own big bedrooms upstairs.

The room at the top of the stairs has a wall bookcase. The boys get right busy and put in their western-animal collections. Dick calls down to me, "Dad, come up and look at our real library."

I tell them, "If you loan a book to your friends, keep a notebook and have them sign their name and promise to return the book in a week."

"Okay, Dad, I will get a notebook and put it here in the book case with a pencil and then I will know who has the book. If they forget to bring it back, I will find them and get it."

"Good idea, Dick. People plan to return a book but sometimes forget."

Mother Auchard's room is the small one off the dining room. There she has no stairs to climb and will be near the bathroom off the kitchen.

Rita is excited. "I love this row of lilacs, and I will plant a chokecherry tree near the backdoor."

"Yes, my dear lady, you shall because I love the syrup you and Mama make from those cherries—so very good on my Sunday-morning pancakes."

Dick and Oscar are anxious to tell Wallace Bean when he comes back for school. Ole brings him in on Sunday. Dick and Oscar find them at the old place.

"Hey, surprise! We are moved to a different house and it's bigger."

Wallace is a little surprised and asks, "Where?"

"Up the street just a little ways, in the music people's house. They are moving away and we are buying their house. Come on, we'll show you."

"Wow! That's a big house."

Oscar chimes in, "It's got a big room upstairs where we can play games and talk without bothering anybody, but no rough stuff there."

Wallace says, "Well, we better not be rowdy or Pa won't let me come stay here no more."

Ole says, "Vallace, you be right, no vay you rough house. You hear dat?"

"Yes, Pa, I hear."

Dick adds, "We won't be wrestling upstairs, just outdoors."

I hear their talk as they are coming in the door. I look over the top of my paper and say, "Hello, Wallace and Ole. Come right in."

Now is the time to talk to Ole.

"We are planning on having Armond come in next fall to high school."

Ole says right away, "Doc, I 'tink' no send Armond to high school. He be a rancher. No need dat."

"Ole, don't think that way about Armond. Every boy needs some more education these days. He will be a better rancher if he goes to high school. Oscar wants to be a rancher also. He wants the general knowledge he will get in high school. For that life a boy needs to learn about business and record keeping. Also, how our government works. He will be much more satisfied by learning these things and getting to know the people who live in this part of Montana."

"Vell, Doctor, I never tought of it dat vay. You may be right. I tink some more. Maybe so. Here, Doctor and Missus, I bring you dis leg of lamb I butcher. I know it make a good roast for you folk."

"Thank you, Ole. All the meat you bring us is the best."

"Vallace, now you behave, don't cause no trouble. I be in to get you next Friday. If snow, I bring sled, okay?"

"Ya, Pa, I behave."

"Yes, Ole, Wallace never gives us any trouble. We

like him to stay with us."

I see the boys smile at one another.

Finally, a long awaited day arrives in March. Everyone who can find some place to get a good view watches the many men helping "heave-ho" the Gilman depot onto the flat car which is hooked up to Engine No. 357. With shouts and blasts of steam, the engine puffs along as the young boys and men run beside that wood frame building (still with the sign GILMAN on its west end).

It comes on the mile of track squeaking and rumbling to the place ready for it just past the grain elevator and the water tank. There is a skiff of snow on the ground but no one notices.

Quickly someone puts up a ladder and rips the name GILMAN from the building. The crowd gives a cheer. We men of Augusta converge on our prize and on Mr. Bob Dyer, the depot agent who appears at the door.

"Howdy, howdy! Welcome to Augusta!" And we shake his hand.

Bob Dyer, our well-liked station agent says, "Thanks. Been waitin' for this day and will remember it a long time."

Busy days follow. I am going ahead on my office project. I study my plans and imagine a day's work in it to make it handy. It will have to last the rest of my dental-practice days. The north side facing the street will have three windows directly in front of the chair. The side waiting room will have a window to the street also. The chair room with the windows will be wide enough for my dental chair's foot and headrest to revolve in a three-quarter circle. On the wall that separates the chair room from the waiting room will be a cabinet for dental instruments and chair supplies.

On the opposite end is the door to the waiting room with the entry door in full view for me to see arrivals from my position at the chair. Heat for water and comfort is supplied by a wood/coal heater that sits between the doors to the waiting room and the lab storage room that is across the entire back of the building.

The lab, where much work will be done, has several windows above an ample workbench that holds my lathe and chuck ready for the electric power. The first work of this project is a concrete foundation. Then floors, walls, roof, and windows. My good lady makes translucent curtains that face the street. A back door opens from the lab room out to the coal and wood shed and a single-seat outhouse. A dental office can be a small building with a special purpose but takes thoughtful planning. As soon as the weather warms up enough to pour foundations, the construction will begin.

Across the street from my office, there is great activity. F.M. Mack is in the process of moving his large general store from Gilman. Because of the size, it has been cut in half, and each piece is moved and put back together. Mack's store and my office will face each other for a long time.

I see Mack at the Masons' meeting. He says, "Doctor, I see you are building an office right across the street from my store. I'm very glad to see that."

"Well, Mr. Mack, that feeling is mutual. We'll be seeing a lot of each other."

"Kenck, don't call me Mister, just 'Mack.' I don't like my first name either."

"Fine, we can agree on one name for each." We shake hands on that and realize we are going to be good business neighbors. Besides Mack, many others are moving their businesses and even their homes to our town. A really big one to come is one of the hotels.

With Dick being a quick helper and learning about electric wiring, the work of the electricity coming to us goes quickly along. He can't do two jobs at once, so I hire Tony to help me build my office. I want it ready when the power is in.

Along with all the exciting happenings, the train crew moves to Augusta. These families add to the social life of the town. The train comes in from Great Falls each evening and leaves for the Falls every morning. Some of the crew are the Riordons, LaSalles, Huotaries, Fosters, and several more moving in soon. These folks are good additions to our town. With our business people, our teachers, and the railroad families, we have an interesting social life. House by house, and business places too, each gets wired and a fuse box. All are given instructions and warnings about the dangers of electricity.

At my regular Montana Dental Association meeting this spring, I order my new dental chair with electrical attachments to be shipped. Also, new lab equipment that I have dreamed of for so long. But I do remember the new electric appliances I want Rita to have.

I'm curious—which things will she choose first. I say to her, "My good lady, which of all the appliances we need will be your first choice?"

"That is no problem. That would be a refrigerator."

"Rita, you are a smart woman, a good wife, and I love you, even though I say goofy things sometimes. And besides that, I will make it possible for you to go find your new electric things."

A new office, a new house, new source of power, many new people. It almost seems like a new town. Besides that, a new hunting cabin in the mountains. Sometimes a fellow's dreams do come true.

So much happened this year, 1925. Can the pace be kept up? It better not. The "hurrider" I go the "behinder" I get. I must have time to absorb the new. So here we go.

"Rita, I'm thinking we should try to find a buyer for the ranch and the Basin. The ranchers I can think of who might be interested are Carmichael, Mosher, and Dick Bean. All run mostly sheep. Some of these outfits would like to have summer pasture closer to home."

"Well, I can say this to you. The first of these you see just ask him if he's interested. If not, he will tell you of someone who is."

"Good idea, Rita. How I do need your quick thinking."

Now that selling is in our thoughts, we will see what happens.

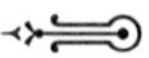

Down the street I walk the short distance to my new office. Every time I see it, I think, "What took me so long?" I have needed it this way for years. Same way about our new house. Right away I make a good-sized sign to put on the side of this new building.

The next thing surprises me—a dental assistant lady. I do not have to search for her either. My perceptive wife has a hand in this. I realize suddenly that Rita has said several times that I spend too many hours doing extra chores at the office and should have someone to sterilize and put away instruments, get the chair ready for the next patient, check on the next day's appointments, and greet people when I'm involved at the chair or in the lab.

Soon a petite lady appears at my door. A cheery voice says, "Good morning, Doctor. I have something special to talk to you about. It's not my teeth. I was talking with your wife at the club meeting yesterday. I told her that I would like to have a job of some kind. I have a tiny house and Fred and I have no kids. She said, 'Ask my husband if he would like an office lady. He spends hours doing office work that someone could learn and do for him.' My name is Jo Huotari and I think I would like to work for you."

"Well, Jo, when I think about it, I would like to be relieved of some of the chores you could learn to do. But I will not be able to pay very much. What do you say about that?"

"Doctor, I really don't expect much pay, and I would like to learn."

"If you want to do it and learn, I will see how it goes by giving you ten percent of what comes into the office. How will that be?"

"Doctor, that is fine with me. I can come as soon as I get a white uniform. What time in the morning will you want me here?"

"How about 8:30? I will build the fire a little earlier."

"Thank you so very much. Within two days I will have a uniform. Goodbye for now and I will see you very soon. Thank you. My husband will be very happy."

One change brings another and another. Now with power available many things in my office are new: my dental chair with its vacuum raising and lowering system, the new electric hand drill, the light over the chair, the electric pump that brings water from the water tank to the chair basin, also the bigger pump from my well tank to the lab for the hand-washing basin, and to the hot water tank which is heated by a pipe system that runs through the stove. But very special is the electric sterilizer and my electric motor for drilling in the lab. No, I won't throw away my old foot drive. If the electricity fails I may need it.

As she said, Jo shows up two days later to learn the work. I also must learn how to let her help. She's quick. After a week Rita asks, "How is Jo working out?"

"She learns faster than I thought she would. It will take a while for the folks who come in to get used to a lady greeting them. A funny one today. A boy came in and Jo said, 'Hello, what do you need?' He opened his mouth but nothing came out. He seemed stunned, no sound. I know what he wants and wait a bit to hear him say it. I turned from the chair where I was working on a patient and I see he is still stuck, mouth open, no sound. I come to his rescue. 'Charlie, what do you want to say?' He comes to his senses and then blurts out his message, 'Seven, seven, seven.' Then he bolted out the door. Jo asked, 'What is that all about?' And I have to explain that it's a code message."

"A code message? But doctor, you don't look worried."

I told her the card club meets at George White's house tonight.

"Doctor, I'm curious. Who are these card players? Or shouldn't I ask?"

"It's okay for you to know, but we don't advertise. It's Sparks, our superintendent; Downie, the principal; me; and sometimes Joe Bush, the sheriff, when nothing's going on in town."

Jo said, "Next time I will know. I'm learning what goes on in this town."

At supper Oscar says, "Dad, you guys should be more kind to Mr. Sparks. The last time after the party he came to school with a shirt that looked like a pajama top."

"Maybe Mrs. Sparks decided to wash all his shirts."

Rita gives a chuckle and changes the subject.

"Husband, this is February 1925. Shall we celebrate?"

"My good lady, we shall. Especially we need to go find more electric things for your kitchen."

"Let's go to Helena. We won't go to Butte this time.

When can you take a few days away?"

"Let's say next Wednesday. I'll tell Jo to put a note on the door that I'll be back on Monday; she doesn't need to come in until then."

That day we catch the train right from Augusta and change trains in Great Falls for Helena, and in Helena we stay at The Harvey. We are glad to take the train and miss having flat tires in the cold and wind of February.

A day of looking at many electrical appliances helps Rita to decide on four basic things—a General Electric refrigerator, Monarch electric stove, an Easy Washer, and an electric iron. We know there are more things we now can use with electric power, but we just buy a few this first time.

"Oscar, this is all I need for now. It will take me quite a while to get used to this many new things along with our new home."

"Rita, my dear good lady, you have been a splendid helper to me for all these twenty years. You de-serve every bit of this and more. Let's go to the Parrot and celebrate with ice cream any way you like it." With a hug and a kiss in our room, we go down to the wonderful Parrot Soda Fountain and Candy Store. The strawberry sundae is so very good, even in February. We buy for Mama and the boys each a box of their wonderful hand-made chocolates.

Home again! The boys love their boxes of candy. Dick doesn't take many days to eat his. We never know about Oscar. He hides his and says, "I make it last a long time. If Dick finds my box, it won't last."

So, now we wait for our shipment of new things to come. In about a week Austin Christian, our depot freight man, drives his wagon into our yard, and with the help of his strong son, Austin Jr., starts to unload our new appliances.

He says, "Doc, this stuff came yesterday so thought I'd get this over before you left for the office."

"Austin, I will help you get these boxes into the house. We have been expecting them so have shoved things around to make space. Surely is good you have a strong helper."

"Yep, he's getting big and husky. Good thing too. I ain't so strong as I used to be when I was cowboyin'. I'm thinkin' to buy me a Ford truck next year. Might save me some work takin' care of my teams all the time. Besides, they're gettin' old like me."

"Austin, you've been freighting a lot of years. It's high time you made it easier on yourself."

We carefully bring in all of Rita's new things.

"Rita, when I come home at lunch, we'll start putting stuff where we had planned, and Dick and Oscar will be here to help this evening."

"Don't worry, Oscar, Mama and I will enjoy just looking at all of them sitting here."

At lunch time the boys are surprised at all the new appliances sitting around.

Dick says, "Good thing I got a little time off now from wiring houses with Del. I can wire our own house so we can plug in everything right where it's needed. Another thing Del was saying to me is that you should have the telephone from the Quinn house moved to your office, and because the phone is in this house already, you can call Mother to tell her when you are going to bring someone to dinner."

"You're right, Dick, I've been meaning to get you working on the phone for the office." Now, at this age, I'm finding that change brings more changes of one kind or another.

This summer the cabin has been quiet. People, including our family, have been busy.

In September, Ed Druckmiller stops by the office.

"Doc, this is some nice office you have here. First thing, if you have time today, take a look at my teeth. What can I do about 'em? They ain't decayed, just a little loose, right?"

"Ed, if you want to, you can save them for a few more years but you have to really want to because you will need to do the salt water treatment every single day and come in about every two months and let me scale the deposits off and see how you are doing."

"Okay, Doc, show me how and I will do it."

"Today I will clean off all the lime deposits and show you just how to use this toothbrush to brush your gums with strong salt water every single day. If you will agree to do it, I assure you that you will save your teeth for a few more years. Just talk to Bob Dyer. He will tell you it really works."

"Okay, Doc, I will try this treatment. Sure would beat gummin', as the old guys say."

"I've got some time right now, so just get yourself in the chair here. I will begin the process and see if we can get the irritation away from your gums so they can begin the process of healing. You will need just this brush and about a half teaspoon of plain salt in a cup of water. If you are faithful to do this, soon your gums will tighten up and your teeth will also tighten up."

"Gee, Doc, that sounds so simple. I sure hope it works."

"Ed, it will work if you are faithful. Never go out on the trail without your bag of salt and a cup as well as one of these brushes I'm giving you today. It's September. Next month we no doubt will be heading into the hills, so I'm sure there will be plenty need for your horses. Stop by the next time you come into town so I can check on your gums to see how you are doing and we will know who all is coming for the hunting party.

October brings a faithful bunch to hunt: [See R Cabin's Log Book list for October 1925.] Eight of us sign the Log Book for that month's hunt. Dick has been kept working so much he will have to wait to try testing the trapping next year at the Benchmark area.

The time for our hunt is, as I said, the last week of October 1925. Some who want to come can't make it. The out-of-town folk who make it are John Nilan and George Hildebrandt both from Helena, Dick Baker from Tacoma, Tom Baker from Augusta, and J.C. Manix, Ed Druckmiller and myself from Augusta. We miss Sam Larkin with his horses. Ed had a hunch that Sam wasn't going to make it so he brought extra riding horses and saddles. That Ed is a terrific planner. [See Log Book for text of hunt]

In November after the hunt, Ed comes by my office to let me check his teeth and gums.

He says, "Doc, my mouth is a lot better. Your salt

J.C. Manix and Dr. Kenck with a bear hide

treatment is doing the job." He is right; his gums have healed.

"Ed, you've made a good start. Don't let up."

"Today, Doc, I saw Dick at the store. He says he finally is getting to a stopping place wiring the town, and soon we can get our grub supply, traps, and warm duds and escape to the cabin."

"Ed, I appreciate that you are going to the cabin with him. I remember what you said once: 'It's better for a guy not to be alone in the mountains.' Besides, Rita and Grandma surely do like to know that you are with Dick."

"Yep, that kid knows those critters. Maybe I can learn from him some of the tricks the Indians taught him about settin' traps."

Dick and Ed spend a week in February getting their outfit ready. After they recheck essentials, they load it all into a wagon and trail the saddle horses. They transfer everything to the four packhorses. They find it takes planning to get all they need on them. Then the horses have to be taken back to the Ford Creek camp where they can be kept for the month.

March 1926 passes slowly for us. We hear the snow in the mountains is unusually deep and the temperature is very low. When the month is over, Dick comes in with beautiful furs, long hair, and whiskers. He says the trapping was okay but getting to the traps was the work. The creeks in the foothills like the Dearborn are much easier. My son is a hunter and trapper!

Also, in March the remaining homes in Gilman are moved to Augusta. One by one the Gilman houses are lifted on to a bed of timbers and trundled just a mile or two. The Bob Dyer house gets moved to the west end of town right near the home of Bill and Charlotte Cunniff. The Orrie Brown house also comes to that end of Main Street. Gilman Hotel becomes the Randall Hotel in Augusta. About every two weeks the house movers, like the Clemons family, slowly and carefully bring another house from the diminishing town of Gilman.

CHAPTER 60

THE BURNING OF DEARBORN CANYON

Spring of 1926. Our own Wallace Bean is set to graduate from high school this spring. He is talking about trade school this fall because the old Bean Ranch isn't big enough to support two families. Time for him to do some looking around about which trade he'd like to learn. The graduation itself was memorable. I handed Wallace his diploma. A fine young man. So glad he has been able to finish school.

The summer is hot and dry, drier than usual. Suddenly we hear the Dearborn is on fire. Started by a careless packer in Black Trail Flats. It raced from there down to Devil's Glen. Six or seven men, including all the Beans, thought they had it contained in the Glen, but it jumped, burning off the Glen in the process. By that time a force of three hundred men had gathered at the end of the road in Dearborn Canyon to fight the fire. They were unable to stop it and had to run from the fire's fury. It chased them out of Devil's Glen and then it raced up Twin Buttes where it crowned. A lot of exhausted, dispirited men came down the Canyon road that day, but they were all happy the fire was finally out.

The fire fighters heard spooky gunshots coming out of Devil's Glen at times all during the fire. Days later after things had cooled off, the men found a burned body, only the skeleton remaining, with some cast iron cooking gear and an old burned rifle. We think it was an old prospector who stopped coming to town a few years back. The other casualty of the fire was Wallace

Bean's broken arm and cracked hip—kicked by a packhorse while ferrying fire fighting supplies. I took him over to Choteau where Dr. Bateman and I cast his arm and then took him home with me after that. Without a mother in the Bean household, Wallace wouldn't get the healing care he needed while one-armed and laid up with a cracked hip.

The burned-out Canyon looks terrible, especially with the Twin Buttes so black and treeless. I wonder how long it will take for the trees to grow back. One old-timer says it takes about forty years, so that puts it almost beyond my time. Even by twenty years it should look better. I'll aim for that.

CHAPTER 61

DICK, OFF TO COLLEGE

Wallace is at our house for a few weeks to help him get used to having his right arm in a cast and a cracked hip that he has to go easy on. Dick is kind enough to help him with bathing and dressing. The sudden loss of one's right hand makes a person develop new strategies, like left-handed shaving. It's a good thing Armond is still home to help Ole with chores. In a few days I hear Dick and Wallace hatching a plan about going to a trade school in Chicago. Dick wants to learn welding. Wallace wants to learn a trade also, but money is his problem. We, Rita and I, decide to loan Wallace the money to attend the trade school with Dick. It's better they go together.

Finally, Bateman takes the cast off. Now, with bags long ready, they will take the train to Chicago and see what they can do to learn welding and other trades.

At the depot Dick says, "Dad and Mother, I will write you and tell you how we make out, and I promise I'll write once a week or close to that."

"Okay, son, I know how busy you will be. I remember the trouble I had when I was there in Dental College so long ago, getting letters written to my mother."

Rita hands each of them a sack of lunch. "Boys eat your lunch today—all of it. Leftovers can make you sick."

Bob Dyer chimes in, "You kids will change trains at the Falls and again at Havre. There you catch the Empire Builder for Chicago."

The train is now coming down the track from the way where it was parked for the night. Goes by with bell ringing and stops by the depot with a blast of steam to show the engine is on the ready. Then agent Dyer can see that the mail sacks are loaded. The boys bid their final goodbyes and climb on board. Ed, the engineer, gives us all a wave, and with a couple of toots from the whistle, the cars go clanging down the tracks for the Falls.

In about ten days the first letter comes.

"Wallace got a job at Marshall Fields days and signed up for night classes. I started welding class right away."

Now we look for the next letter but we won't be surprised if it's more like two weeks.

CHAPTER 62

A CUT THUMB, A BROKEN JAW, & GREEN TEETH

Fall days are shorter, air is cooler, wind is picking up. Hunting is on my mind. Maybe we'll have a good turn out at the cabin come October. I'm sure of Hildebrandt. Sam Larkin comes in and talks. He's not sure he'll make it. The cabin gives us guys a forward look, especially me. Mountain air and sounds—elk bugle, quaking aspen chattering in the daytime breeze, the silence of first fall snow. All these things stir the wild in us—give us a whole new look at life.

The rest of the year I'm a useful part of this growing town. Newcomers from everywhere. Besides the Gilman people with their houses, others are moving in. Mr. Quinn builds a garage right on the main street. His advertisement in *The Tribune* for a mechanic is answered by John Gort of Conrad who read the paper and got the job.

He brings his family from Conrad, and at first they live in the vacant print shop behind the garage. Now they have moved into the Quinn house we recently had. They have three little ones, two girls and a boy—Marie, Anna, and Anthony. Mrs. Gort is a good cook. Her special is sauerkraut. She sells it to those who want kraut with lots of juice for physic. September is her kraut time, slicing every head of cabbage she can get.

Today is a busy one for Christina Gort, but suddenly I hear her alarmed voice at my office door. "Missy Jo, where is the doctor!?"

Jo answers quickly, "He's here." I come right out

from my work bench.

"What happened?" Cristina is carrying young Anthony with a towel around his hand.

"Oh, Doctor, he tried to help me make kraut. His thumb he sliced it in the cutter!"

"Anthony, come back here and let's take a look at your hand."

He is sobbing and shivering. I talk to him all the way through to get him relaxed.

"We'll fix your thumb so it will quit hurting and heal fast."

After carefully washing the bloody hand and thumb I see where the cut is. It has already clotted and the two cut surfaces have started to stick together. I bathe the area with iodine and glycerin, make a cast-like bandage to hold the pieces together, and then bandage his whole hand.

I explain to his mother, "Mrs. Gort, here is a packet of aspirin. If he hurts so bad he cannot sleep, give him an aspirin with a drink of water. It may help."

"Oh, Doctor, thank you so much. I thought the end of his thumb would have to come off."

"The cut is so clean and it has already started to mend. I think it will heal and he will still have a complete thumb. Bring him over tomorrow. We will look and make sure it's okay."

"Doctor, when my sauerkraut is cured I bring you big jar."

"That's nice of you. It is one of my favorites."

At supper Rita says, "Jo came by and told me about the Gort boy getting his thumb almost cut off in the kraut cutter."

"Yes, that was one scared little guy. I asked him if he was trying to help his mother. He said, 'I guess she don't need me.'"

The next morning another serious case appears at my door, a total dental problem. It's Little Joe White. I hardly know him. His talk is painful. At first I cannot imagine what has happened to him. His face is swollen. Finally, after much effort, he is able to tell me. He's been working up at Glacier Park all summer. Some dude got drunk and hauled off and really hit him in the jaw, not once but twice. The guy had been drinking and decided to act out when the bartender refused to give him another drink.

Joe says, "Us guys decided to take him out of the saloon. I got in the way, I guess. The next day the boss told the dude he has broken my jaw and he will have to pay for me to go get it fixed." Little Joe gives me the man's address and I'm to send him the bill.

I tell Jo, "Put this address in our file. We need to send him the bill for fixing Little Joe's jaw."

To Little Joe I say, "Is your mother here in town with you?"

"Yes, she picked me up at the Falls when I come there on the train. My boss called her. Told her to meet the train." As we talk, Mrs. White appears at the door. I tell her what I need to do to repair the jaw and that it will take over three hours. "You can wait here if you want, but if you have something you can do or someone to visit, you'll have time for that. When you come back, I will tell you how you can care for Little Joe's broken jaw."

She says, "Thank you, Doctor. I certainly can keep busy, and I will be back in a couple of hours."

We get busy and take x-rays of his jaw bone and tooth structure to find the broken bones and plan on how much we need to move the bones that are broken. I clean his whole mouth with antiseptic solution. I also put in pain medicine where I have to move the jaw and then bands around four upper and four lower teeth in opposite positions. Each band has an eye on the cheek side that I can thread in a steel wire to lace the upper and lower teeth together.

When his mother comes back I tell her how to fix food for Little Joe.

"Fix all food that can be reduced to a liquid, like eggs in milk for a custard. Any food that can be cooked until very soft can be sucked through the teeth. Use your imagination and think how it can be made soft. He needs lots of food to make his bones mend."

"Thank you very much, and I will see that he comes in to his appointments."

I explain to Jo, "This has been a full day's work. When we get cleaned up from this job, I think we should take the rest of the day off ."

Jo sighs and says, "Yes, we need to recover."

Rita says when I get home, "It's a good thing you had a helper today. When Jo came by at noon she explained what you had to do. Poor Little Joe to get smashed up like that. He is the last person who would pick a fight."

"Yes, I know that he will suffer a lot for a few days, but then he will begin to feel better. I gave him some aspirin to help through the worst of it. One good thing about the mouth is that the tissues heal fast. Also Little Joe will learn that he can talk by moving his tongue and lips to make the words understood."

By mid-October of 1926, I hear from all who plan to come hunting again. Dick and Wallace are managing a letter about every two weeks. Little Joe is healing fast and can talk with his teeth tied together.

After another dry summer and fall, a hunting trip in the mountains will seem special and different. A few of us will get together at the cabin. From Augusta there are J.C. Manix, Tom Baker, and Ed Druckmiller. From Lewistown it's Dick Baker, from Tacoma it's Dr. Wright, and from Helena John Miller and George Hildebrandt. Enough guys to make a good story-telling party.

Game is scarce, but we find enough to string some up and not feel skunked. We always get some firewood and do some clean-up work around the cabin. We decided an outhouse should be our next project. It should be put on the slope behind the cabin and have it open in front where we can have a view of the mountain across the valley. They all agreed that the open front with the view was a definite plus. Now I must get back to real life and find out how the boy with the broken jaw is doing.

Monday morning Little Joe is the first to come in. He is smiling and looking so much better. I say to him, "You don't look like you have been on a liquid diet."

He has a big grin and says in the strange language of broken-jaw dialogue, "My mom figured it all out and made the grub I could eat."

I say to him, "You have a smart mother. You look like she has fed you plenty good."

"Doc, how long?"

The Outhouse

"It's been a bit over a month that I wired your jaws shut. It will probably be about two more weeks. When I take the wires and the bands off, you will really have to be very careful. No hard chewing for three weeks."

"This time I will come back in two weeks."

By mid-November, 1926, it's time to send a statement to that man who broke Little Joe's jaw.

"Doctor, this record card seems a bit detailed," says Jo Huotari.

"Yeah, right. Just list the main process."

The bill looks like this:

1. Six x-rays
2. Clean & prep all teeth and gums
3. Impressions
4. Eight bands with wiring
5. Installation
6. Check-ups

TOTAL $150.00

"Here in the book is the address in Chicago."

"Jo, besides getting the statement ready, make another copy on a card with the address to put in my wallet, because if he doesn't answer by January or February, I will find him in person. I plan a business call in Chicago early next year."

"Okay, I'll have it ready for you when I finish typing."

Later in the day a teenage boy comes to my door.

"Howdy, young man. What brings you to see me?"

He says, "My mom made me come and talk to you."

"What is the problem?"

"She doesn't like the color of my teeth. She says, 'You have to go see Dr. Kenck.'"

"Who is your mother. And what is your name.?

"I am Donald Butler, and my mother is Mrs. Butler."

"So, you are the son of the lady who runs the other hotel in Gilman?"

"Yes, sir. We live in the hotel. My dad is working in the Falls."

"Donald, come right in and sit in the chair and let me have a look at your teeth."

This young boy acts a bit fearful, like something will be painful.

"Donald, don't be afraid. What I do will not hurt. I will help you to have a well mouth. Right now it's really sick."

I run the explorer around the whole mouth. I find very little decay, just a set of teeth completely covered with a greenish plaque.

"Donald, I see you do not brush your teeth very often."

"No, it hurts too much."

"Your mom was right to send you in. Your mouth will make you sick if something isn't done."

"I don't know what to do."

"Donald, today I will clean all of your teeth and remove the green plaque and the lime deposits. Then I will give you some toothbrushes and show you how to brush your teeth and gums. Will you do this to have your mouth well and a nice smile?"

With a shy smile he answers, "Yes, sir, I will."

After about an hour of scraping, rinsing, and spitting, I put on the chuck with the polishing brush and smooth the surfaces of all his teeth.

I say to him, "Now run your tongue around and feel how smooth your teeth are. You actually have nice teeth." I hold up the hand mirror. He can't stop smiling.

"Tell your mother that I'm glad she sent her boy to me. It will make a big difference in how he feels and looks. Donald, promise me that you will follow the directions I gave you and come in one month from now. I need to see how your gums are healing. Will you do that?"

"Yes, sir." His whole attitude has changed!

"Go now and show your mom." I know he will run the whole mile to Gilman to show his new smile to his mom.

A few days later Mrs. Butler comes to see me.

"Doctor Kenck. I want to thank you for saving Donald's teeth and his health. I have tried to get him to brush his teeth but he kept saying, 'It hurts too much,' so that is why I demanded that he come to you."

"You were wise to do that."

"I want to pay for the work. I have no idea how much you charge but somehow I will save up and pay it."

"Mrs. Butler, for this you need not pay me anything. To see Donald smile is pay enough. Please see that he follows my instructions about brushing his gums and teeth with salt water."

"Thank you, Doctor. I will certainly do that and remind him to come in as you asked."

Winter starts early in 1926. By Christmas we have had some snow but mostly severe cold and wind. Oscar has been helping Uncle Will with cattle feeding. In between times we have been talking to him about what he wants to do, whether to go to college or not. Rita and I are much in favor of him going to Bozeman Agriculture College. We try to help him see the reasons.

My second son is a shy one and would just as soon not expose himself to the college challenge. Even so, we keep working on that because we know how Rita's brother Will has excluded himself from society. We truly want Oscar to have a bit more of a social life. Finally, we do persuade him to go to Bozeman and see the school. After looking around and hearing about the offered courses, he decides that he should really learn the business part of raising cattle. He will start in January.

Christmas 1926 without Dick is rather lonely. We are glad that Armond is with us weekdays. We find a girl who needs a place to stay—Minnie Moran from out by the Half Way House has come into town for high school. She is willing to sleep with Grandma so she can wake her up when she fails to breathe sometimes. After Oscar leaves for agricultural school in Bozeman, Oscar writes he's learning a few extra things, like wrestling, and that he will be able to take Dick down when they get together again.

Oscar graduates from college

CHAPTER 63

RIDING "THE EMPIRE BUILDER" TO CHICAGO

February 1927 rolls around, and we get no response from the man in Chicago who broke Little Joe's jaw, so I have decided to make a trip there for three reasons: collect that payment for the broken jaw and see how Dick and Wallace are getting along at school. Also, I am going to my old Dental College to see if that professor I had is still around. I want to ask him if he will come to our State Dental Convention when it's my turn to be president. I hope he's still around then. He's a good speaker. Dick and Wallace will be surprised when they see me.

"Rita, I will be gone no more than a week. Jo will put a note on the office door. Get Armond to do any chores for you. Tomorrow is the day. I asked Austin

Christian to stop by and pick me up in the morning."

"My dear husband, take care and tell Richard 'Hello' for me. Of course, Mama, Armond, Minnie, and I will manage. Be careful and we will look for you back in about a week."

Early next morn Rita and I stand together in the shelter of the front porch. With my arms around her I say, "Goodbye, my dear. I wish you were going with me. Let's plan something for just you and me this spring, my sweet wife." Austin arrives and gives me a ride to the depot.

"Don't mention it, Doc. When do you expect to come back?"

"I better be back in a week 'cause I promised my

missus."

"Well, I'll be watchin' for you. Hope you have a good trip."

Bob Dyer pops his head out the door of his office. "Hey, Doc, looks like you expect to be away a few days."

"Yep, gotta do a few things in Chicago."

"Okay, I'll issue a ticket to Chicago and back. Change in the Falls for Havre. Catch The Empire Builder there. You want a sleeper?"

"Yes, I don't much like to sit up all night."

"Same coming back, you will need it."

Several get on at Great Falls and at Fort Shaw and Sims. And so the trip goes on in the warm railroad car. By mid-afternoon we are in Havre ready to climb aboard the new Empire Builder. Such luxury! By nine p.m. we are notified that the Pullman birth is ready. So, after a light supper in the dining car I retire to the Pullman.

Next thing I know the porter is calling, "Next stop, Minneapolis! Breakfast is now being served in the dining car!"

After finding my way around Chicago, I'm glad to get home to report to Rita.

I'm off the train exactly a week from the day I left. Bob Dyer comes right out to meet me, and Austin is there with his freight truck. Bob yells over the sounds of the steam pressure being put out by engineer Ed Reardon, "Welcome home from the 'Windy City'!"

"Yeah, it was windy and mighty cold too." I'm sure glad to pile into Austin's truck.

"Yes, Austin, the good thing about going to such a big city is coming home."

"Welcome home," comes from all voices as I come in the front door. Everyone is looking at me with 'question' eyes.

"The answer is, 'Yes, no problem. The man who hit Little Joe happened to be home. He even apologized for his bad behavior.'"

Armond could wait no longer. "How is Wallace? Did you see him?"

"Yes, yes, but let's eat. I smell supper and I'm hungry."

Rita chimed in, "Somehow I knew you would be

home tonight so we waited to hear the train whistle."

"I am so glad to be home at my own table. Rita, you are the best cook."

And my answer to Armond is, "Yes, I saw him at Marshall Fields where he works days and then goes to college evenings. He showed me a lot of the store. His job is to unpack new household goods. Dick likes the electronics classes. But I'm sure hungry, so when I get my good supper eaten, I will tell you more."

Later, after the good stew, I begin on some of the details of the trip.

"The Empire Builder that I caught at Havre is one classy train. The Pullman sleeper car is very comfortable. I slept in an upper birth both ways. I think that is the best. It's farther away from the rail noise. The attendants see to our comfort. Grand Central Station in Chicago is huge and sounds echo all over from the stone walls. A public address loudspeaker voice is continually telling which trains are leaving and arriving on which tracks. Traveling by myself is lonely. Lots of people but everyone keeps to himself. The train crew are pleasant and helpful.

"After I looked up the man who owed me, I went to the Dental College, and I was astonished at the size and modern equipment. Of course, I should have expected that. It's been over thirty years since I was there. The best thing though was the young professor was still there except just 'a bit' older than I am. He will be glad to come to Montana. He said, 'I have often wondered how you are doing in the profession you chose.' We had a good visit."

After all had gone to bed. I say to Rita, "When I talked to Wallace at the store I asked him if he had seen anything special that would be nice for me to bring home to you because it is close to your birthday. He said, 'Yes, let me show you.' So in a few days it will come on the train. I want to surprise you. Can you wait?"

"Of course I can wait but I will have fun guessing. Then I will see if I can still out guess you."

"Rita, my good lady, I realize we can still play our private games."

Wow! It's nice to be home.

Three days later Austin comes by my office.

"Doc, this box of stuff come last night. Where do you want me to unload?"

"Good, Austin, just go ahead and leave it off at the house. Rita doesn't know what it is so I'll open it when I come for lunch."

"Is it okay if I tell her that?"

"Yes, Rita and I have fun with our guessing games, so just say I will open it when I get there for lunch."

Jo gets curious. "What's this all about?"

"I used some of the money I collected to buy something for Rita's birthday this month."

"If it's something from Chicago, it must be special."

"Yes, it is a new product. A whole new idea of cookware made of heavy metal called aluminum. Rita is cooking with pots and kettles that her mother gave her. Some cast iron and some enameled steel. This is quite different, lighter than cast iron. Anyway, you will see. Stop by and take a look."

"I'm sure curious. I've cooked forever with my mother's old cast iron kettles."

At lunch time I drag the box into the kitchen, open it, and one by one take out the shiny new polished kettles. Rita is in awe of such a beautiful set of cookware. She is fascinated with the three kettles that fit together on one burner. There are lids that fit each one-third-shaped kettle and a special handle that can be used on every kettle. Also, there are regular sauce pans, each with lids, and a frying pan with a tight, heavy lid.

Rita exclaims, "I could not have guessed this wonderful set of cookware. This will be fun to find out how to cook with it."

"Yes, Rita, and here is a booklet to tell you exactly how."

"I'm a little old to learn, but it will be a pleasure to try something new. Thank you, my dear husband, for this new cook set. I must read the instructions."

"Wallace showed me this new cookware and said he had helped the sales person who did the cook show. He said, 'I thought about Mrs. Kenck and wanted her to have a set like that.' So, Rita dear, give some credit to Wallace."

While in Chicago I missed a school-board meeting. Soon F.F. Sparks comes in to my office. "I seldom get away from the school, but I wanted to make a special effort to talk with you since I didn't get to see you last week. The job does keep me busy and more so with a girls' basketball tournament in March."

"Tell me about it. Sounds very interesting."

"Yeah, our school has some girls who play aggressively and will someday win a tournament. Since Augusta hosts the tournament every year, we should win some of the time."

"When is it scheduled?"

"It's got to be at the end of the spring quarter. That would be a time when all the invited teams can come. H.P. Lewis, the superintendent at Conrad is eager for Augusta to have the tournament. He has a tough team to beat and he wants to show them off."

"I say, let's go for it. You will have to contact all the schools. It's a lot of extra work for you, but I'm sure the kids and everyone in town will do their best for such an event."

"I'll assign all the different jobs to students. They need to be involved."

"By the way, Sparks, how is your new house coming?"

"Before long we will be moving in. And another thing, I'm having a log cabin built near it."

"I think I know why, but tell me."

"With a family as big as mine I need a place where I can have a bit of quiet and a place where we can hold our '777' meetings. Those are important."

"How many children do you have? Every once in a while I hear the name of one I haven't heard before."

"Last count was six but we think there is another on the way."

"With more children you do need a bigger house and a cabin for some quiet."

"I hear your trip to Chicago was a success. I know how it is in a big city when you don't know anyone. I'll see you at the next board meeting."

"Just a minute. There's something I want to talk to you about."

"Okay, I'm not in a big hurry anyway. My missus is always late getting dinner."

"It's about you coming up to Benchmark for a few days to R Cabin and doing a little fishing."

"How is fishing there? Which creek or river is it?"

"It's the South Fork of Sun River. Sometimes it's a creek and sometimes it's a river. Fishing is pretty good there for several kinds of trout. The story behind those fish is about thirty years old."

"You must have come west in a covered wagon."

"No, Sparks, I came flying in by stork in 1875. I landed in Helena my first stop. But about the fish in the South Fork of the Sun. In '03 another fellow and I got barrels of fingerlings from the fish hatchery and packed them in on packhorses in five-gallon cans to plant in Wood Lake and in the South Fork."

"That's a good story, but why?"

"It's the falls of the Sun. The fish couldn't get up to spawn. So, that's how a couple of other fellows and I decided to get fish into the South Fork."

"Good story, Kenck. You got me hooked. You figure out some time when we can both get loose, and I'll be glad to see you there and catch a few."

"It's a done deal. We will go as soon as we can make the time."

CHAPTER 64

THE PINNACLE OF ALL OUR DREAMS

As Rita and I come into the 1930s, we realize we have reached the pinnacle of all our dreams: a home we are proud of, a practice that supports us, two fine sons who are making us proud of their achievements, a cabin in the mountains where we can entertain our friends, and much more that I cannot list. The coming years should bring satisfaction.

Before I go further, I want to tell you that there will be a copy of the cabin guest book included because I cannot give all the details as they happened. Just look through the list and you may find your own name written there and many interesting notes other guests have added.

Since the '30s have begun with a down note because of the crash of the stock market, we can expect hard times, but we Montana folk can help one another and make it through.

The building of Gibson Dam is keeping a fair-sized population here, which gives our town business support even though our ranchers are struggling with low prices for their beef. The worst result is that the train schedule has now changed. The engine and train crew are based in the Falls and make a midday trip to Augusta and then back to the Falls. The loss of these folk as residents is sorely noticed. For me it means the loss of a good office girl, Jo Huotari.

"Rita, my good lady, since we are alone now and with school out for the summer, let's you and me try out that new road the Conservation Corps boys have built and drive out to the cabin."

"Yes, I would like to do that. I need to see if I could give some of my excess pots and pans to the cabin since I have that new set you brought from Chicago."

A summary of the 1930s must include the marriage of Dick to Mary Geldrich and the subsequent birth of a boy, R.C. Junior, and a girl, Arlene—thus fulfilling another dream of grandchildren. Another desire is for Oscar to acquire a ranch of his own.

This happens after Will Auchard acquired a portion of the ranch at the death of his father, Richard Auchard, and then left in his will to his sister, Rita, and his nieces and nephew. [Almost fifty years ago Oscar bought out sixteen shares of the Auchard Ranch to make it his own. First, having only milk cows, he shipped cream to Great Falls on the train to earn the money to buy Hereford beef cattle. Oscar sold to livestock yards in Spokane, Washington, and even to Japan.]

Dick Kenck, Montana State Trapper

Oscar Kenck

Arlene and Richard Jr., children of Dick and Mary Kenck; grand-children of Dr. and Rita Kenck and Peter and Mary Geldrich

Left: *Arlene Kenck: grand-daughter of the Kencks and Geldrichs; high school graduation in 1955*

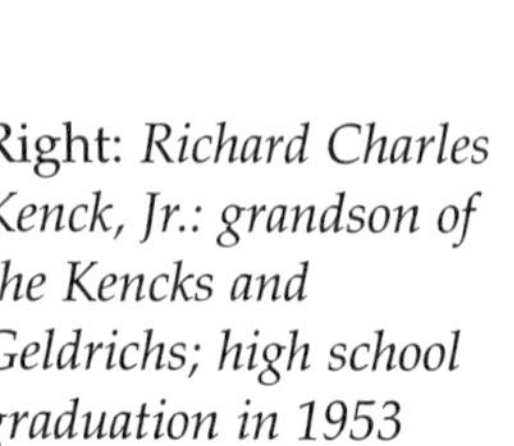

Right: *Richard Charles Kenck, Jr.: grandson of the Kencks and Geldrichs; high school graduation in 1953*

OBITUARY

Dr. O. A. Kenck, one of Montana's first dentists, practiced in the state sixty-two years. Born in 1875, he died at the age of 89 in 1964 while still residing in Augusta. Dr. Kenck attended Helena schools and had the distinction of being the third graduate of Gonzaga University in Spokane. He was honored there on the 65th anniversary of his 1895 graduation. After receiving his dentistry degree from the Chicago College of Dental Surgery, he returned to Montana to practice his vocation, which began in a horse-drawn wagon. He served first in Helena and then in Augusta and Choteau. Since there was often no medical doctor available, Dr. Kenck frequently was called upon to serve as one—particularly at births and then during the influenza epidemic. He married Rita Auchard in 1905, and together they became parents of two sons, Oscar and Richard (Dick). His beloved wife Rita passed away in 1975; their son Dick died in 2001; and their son Oscar died in 2002.

APPENDIX

The following is a list of the honors bestowed upon Dr. O.A. Kenck during his life—taken from the life story of R.C. [Dick] Kenck:

Graduate of Gonzaga University, June 1895

Graduate of Chicago School of Dentistry (D.D.), 1898

Montana Dentist of the Year, 1931

Honorary Degree from the American Medical Association

Honored by Presidents Wilson and Truman for his work for promoting war bonds

Silver Beaver Award from the Boy Scouts for over twenty years of service

Augusta School Board Chair, 1923-1963

Served all the offices of both the Masons and the Eastern Star Lodge

Life-time member of the Woodmen of the World

Resources for the Writing of Montana Treasure: Dr. O. A. Kenck— His Life and Times:

Montana Historical Society (numerous data)

Gonzaga Archives (early days of Gonzaga)

In the Shadows of the Rockies: Family stories of the people of Augusta

Dearborn Country

Teton Country

Many personal accounts of the people of Augusta

Family genealogy book collected and written by the descendants of Richard Auchard

Augusta High School records collected and distributed, Connie Randall

Tale of Two Towns, Jeffry Cunniff

LOG BOOK excerpts from the guest book kept at "R Cabin" at Benchmark.

OUR CAMP   PLEASE REGISTER:

Everett White and Charlie Gassman camped on this spot April 1908

Cabin Roof:
30 feet long
33 feet wide
North Slope: 18'
East Slope: 15'
Reroofed, August 1945
Re-caulked windows with cement-stucco June-October 1949

(Note: The following people are all from Montana unless otherwise noted.)

JULY 1924
In camp at building of this cabin

Mina Vandenburg, Helena
A.L. Vandenburg
Earl Vandenburg, Great Falls
Rita Kenck, Augusta
Ed Druckmiller, Augusta
Sam Larkin, Augusta
O.A. Kenck, Augusta
Oscar, Augusta
Goalman White, Augusta

OCTOBER, 1924
S.N. Larkin, Augusta
Tom Baker, Augusta
R.D. Wright, Augusta
Ed Druckmiller, Augusta
O.A. Kenck, Augusta
Fred Swanson, Augusta
R.E. (Red) Mahood, Cascade
J.C. Manix, Augusta
Geo. Hildebrandt, Helena

1925
Roy A. Oliver (Stub), Wisdom
R.D. Wright, Augusta
O.A. Kenck, Augusta
J.C. Manix, Augusta
Tom Baker, Augusta
John Nilan, Helena
Geo. Hildebrandt, Helena
Ed Druckmiller, Augusta

MARCH 1926
Ed Druckmiller
R.C. Kenck
Trapped for a month

OCT 1926
R.S. Baker (Dick) Lewiston
O.A. Kenck, Augusta
R.D. Wright, Augusta
J.C. Manix, Augusta
Tom Baker, Augusta
John Nilan, Helena

Geo. Hildebrandt, Helena
Ed Druckmiller, Augusta

1927
R.S. Baker (Dick)
O.A. Kenck
Geo. Hildebrandt
J.C. Manix
John Manix
T.F. Bergeron (Joe Bush)
S.N. Larkin
Oscar A. Kenck Jr.
R.B. Wellman
Dr. C.H. Dulaney
Thos. Baker
G.G. Christian
Oscar Christian
L.A. Miller

1928
R.S. Baker (Dick)
O.A. Kenck
R.D. Wright

S.N. Larkin
J.C. Manix
R.E. Mahood
Geo. Hildebrandt, Helena
W.D. Vaughn, Augusta
C.H. Dulaney
H.E. Vincent
Russell Hermanson, Brady
T.F. Bergeron (Joe Bush)
Fred Huotari
Bert Foulger
Meyers
H.S. Doolittle
Oscar Kenck
C.H. Pings
Ed Druckmiller
R.C. Kenck

OCTOBER 15, 1929
J.C. Manix (Joe), Augusta
R.D. Wright
R.S. Baker (Dick), Lewiston
Dr. J.A. Wright, Havre

H.E. Vincent, Augusta
Geo. Hildebrandt, Helena
C.H. Dulaney, Augusta
Clyde Burgess, Helena
Bill Whitman (Chef), Augusta
C.H. Pings, Augusta
W.D. Vaughn
Rex E. Woods, Nov., stayed all winter to March 1930
Ben Griffith, Denver, Colorado
David Griffith, Denver, Colorado
Dick Kenck, Augusta, Trapped all winter, went out first April. –55 below for nearly 2 weeks. First snow Dec 13, 5½ feet on level in front of cabin. Then rained & dropped to 18″ & froze.

OCTOBER 15, 1930
Byron De Forest
L.A. (Lon) Smith
J.C. Manix (Joe)
Tom Baker
R.S. Baker (Dick)
Geo. Hildebrandt
O.A. Kenck
Chas. Sparks
Walter James Manix
J.A. Cunniff
W.D. Vaughn
R. Percy Abbey

OCTOBER 15 1931
R.S. Baker (Dick)
Byron De Forest (Aqua River)
J.C. Manix (Joe)
R.D. Wright
O.A. Kenck

OCTOBER 15TH 1932
Looking back from 1945,

this strikes me as one of
my best trips to date—
R.D.Wright
Roy A. Oliver (Stub), Wisdom
C.R. "Mud" Townsend, Ely,
 Nevada.
L.A. (Lou) Smith, Bull
 Cook, Lewiston
R.D. Wright, Tacoma,
 Washington
T.H. Buirose (?), Dillon
Byron DeForest, Water Boy
W.D. Vaughn (Wick)
 Boulder City, Nev.
W.J. Romisa (Bill), Dillon
R.D. Surry (Dave), Dillon
J.C. Manix "Joe", Augusta
O.A. Kenck (Oakie), Augusta
Joe Bergeron (Joe Bush)
John Arps
June Arps
Peter Geldrich Sr.
Peter Geldrich Jr.

Paul Hearney
Dick Kenck
Clyde Burgess

OCTOBER 1933
Oct 12 Rita Kenck
Oct 12 O.A. Kenck

JULY 1934
THE YEAR THE BIG FISH
Thom. Baker
Oscar Christian
G.G. Christian
June Baker
Pearl Christian
Peggy Baker
Barbara Baker
Helen Baker
H.M. Downie
Mrs. H.M. Downie
E.O. Christian
Nancy Sparks
Earl Christian

Esther Cunniff
Sara Ann Costely

JULY 14 1934
John C. Norman
Myra C. Norman
Arthur Swanstein
Hortence Swantein
Mrs. O.A. Kenck
W.J. Auchard
R.C. Kenck
Mickey Kenck
O.A Kenck
Bill Rush (with the federal
Biological Dept) was kicked
by a packhorse near the
west fork and had his leg
broken at the knee. A. Rang
in from Benchmark met us
going home. O.A.K. ? back
taking a forest Service
horse, met Dr. Niles. Took
them along, round Rush-

splinted him with materials at hand, made a six foot stretcher & started for Benchmark, more men kept arriving to assist, by the time we reached Bench-mark there were 11 men on the job, had to ford the river 5 times, the stretch with Rush & poles & splints weighed some 250 lbs. At Benchmark we loaded him into Ranger Martin's car and took him to Helena. Among those coming to meet the stretcher were Colin Chisholm and Herb Calabaugh. Rita, Mickey and the Forest Service cooks fed some 18 people last night.

JULY 20-25 1934
O.A. Kenck

Rita Kenck
Oscar Kenck

JULY 22 1934
Mickey Kenck
Dick Kenck
Clarence Sharp

NOV. 3 1934
Oscar Kenck
Wm. E. Kristiansen,
    Philipsburg, out Nov. 9

NOV. 10, 1934
H.E. Vincent, Augusta
W.O. Christian, Augusta

FEB. 1, 1934
Mr. & Mrs. Carl Fender
J.E. Druckmiller

FEB. 28, 1934
Mr. & Mrs. Carl Fender

NOV. 11 & 12, 1934
Tom Baker Jr., Lewiston
Tom Baker, Lewiston
Mack Brown, Lewiston
Joe Westfall, Lewiston

Nov. 25, 1934
O.A. Kenck
Chuck Geldrich
Oscar Kenck
Dick Kenck

NOV. 25, 1934
Thomas Sangray
Fred Bernier
Gene Hungerford, Butte
Roy Garuth, Butte

DEC. 12, 1934
Ed Druckmiller

AUG. 3, 1934
Mrs. J.C. Manix

J.C. Manix (Joe)
Mrs. O.A. Kenck
O.A. Kenck

SEPT. 8, 1934
James Christian
Walter Cox

Jan. 7, 1935
Bruce C Neal
Lima Neal

Our elk? ? Work someone at Benchmark, 4 am hill above Benchmark cabin & at Andy Cabin 15 on the hill & of? Below the lake 28 inches of snow in bottom, very few elk sighted. Hill north of Blos-som (?) Ranch (?) lots of feed sighted but no sign of any large bucks.

JUNE 23, 1935
R.J. Dyer
Mrs. R.J. Dyer
Orin Waltrutt
George Doris
Mrs. HW Mitchell
Mrs. Omar Halvorsen &
   children
JUL 14 1935
Mr. & Mrs. Oscar Christian,
   Augusta
Graydon Christian
Esther Cunniff
Mr. & Mrs. Elton Christian,
   Calif.
P. Bass Christian, Calif.
Wally & Don Christian,
   Calif.

JULY 22 TO 29, 1935
Geo. Hildebrandt
Mrs. Geo. Hildebrandt
Mrs. Rita Kenck

O.A. Kenck
R.C. Kenck, July 27-28
Mrs. R.C. Kenck

AUG. 11-15, 1935
Sam Casey, Lewiston, Mt.
Tom Baker, Lewiston, Mt.
Arthur Stuart, Lewiston, Mt.
Bob Baker, Lewiston, Mt.

AUG. 18, 1935
Mina Vandenburg
Ady Brandt
Rita Kenck
O.A. Kenck

AUG. 22, 1935
Mrs. F.N. Swanson
Marion Swanson
Helen Parsons
Betty Quigley, Chicago, Ill.

AUG. 25, 1935
G.W. Swanson
Erick Englund

SEPT. 8, 1935
Byron DeForest
Mrs. Byron DeForest
Katherine DeForest
The old cabin looks natural

OCT. 14, 1935
(Bull Calf) Byron DeForest
Geo. St. Peter (Lewiston)
Tom Baker
J.C. Manix, Boulder City,
   Nev.
O.A. Kenck

NOV. 23, 1935
R.C. Kenck
O.A Kenck Jr.
O.A Kenck

NOV. 29, 1935
H. Potter
Ballie Buck

JUL. 3, 1936
Mina Vandenburg
Myrtle Buck, Augusta
Rita Kenck
Ballie Buck
O.A. Kenck

AUG. 16 TO 20, 1936
Mr. & Mrs. C.H. Pings (Spokane,
   Wash.) Surprise party
Miss Erma Baltus, Madison,
   Wis.
Clifford Christian, Boulder
   City, Nev.

CHINESE WALL TRIP:
J.C. Manix, Boulder City, Nev.
R.D. Wright, Tacoma and
   Coulee Dam, Wash.

O.A. Kenck

J.R. Krutan, Glendale, Calif.

J.E. Druckmiller, Augusta

Goalman White, Augusta

AUG. 19-20, 1936

Mr. & Mrs. Osmond Manus
& Tommy Boy (5 mos.),
Augusta

Mr. & Mrs. Mickey Thomas,
Parker Dam, Calif.

Phil Pings, Augusta

AUG. 27, 1936 TO AUG. 30

Maude Dissly, Lewiston

Mrs. R.J. Dyer, Augusta

Robert James Dyer Jr.,
Augusta

Angela Dyer, Augusta

AUG. 29, 1936

Dorothy Kraber

2722 Central, Great Falls

Kay Kraber

Earl F Kraber

R.J. Dyer, Augusta

SEPT. 7, 1936

Mrs. Geo. Hildebrandt,
Helena

Geo. Hildebrandt

Rita Kenck

O.A Kenck

OCT. 14, 1936

J.C. Manix

Geo. St. Peter

Tom Baker

Byron De Forest

OCT. 15, 1936

Dr. O.A. Kenck

NOV. 20, 1936

Sam Woods

R.C. Kenck

JAN. 9, 1937

Chas. A. Gassman, Augusta

JUL. 9, 1937

Jack McManus, Augusta

Jim McManus, Augusta

Margaret Ann McManus, 3
yr., Augusta

Ruth Mary McManus, 11
yr., Augusta

Mr. & Mrs. Carl Neufelder
& son, Butte

Mr. & Mrs. Walter
McManus, Augusta

Sara Manix, Augusta

JUL. 25, 1937

Leonard Stewart, Great
Falls

Austin J. Christian, Augusta

Wallis C. Stoner, Great Falls

Larry, Carl Christian

Margie Burris, Augusta

Loretta Christian, Augusta

Mrs. W.C. Stoner, Great
Falls

Mrs. Rosetta Christian,
Augusta

Aug. 19-25, 1937

Elizabeth Sorenson

Helen Lasmis

Mrs. Margaret O'Day

Armand Bean

Oscar Kenck Jr.

Sept. 12, 1937

Rita Kenck

Mina Vandenburg

Addie Baldwin

R.C. Kenck, 23 months old,
walked most way in from
Benchmark

O.A. Kenck

Nov. 25, 1937

Charles Blakely

Oscar Kenck
Wm. Anderson, Sun Lodge
O.A. Kenck
Dick Kenck
Glen E. Bliss

MAR. 17, 1938
Alex Gagnier, stopped and
    had coffee

MAY 28-30, 1938
Dave Morrison, Lewiston
Art Stuart, Lewiston
Trig Haugen, Lewiston
"Whitey" Nelson, Lewiston
Tom Baker, Lewiston
28 - 40 fish
29 - 50 fish
? ? lost count of fish

OCT. 28 TO 30, 1938
HUNTING TRIP
Jack McManus

W.J. McManus
Jim McManus
R.J. Dyer
E.H. Olson
Nov. 19, 1938
Marvin Griesen
Bob Eberhart

JUNE 5-9, 1938
Grandpa Tom Baker (47)
Oscar Christian (54)
Pearlie Christian (47)
Verna Manix (44)
Grandma Verne Baker (47)
Too much candy
Callers:
Rita Kenck
O.A. Kenck

JUN. 12, 1938, ALL FROM
    GREAT FALLS
Earl Clark
Ethyl Larkin Clark

Robert Clark
Billie Clark
Jay Larkin Sulser
Sidney Sulser

AUG. 15, 1938
Mrs. R.J. Dyer
Emerson Miller, Missoula

AUG. 21, 1938
Gurley Kraber
Bertha Elizabeth Dyer
Earl Kraber
Kathleen Kraber

NOV. 27, 1938
Wm. A. Castle
Albia Laws
O.A. Kenck
Ed Druckmiller
R.J. Dyer
Mrs. R.J. Dyer
Floyd Barnard Jr.

Angela Dyer

SEPT. 10, 1939
Sadie B. Bryson
Ann Ulligard, Mayville, ND
Rita Kenck, Augusta
O.A. Kenck, Augusta

SEPT. 20, 1939
Tom Baker